NUCLEAR COMMAND, CONTROL, AND COMMUNICATIONS

Other Titles of Interest from Georgetown University Press

Arms Control for the Third Nuclear Age: Between Disarmament and Armageddon
David A. Cooper

China's Strategic Arsenal: Worldview, Doctrine, and Systems
James M. Smith and Paul J. Bolt, Editors

The End of Strategic Stability? Nuclear Weapons and the Challenge of Regional Rivalries
Lawrence Rubin and Adam N. Stulberg, Editors

The Future of Extended Deterrence: The United States, NATO, and Beyond
Stéfanie von Hlatky and Andreas Wenger, Editors

Hacking the Bomb: Cyber Threats and Nuclear Weapons
Andrew Futter

NUCLEAR COMMAND, CONTROL, AND COMMUNICATIONS

A PRIMER ON US SYSTEMS AND FUTURE CHALLENGES

JAMES J. WIRTZ AND
JEFFREY A. LARSEN, EDITORS

GEORGETOWN UNIVERSITY PRESS | WASHINGTON, DC

© 2022 Georgetown University Press. All rights reserved. No part of this book may be reproduced or utilized in any form or by any means, electronic or mechanical, including photocopying and recording, or by any information storage and retrieval system, without permission in writing from the publisher.

The publisher is not responsible for third-party websites or their content. URL links were active at time of publication.

Library of Congress Cataloging-in-Publication Data

Names: Wirtz, James J., 1958– editor. | Larsen, Jeffrey Arthur, 1954– editor.
Title: Nuclear command, control, and communications : a primer on US systems and future challenges / James J. Wirtz, Jeffrey A. Larsen, editors.
Description: Washington, DC : Georgetown University Press, 2022. | Includes bibliographical references and index.
Identifiers: LCCN 2021036063 (print) | LCCN 2021036064 (ebook) | ISBN 9781647122447 (paperback) | ISBN 9781647122430 (hardcover) | ISBN 9781647122454 (ebook)
Subjects: LCSH: Command and control systems—United States. | Nuclear weapons. | Deterrence (Strategy) | United States—Armed Forces—Communication systems. | United States—Military policy.
Classification: LCC UB212 .N86 2022 (print) | LCC UB212 (ebook) | DDC 355.3/3041—dc23
LC record available at https://lccn.loc.gov/2021036063
LC ebook record available at https://lccn.loc.gov/2021036064

23 22   9 8 7 6 5 4 3 2   First printing

Printed in the United States of America

Cover design by Jeremy John Parker
Interior design by BookComp, Inc.

CONTENTS

List of Illustrations — vii
List of Abbreviations — ix
Foreword by Rebecca K. C. Hersman — xi
Acknowledgments — xiii

Introduction: Assuring Control of the Nuclear Force — 1
James J. Wirtz

PART I

1. Deterrence: The Role of Nuclear Command, Control, and Communications — 15
   James J. Wirtz

2. NC3 during the Bomber Age: 1945–57 — 35
   James Clay Moltz

3. NC3 during the Missile Age: 1957–91 — 49
   James Clay Moltz

PART II

4. US Nuclear Command, Control, and Communications: An Overview — 71
   Jeffrey A. Larsen

5. Space Architecture for NC3: Systems and Technologies — 93
   Matthew R. Crook

PART III

6. Cyber Operations and Nuclear Escalation: A Dangerous Gamble — 121
   Jon R. Lindsay

7. Technology Threats to NC3: Past Lessons and Current Challenges — 145
   Wade L. Huntley

8   Technology Threats to NC3: A Future Scenario   161
    Wade L. Huntley

PART IV

9   NC3 Modernization: Progress and Remaining Changes   185
    Michael S. Malley

Conclusion: US NC3 at a Critical Juncture   209
    Jeffrey A. Larsen

List of Contributors   221
Index   223

ILLUSTRATIONS

FIGURES

1.1.	US Nuclear Weapons Stockpile, 1945–2020	25
4.1.	US Nuclear Command and Control System	81

TABLES

5.1.	Typical Circular Orbit Velocities and Altitudes	96
5.2.	Electromagnetic Radiation Characteristics	99
5.3.	Common Uses of the Infrared Spectrum	100
6.1.	Comparison of Operational Factors in the Nuclear and Cyber Domains	128
6.2.	Comparison of Strategic Factors in the Nuclear and Cyber Domains	131
6.3.	Comparison of Proliferation Factors in the Nuclear and Cyber Domains	132
6.4.	Acknowledged Nuclear Weapons, State Nuclear, and Cyber Capabilities	135
6.5.	Cyber-Nuclear Escalation Mechanisms by Actor and Timing	137

ABBREVIATIONS

AEC	Atomic Energy Commission
AEHF	Advanced Extremely High Frequency
AFB	Air Force Base
C2	command and control
C2BMC	Command, Control, Battle Management, and Communications
C3	command, control, and communications
C3I	command, control, communications, and intelligence
DDoS	distributed denial-of-service
DEW	Distant Early Warning
DOD	Department of Defense
DSP	Defense Support Program
EHF	extremely high frequency
EMP	electromagnetic pulse
FAB-T	Family of Advanced Beyond Line-of-Sight-Terminals
FLIR	forward-looking infrared
GAO	Government Accounting Office / Government Accountability Office
GEO	geosynchronous orbit
GHz	gigahertz
GPS	Global Positioning System
GSO	geostationary orbit
HEO	highly elliptical orbit
ICBM	intercontinental ballistic missile
ITW/AA	Integrated Tactical Warning and Attack Assessment
JADC2	Joint All Domain Command and Control
JCS	Joint Chiefs of Staff
LEO	low earth orbit
LIDAR	light detection and ranging
MEO	medium earth orbit
MHz	megahertz
MILSTAR	Military Strategic and Tactical Relay
MIRV	multiple independently targetable reentry vehicle
MUOS	Mobile User Objective System

MX	Missile Experimental
NATO	North Atlantic Treaty Organization
NMCS	National Military Command System
NC2	nuclear command and control
NC3	nuclear command, control, and communications
Next-Gen OPIR	Next-Generation Overhead Persistent Infrared
NLC3S	National Leadership Command, Control, and Communications System
NORAD	North American Air Defense Command / North American Aerospace Defense Command
NSC	National Security Council
NSDD	National Security Decision Document
OPIR	Overhead Persistent Infrared
PAVE PAWS	Precision Acquisition Vehicle Entry Phased Array Warning System
SAC	Strategic Air Command
SACCS	Strategic Automated Command Control System
SAGE	Semi-Automatic Ground Environment
SALT	Strategic Arms Limitation Talks/Treaty
SATCOM	satellite communications
SBIRS	Space-Based Infrared System
SDI	Strategic Defense Initiative
SHF	super high frequency
SIOP	Single Integrated Operational Plan
SLBM	submarine-launched ballistic missile
SSB	single side-band
SSBN	nuclear-powered ballistic missile submarine
START	Strategic Arms Reduction Talks/Treaty
STRATCOM	US Strategic Command
TACAMO	Take Charge and Move Out
UFO	Ultra High Frequency Follow-On system
UHF	ultra-high frequency
WCDMA	Wideband Code Division Multiple Access
WGS	Wideband Global SATCOM
WMD	weapon(s) of mass destruction

FOREWORD

Comprising more than two hundred subsystems, touching all three legs of the triad of nuclear delivery systems, and requiring a fully integrated infrastructure of space-, ground-, air-, and sea-based capabilities, nuclear command, control, and communications (NC3) is the most complex and yet least-known component of the nuclear weapons complex. Moreover, the safety, security, and reliability of the NC3 system of systems is increasingly viewed as fundamental to the functioning of nuclear deterrence in US national security. As Adm. Charles R. Richard, commander of US Strategic Command, has stated, "The NC3 is as important to the strategic deterrence mission as the delivery systems and the weapons complex and we are in equal need to recapitalize it alongside the delivery systems."[1]

Today, with the attention paid to nuclear command and control and the broad consensus on the importance of NC3 modernization, it is hard to imagine that this has not always been the case. Yet, as this edited volume makes clear, the history of the US nuclear command and control system reaches back to the beginning of the atomic age and reflects similar periods of crisis, neglect, and renewed attention that characterize the broader nuclear enterprise.

This book offers a primer on how the US NC3 architecture has evolved and the role it plays in enabling deterrence while assuring positive and negative controls over nuclear weapons. The book lays out the historical foundation for the NC3 system, carefully walks through its components, and offers insight into the challenges facing NC3 in an increasingly digitized world. Such a system cannot escape the growing dangers that lie in an increasingly contested and congested space domain or in the ubiquitous and risk-laden cyberspace through which so much of NC3 must travel.

The nature of crises confronting US commanders and their NC3 systems has evolved. In earlier years, concerns about a bolt-from-the-blue nuclear attack that could create severe time constraints and require the system to respond under the most dire of circumstances drove perceptions of risk and system requirements. In today's security environment, the US NC3 system must accommodate more complex multipolar challenges, a rapidly evolving technological environment, and the realization that nuclear use could emerge not only from Russia but also from China, North Korea, or even some other state armed with nuclear weapons in the future. Today a sudden nuclear exchange seems unlikely, even as the risks of nuclear escalation from conventional or subconventional crises or conflicts between nuclear-armed states appear to be increasing. This, in turn, raises important questions about the integration of conventional and nuclear C3 systems and the management of crises with conventional and strategic elements that may unfold in today's complex digital information environment.

The future NC3 architecture will be called upon to provide a multisource, multipolar, all-domain situational awareness that does not solely detect adversary aggression but rather predicts it. Discussion of this changing security environment and contemporary developments in NC3 modernization fills the later sections of the volume. As these chapters make clear, while progress has been made in centralizing control and leadership over the system and building political support for its modernization, difficult challenges remain. The adage "We cannot know where we are going if we don't know where we have been" applies to nuclear command and control, NC3, and indeed to the broader strategic nuclear deterrence mission. In this volume, the reader can trace that path from the program's earliest beginnings to the future risks and challenges that will shape the architecture of the future, and in doing so better serve our understanding of the NC3 mission and the requirement to steward it effectively.

—Rebecca K. C. Hersman, director of the Project on Nuclear Issues at the Center for Strategic and International Studies

NOTE

1. Robert Ackerman, "NC3 Looms Vital to Strategic Modernization," AFCEA *Signal*, January 7, 2021, https://www.afcea.org/content/nuclear-c3-looms-vital-strategic-modernization.

ACKNOWLEDGMENTS

This volume had its genesis at The Blind Tiger restaurant in Shreveport, Louisiana, and many talented officers and officials motivated our exploration of nuclear command, control, and communications (NC3). Richard Mihalik, Rodney Mack, and Ernesto Hernandez of Air Force Education and Training Command recognized that education is key to preparing operators of the newly designated NC3 weapons system for the challenges ahead. Col. Mark Jablow USAF, the first commander of the NC3 Center at Barksdale Air Force Base, also embraced education as an enabler for his command, while Russell Mathers, Michael Tichenor, John Langston, Brian Hill, and Col. Pamela Bruner USAF, from the center helped bridge the divide between academics and policy. We also benefited from the expertise and bureaucratic savvy supplied by Mohsen Parhizkar, Lt. Col. Jason Rossi USAF, and Harold "Skip" Comacho from the Nuclear Weapons Center at Kirtland Air Force Base; from Todd Sriver, USAF Headquarters; and from Col. Amanda Kato USAF, and her team at the NC3 Integration Division at Hanscom Air Force Base. Col. Tim Sands USAF, a military associate dean at the Naval Postgraduate School (NPS), served as our guide to Air Force NC3, while Capt. Edward "Tick" McCabe USN, who held the air warfare chair at NPS, provided us with insights drawn from his experience as an NC3 operator. We received additional support at NPS from Angela Archambault, Peter Boerlage, and Christopher Smithro.

Three of our authors participated in a workshop, "NC3 Systems and Strategic Stability: A Global Overview," at Stanford University in early 2019 cosponsored by the Nautilus Institute, Technology for Global Security, and Stanford's Preventive Defense Project. We thank Peter Hayes and Philip Reiner for their invitation to this event, which helped focus our thinking on this set of issues.

The views expressed in this publication are those of the authors and do not necessarily reflect the official policy or position of the Department of Defense (DOD) or the US government. The public release clearance of this publication by the DOD does not imply DOD endorsement or factual accuracy of the material. That said, approval for publication as amended did not alter this book's fundamental findings or observations.

INTRODUCTION

ASSURING CONTROL OF THE NUCLEAR FORCE

James J. Wirtz

During the afternoon of March 11, 1958, a US Air Force B-47E Stratojet took off from Hunter Air Force Base in Savannah, Georgia. The plane, piloted by Capt. Earl Koehler, was on a routine training mission to Bruntingthorpe Air Base in England. To create a realistic training mission, the plane carried a Mark 6 nuclear weapon, although the crew stored the nuclear core of the weapon in a separate compartment. The fact that the aircraft was transporting a disassembled nuclear weapon might strike contemporary readers as strange, but the Cold War was tense in 1958. Planners did not think it was prudent to forward deploy a mission-capable bomber without its wartime nuclear armament.

As the plane headed north over South Carolina, Koehler noticed that the Mark 6 was not locked into place on the bomb rack. Standard practice called for unlocking bombs in case they had to be jettisoned in an emergency on takeoff; now the locking pin that was controlled from the cockpit was not working. Koehler then asked the aircraft's navigator, Capt. Bruce Kulka, to crawl back into the bomb bay to insert the locking pin by hand. Kulka had never performed this task before and had no idea what the locking mechanism looked like or where it was located. As he was searching around the compartment, he accidentally pulled the manual bomb release, and the Mark 6 fell onto the bomb bay doors with Kulka sitting on top of it. A few moments later, the bomb bay doors gave way, dropping the bomb onto the South Carolina countryside and leaving Kulka hanging on for dear life fifteen thousand feet in the air.[1]

When the bomb hit the ground near Walter Gregg's family farm outside Mars Bluff, South Carolina, its high-explosive detonators went off, injuring the Gregg family and destroying their house. No nuclear yield or contamination occurred, however, because the weapon's nuclear core remained safely on board the B-47.[2] The fact that this "normal accident," an unanticipated

1

human-machine interaction, produced modest consequences has generally consigned the event to the realm of nuclear folklore and urban legend.[3] Nevertheless, the "Mars Bluff incident" also is an example of a failure in nuclear command, control, and communications (NC3) in the sense that the weapon was dropped without authority or even the knowledge of a chain of command that led directly to the president of the United States. The bomber crew, the US Air Force, and the overall US nuclear command structure lost negative control of the nuclear weapon, dropping it on the Gregg family. Scholars have not always considered nuclear accidents from this perspective, but all accidents and mishaps involving nuclear weapons and their associated delivery vehicles constitute some sort of breakdown in NC3.

Events such as the Mars Bluff incident help explain why concerns about NC3 systems and procedures entered popular culture and political discourse. For example, Hollywood has embraced the unauthorized use of nuclear weapons—a breakdown in NC3—as a major story line of the nuclear age, turning several novels into widely seen movies. In the 1964 movie *Fail-Safe*, an onboard equipment malfunction causes a flight of US bombers to receive orders to attack Moscow instead of standing down following a false alarm.[4] In the 1965 film *The Bedford Incident*, a US Navy destroyer accidentally attacks a Russian submarine with a conventional torpedo when a crewman misinterprets a command, leading the sinking submarine to return fire with its nuclear-armed torpedoes.[5] Scholars would come to describe this kind of incident as "inadvertent escalation," whereby close interaction of opposing forces leads to the outbreak of hostilities without permission or even knowledge of the chain of command.[6] In Stanley Kubrick's 1964 black comedy *Dr. Strangelove or: How I Learned to Stop Worrying and Love the Bomb*, a fictional US Strategic Air Command general launches his squadron of nuclear-armed B-52s to attack the Soviet Union, which highlighted the possibility that NC3 systems could be defeated by insider threats.[7] More recently, the 1983 film *War Games*, in a way that was decades ahead of its time, tells a story of how a young computer hacker inadvertently corrupts the computer system controlling the US nuclear deterrent. The hacker accidentally gives control of US nuclear forces to the computer, thereby terminating the ability of proper authorities to exercise command and control of the nuclear arsenal. The 1984 film *Terminator* tells an even more contemporary tale by identifying the emergence of the "singularity," the moment when computers gain an intelligence far superior to humans, as the ultimate threat to NC3.[8] The film reflects today's concerns about the perils of artificial intelligence and machine learning; the fictional "Skynet" defense network becomes self-aware and turns the world's nuclear weapons against its human inhabitants.

NC3 also has raised a variety of issues and concerns for scholars and officials over the course of the nuclear age. With the Japanese surprise attack on Pearl

Harbor reverberating strongly within US strategic culture in the first decades of the Cold War, policymakers became concerned about the possibility of a "bolt-from-the-blue" attack, especially a "decapitation" strike directed against the NC3 system. In her classic study of the intelligence failure surrounding the attack on Pearl Harbor, Roberta Wohlstetter made the case that it was imprudent to bank on warning of a strategic surprise attack and that the lesson for the US nuclear deterrent and NC3 structure was clear.[9] Systems and procedures involving nuclear weapons, NC3 systems, and the officers and officials who operated and commanded them had to be designed and housed in ways that would survive a nuclear attack. It was not prudent to count on strategic or even tactical warning of a nuclear attack as a way of preserving one's ability to retaliate with a nuclear force.[10]

As the Cold War dragged on, the Soviets increased their prompt hard-target kill capability, further calling into question the ability of the NC3 system and key personnel to survive a so-called decapitation attack—that is, an attack designed to sever the connection between the nuclear deterrent and legitimate authority. In response, the United States attempted to complicate the problem faced by the attacker by placing increased emphasis on redundancy, mobility, and dispersion of NC3 systems and critical command nodes. For instance, the US military maintained a C-135 aircraft on continuous airborne alert as a nuclear command post from February 1961 to July 1990.[11] There were doubts, however, that even such demanding efforts would preserve US NC3 systems in the face of an all-out Soviet nuclear attack. Some critics warned that the United States had adopted a de facto "launch-on-warning" strategy to counter the risk of the loss of NC3 networks following a massive Soviet decapitation attack.[12] Critics suggested that by turning the NC3 system into a "hair trigger," which could respond to warning of an attack before nuclear weapons actually detonated on American soil, one could negate an opponent's counterforce threat but not without the risk of potentially cataclysmic results if the hair trigger were activated in the wake of a false alarm or technical glitch.

When the situation of mutual assured destruction emerged between the superpowers, which made it increasingly unlikely that one side or another could reduce damage suffered in a retaliatory attack following an even partially successful decapitation strike, scholars became increasingly concerned about different types of problems that might lead to a breakdown of NC3 and then nuclear war. Paul Bracken, for instance, noted that Soviet and US NC3 systems were in fact tightly coupled, creating a situation in which changes in the alert status of one nuclear force could produce a "ratcheting effect," leading the opponent to raise its alert status. Bracken likened the situation to the competitive mobilizations that occurred on the eve of World War I, which seemed to escape the control of political authorities.[13] Bracken's concerns were not far-fetched.

In November 1983 Soviet officials apparently mistook Able Archer 83, an NC3 exercise by the North Atlantic Treaty Organization (NATO), for actual preparation for a nuclear conflict and began placing their nuclear forces on a heightened state of alert. NATO officers noticed the change in the Soviet nuclear alert posture but bravely decided not to respond in kind by alerting NATO or US nuclear forces. President Ronald Reagan and several members of his administration were deeply shaken when they learned about the events surrounding Able Archer 83 and realized that this ratcheting effect actually had taken place.[14]

Scholars also identified tight coupling between nuclear weapons, associated delivery systems, and NC3 technologies and procedures as something that could undermine operation of the overall nuclear enterprise. Tight coupling of various systems and procedures with highly dangerous components such as nuclear weapons can lead to normal accidents when humans unknowingly or knowingly operate systems outside of expected parameters or otherwise create conditions that the system was not designed to tolerate. Under these circumstances, adding safety systems and procedures only makes matters worse because it introduces additional complexity and unanticipated variations in operational conditions.[15] The 1979 accident at the Three Mile Island nuclear power plant and the 1986 nuclear disaster at Chernobyl in northern Ukraine, for example, occurred when technicians lost situational awareness as they tested safety systems at both reactors. Additionally, bureaucratic imperatives; a breakdown in principle-agent relations, which manifests when subordinates (agents) fail to adhere strictly to standard operating procedures set by superiors (principles); and a general lack of attention to detail can cause personnel to operate systems outside of expected parameters, which in hindsight turns what should be routine, safe operations into a game of Russian roulette. Personnel can become desensitized to the risks they are running as equipment is routinely operated out of specifications or as procedures are developed on the fly. The *Challenger* disaster, for example, occurred when officials operated the space shuttle knowingly in conditions outside of engineering specifications.[16] The fact that experienced professionals would operate a high-visibility and high-risk system in such a way gives many observers pause about the ability of organizations and the personnel who populate them to maintain safety and control of systems that can fail disastrously—systems such as NC3 and its associated nuclear weapons.

New twenty-first-century technologies also have raised the specter of inadvertent escalation, a term that is alternatively used to describe two types of situations. On one hand, it can occur when opposing military units operate in close proximity to each other, creating a situation in which aggressive maneuvering, a high alert status, or accidents or unauthorized actions can lead to the unintended eruption of hostilities. The scenario contained in the movie *The Bedford Incident*, for instance, reflected this type of inadvertent escalation, creating an outbreak of conventional hostilities that quickly led to the use of nuclear weapons. On the other hand, inadvertent escalation can occur when conventional operations degrade an opponent's nuclear forces, dedicated NC3 systems, or dual-use (conventional and nuclear) command, control, communication, surveillance, or reconnaissance systems, leading to the target's assessment that conventional hostilities might be a prelude to nuclear war.[17] The escalation dynamic here not only is based on the inadvertent creation of a "use-it-or lose-it" situation, whereby the target's nuclear capabilities are eroded by conventional combat, but also on the perception that the conventional attrition of NC3 systems is actually a prelude to nuclear attack.

As a practical matter, the lines between unconventional, conventional, and nuclear war might be distinct in theory but difficult to recognize on the battlefield. So-called left-of-launch attacks using cyberweapons or insider threats can offer an unconventional way to undermine confidence in NC3 or the overall integrity of a nuclear force. The emergence of long-range, conventional precision-strike capabilities and hypersonic weapons that can take out hardened targets offer a possible "conventional" method of destroying weapons or installations that once required nuclear warheads. Nevertheless, prudence dictates that deliberate unconventional and conventional attacks on NC3 might best be treated as a form of nuclear war, especially if the attacks cannot guarantee that the opponent will not use nuclear weapons in response.[18] Still, new technologies—swarms of autonomous vehicles, cyberattacks, or cryptological penetrations produced by breakthroughs in quantum computing—are increasingly depicted as a way to degrade NC3 and its associated nuclear forces.

NC3 itself did not create this Pandora's box of nuclear accidents, inadvertent nuclear war, human incompetence, treachery, and organizational pathologies. NC3, however, is the key that can keep that box closed. NC3 also provides the key that can get that box to open.

NC3 DEFINED

In the course of recently "scrubbing" its official NC3 policy documents, the US Air Force has updated two important definitions. The first update involved the definition of nuclear command and control (NC2) as "the exercise of authority and direction by the President to command and control United States Military nuclear weapon operations."[19] Air Force Instruction 13-550 then goes on to state that NC2 consists of five mission-essential functions: force management, planning, maintaining situational awareness, decision-making, and force direction:

1. *Force management* is the set of Command, Control, and Communications (C3) activities relating to the assignment, training, deployment, maintenance, and logistic support of nuclear forces and weapons, before, during, and after any crisis.
2. *Planning* is the set of C3 activities relating to the development and modification of plans for employment of nuclear weapons and other operations in support of nuclear employment.
3. *Situation Monitoring* is the set of C3 activities relating to the collection, maintenance, assessment, and dissemination of information on friendly forces; adversary forces and possible targets; emerging nuclear powers; and military, political, environmental, and other events.
4. *Decision Making* is the set of C3 activities relating to the assessment, review, and consultation regarding consideration for use or movement of nuclear weapons or the execution of other nuclear control orders.
5. *Force Direction* is the set of C3 activities relating to the implementation (preparation, dissemination, and authentication) of decisions regarding the execution, termination, destruction, and disablement of nuclear weapons.[20]

The president is not involved in all of these essential functions on a daily basis, but each of these capabilities has to be continuously maintained, even in the aftermath of a nuclear attack, if effective command and control is to be executed.

NC3 is the second important definition provided by the secretary of the Air Force. It is the means to execute the five mission essential functions embodied in NC2. According to the Air Force instruction, "NC3 provides an integrated system comprised of facilities, equipment, communications, procedures, and personnel."[21] NC3 is the backbone of the National Military Command System (NMCS), which maintains continuous, survivable, and secure command and control of nuclear forces. The NMCS provides senior officers and officials with a secure and collaborative environment that facilitates situational awareness and selection of appropriate actions leading to national level decision-making. It also provides a means to monitor force execution and to assess ongoing events across the range of military operations.[22]

Although the president, as commander in chief of the US military, is the sole authority when it comes to ordering the use of a nuclear weapon, scores of officers would be involved in executing that decision. In other words, someone who actually employs a nuclear weapon is acting on the authorization of the president, but there is no direct means of communication between the White House and, for example, a submarine carrying nuclear-armed ballistic missiles. Nor is there a "nuclear button in the Oval Office." Instead, the briefcase (otherwise known as "the football") that always accompanies the president carries authentication codes that would allow the commander in chief to access the NMCS during a crisis. Once the NMCS is alerted, authorized participants would come online to build situational awareness and to identify or confirm options. Once any consultations are completed, an order to employ a nuclear weapon would be converted into a so-called emergency action message—that is, an alert or execution message—to the operational force. For example, Strategic Command in Omaha, Nebraska, or the airborne E-6B command post would generate an emergency action message that would then be received by officers who in fact do have their fingers on the nuclear trigger. Authentication procedures involving at least two people are used as the emergency action message is generated and then travels through the chain of command. Jeffrey Lewis and Bruno Tertrais have described the final step in the process involving an order to employ a submarine-launched nuclear weapon: "Once the order [emergency action message] is received, the captain of a nuclear-armed submarine and his executive officer would open a double safe (requiring that both enter their own combination) containing a Sealed Authentication System card as well as the 'fire control' key used to launch the weapons. The launch of submarine-launched ballistic missiles would involve the participation of four persons: the captain, the navigation officer, the missile officer, and the launch control officer."[23] Getting the emergency action message into the hands of launch-control officers is the end result of an NMCS process that begins with providing the president with the situational awareness required to take appropriate action.

THE TWENTY-FIRST-CENTURY CHALLENGE

NC3 is the key enabler of any effort to incorporate nuclear weapons into a national defense strategy because it provides positive and negative control of a nuclear force. In other words, NC3 must be able to exercise *positive control* (the ability to fire weapons) by employing the force when directed by legitimate authority. NC3 also has to maintain *negative control* every minute of every day by preventing the unauthorized, inadvertent, or accidental use of nuclear weapons under all circumstances. On balance, this negative control has worked well, particularly in light of the inherently hazardous operations undertaken involving the high explosives and plutonium carried by ballistic missiles loaded with hundreds of thousands of pounds of solid rocket propellant and by bombers filled with tons of jet fuel. It is perhaps a wonder that incidents involving loss of negative control are so few and far between. Nevertheless, the importance of NC3 in international politics in general and nuclear deterrence in particular often is given short shrift by strategists. In response, this edited volume offers an overview of the history, strategy, and technology associated with NC3 and how a changing technological and strategic environment is creating an increasingly challenging operational setting for the US strategic deterrent.

As the preceding paragraphs demonstrate, concerns about the security of nuclear forces and command and control systems are not new. During the Cold War, observers worried that nuclear infrastructure and command networks could be penetrated, corrupted, destroyed, or spoofed, leading to a loss of positive control or negative control. Everything from Spetsnaz attacks to insider threats to even nuclear attack itself constituted a potential threat. Additionally, there has always been a bit of unease created by the presence of computers or any sort of electronic automation in the NMCS, although the nuclear enterprise provided a great impetus to advances in computers, networks, and software. In the past, corrupted computer hardware and programming often was depicted as an anomaly brought about by operator error. Today, however, the problem has changed. Despite the fact that computers have been with us since the dawn of the nuclear age, today's nuclear weapons and command and control networks were created in an analog era, and the NC3 system still largely relies on analog technologies and techniques. Nuclear weapons now exist in a "cyber context," which includes, according to Andrew Futter, "the security implications of a more extensively digitized global nuclear order and a greater reliance on information technology throughout the nuclear weapons enterprise."[24] Those mostly Cold War nuclear systems also face the threat of "cyber operations: measures designed to attack, compromise, destroy, disrupt, or exploit activities involving computers, networks, software, and hardware/infrastructure, and the people who engage with them."[25] When combined, cyber context and operations seem to open the door to everything from normal accidents to deliberate sabotage, undermining confidence in the security of the nuclear forces controlled by governments around the world. Nuclear arsenals, or deterrent policies and concepts for that matter, were designed without cyberthreats in mind.

So far, the impact of this cyber challenge on existing nuclear forces and infrastructure has been limited. Air gaps, analog technology, and obsolete hardware and computer coding actually constitute a hard target for hackers. Nevertheless, as programs continue that will eventually modernize the US delivery systems associated with each leg of the nuclear triad (bombers, intercontinental ballistic missiles, and submarine-launched ballistic missiles), these antiquated analog systems will be digitized, creating a host of potential problems. Already elements of the nuclear infrastructure—delivery systems, warning sensors, manufacturing plants, and so on—are within reach of offensive cyber capabilities, although states currently seem to lack political motives to execute these types of operations. Modernization will inevitably bring NC2 within closer reach of hackers. Policymakers recognize this problem, but they have failed to devise a way to utilize information-age technologies while reducing cyber vulnerabilities.

THE WAY AHEAD

Our volume describes the NC3 "weapons system," the relationship between NC3 and deterrence, and the contemporary challenges faced by this vital component of a nuclear force, especially the problems created by an emerging cyber context and other nonkinetic threats to the security of the NMCS in the United States. The US NC3 system is a system of systems that has been cobbled together over the decades with little regard for simplicity or appropriate interoperability and is thus in dire need of overhaul, modernization, and rationalization. The problem includes, but is not limited to, the fact that the world has entered a digital age. A system that must work correctly, at all times, and under all circumstances on such a large scale is simply bound to break down occasionally.

Although our discussion of the role, status, and challenges created by NC3 in US national security strategy will be accurate as presented, it is important to explain at the outset that there are limits to our theoretical musings and empirical forays. The US NC3 system is one of the most highly classified areas within the US defense establishment, making it impossible to discuss several key issues. For instance, exact operational capabilities remain classified, especially the way systems will degrade when subjected to nuclear attack. Similarly, issues related to continuity of government and launch authority are closely guarded secrets, despite the fact that several intriguing operational procedures have been acknowledged by US officials over the years.[26]

Our volume unfolds in three parts. Part I highlights how NC3 is a key enabler of deterrence strategies, explaining why maintaining positive and negative control of nuclear forces under all circumstances is both a critical and an extraordinarily demanding task. The authors explain the role played by NC3 in creating both capability and credibility that are central when it comes to adopting a deterrent strategy as the basis of national defense. Paradoxically, part I also explores how a robust and enduring NC3 system actually serves as a sort of "force multiplier" when it comes to deterrence by expanding the potential circumstances in which nuclear weapons can be employed to achieve deliberate military or political outcomes. The volume then describes how technological and military developments over the course of the Cold War challenged contemporary NC3 systems, leading to the evolution of the philosophies that are reflected in today's command systems and structures. Our contributors thus illustrate two important facets of strategic nuclear history by exploring how concerns about NC3 helped shape the creation and operations of US nuclear forces and how the emergence of new forces and operations shaped the development of NC3.

Part II describes the NC3 weapons system in the United States. It offers a big-picture overview of how the system is meant to work and how NC3 interfaces with the US nuclear triad. It describes the relationship of NC3 to current US nuclear doctrine and deterrence strategy, utilizing recent strategy documents (such as the National Security Strategy and the Nuclear Posture Review) issued by the Donald Trump and Barack Obama administrations. Part II also describes the satellites, space-based systems, ground systems, sensors, and receivers that act as the backbone of the NC3 system by providing intelligence, surveillance, reconnaissance, and communications to officers and policymakers. Our contributors also explain how these space-based and ground-based surveillance and communication systems are constrained by the physics involved in orbital mechanics and signal propagation across the electromagnetic spectrum, creating an operational environment for NC3.

Part III illustrates the challenges facing the largely analog NC3 system as it is increasingly surrounded and immersed in digital systems, cyberthreats, and other nonkinetic challenges. The section incorporates a series of scenarios and vignettes to illustrate the political, kinetic, and electromagnetic threats that could create a "mission kill" of the NC3 system at levels of violence far short of nuclear warfare. In other words, even though the NC3 system is designed to survive and to continue to maintain positive and negative control over the nuclear force in a nuclear environment, nontraditional threats are emerging that create a host of problems that are not easily or cheaply addressed. Part III also assesses current policy guidance and initiatives intended to address these emerging issues, while describing how the policy, politics, and technology of NC3 modernization are evolving rapidly.

The following chapters thus provide a primer on NC3. They describe what it is, how it works, how it relates to broader NC2, and what components make up the US system. It also describes how concerns about NC3 shaped the evolution of the US nuclear force posture, the challenges facing the system, and today's requirements for modernizing the NMCS. Our contributors fill a descriptive niche that allows the reader to better understand not only how NC3 contributes to national security strategy but also the challenges facing the NMCS as the information revolution continues to unfold.

NOTES

1. Eric Schlosser, *Command and Control: Nuclear Weapons, the Damascus Accident, and the Illusion of Safety* (New York: Penguin, 2013), 186. Kulka survived the ordeal.

2. Schlosser, 185.
3. Charles Perrow, *Normal Accidents: Living with High-Risk Technologies* (New York: Basic Books, 1984).
4. Eugene Burdick and Harvey Wheeler, *Fail-Safe* (New York: McGraw-Hill, 1962).
5. Mark Raskobivch, *The Bedford Incident* (New York: Atheneum, 1963).
6. Barry R. Posen, *Inadvertent Escalation: Conventional War and Nuclear Risks* (Ithaca, NY: Cornell University Press, 1992).
7. Kubrick's inspiration was Peter George, *Two Hours to Doom* (London: T. V. Boardman, 1958).
8. Phil Torres, *The End: What Science and Religion Tell Us about the Apocalypse* (Durham, NC: Pitchstone, 2016).
9. Roberta Wohlstetter, *Pearl Harbor: Warning and Decision* (Stanford, CA: Stanford University Press, 1962).
10. Warner R. Schilling, "Surprise Attack, Death and War," *Journal of Conflict Resolution* 9, no. 3 (September 1965): 385–90.
11. James J. Wirtz, "Ground Alert for Looking Glass: SAC's New Emphasis on Strategic Warning," *Defense Analysis* 7, no. 1 (1991): 104–7.
12. Bruce G. Blair, *The Logic of Accidental Nuclear War* (Washington, DC: Brookings Institution, 1993).
13. Paul Bracken, *The Command and Control of Nuclear Forces* (New Haven, CT: Yale University Press, 1983).
14. Nate Jones, ed., *Able Archer 83: The Secret History of the NATO Exercise That Almost Triggered Nuclear War* (New York: New Press, 2016).
15. Scott D. Sagan, *The Limits of Safety* (Princeton, NJ: Princeton University Press, 1993).
16. Steven J. Spear, *The High-Velocity Edge: How Market Leaders Leverage Operational Excellence to Beat the Competition* (New York: McGraw-Hill, 2009).
17. Posen, *Inadvertent Escalation*; James Acton, "Escalation through Entanglement: How the Vulnerability of Command-and-Control Systems Raises the Risks of an Inadvertent Nuclear War," *International Security* 43, no. 1 (Summer 2018): 56–99.
18. James J. Wirtz, "Counter Proliferation, Conventional Counterforce and Nuclear War," *Journal of Strategic Studies* 23, no. 1 (March 2000): 5–24.
19. Secretary of the Air Force, "Air Force Nuclear Command, Control, and Communications (NC3): Air Force Instruction 13-550," April 16, 2019, 4, Department of the Air Force E-Publishing, https://static.e-publishing.af.mil/production/1/af_a10/publication/afi13-550/afi13-550.pdf.
20. Secretary of Air Force, 5. Emphasis added.
21. Secretary of Air Force, 4.
22. Secretary of Air Force, 5.
23. Jeffrey G. Lewis and Bruno Tertrais, "The Finger on the Button: The Authority to Use Nuclear Weapons in Nuclear-Armed States," CNS Occasional Paper 45, February 2019, https://nonproliferation.org/category/topics/cns_papers.
24. Andrew Futter, *Hacking the Bomb: Cyber Threats and Nuclear Weapons* (Washington, DC: Georgetown University Press, 2018), 4.
25. Futter, 4.
26. See "US Strategic Command Command Center," Federation of American Scientists, accessed August 31, 2021, https://nuke.fas.org/guide/usa/c3i/cmdctr.htm.

PART I

ONE

DETERRENCE: THE ROLE OF NUCLEAR COMMAND, CONTROL, AND COMMUNICATIONS

James J. Wirtz

In contemporary discourse on national security, the terms *strategy, deterrence,* and *NC3* (nuclear command, control, and communications) not only are described as things that contribute to achieving policy objectives, but they also seem to appear as policy objectives themselves. Policy documents also call for more and better strategy, deterrence, and NC3, but they rarely get down to first principles to explain how these concepts are interrelated or what makes their achievement desirable. Deterrence is in fact a type of strategy, and NC3 is a critical enabler of deterrence because it helps to produce wonderfully paradoxical effects. NC3 helps to guarantee nuclear retaliation following the total failure of the strategy of deterrence, which in turn reduces the likelihood that deterrence will fail in the first place. NC3 also enables a strategy designed to gain political-military benefits from a nuclear arsenal without actually having to use nuclear weapons on the battlefield, which is referred to as a deterrence strategy. In a sense, by ensuring that nuclear weapons can always be used, a functioning and credible NC3 system creates a situation in which political benefits can be gained from nuclear weapons without having to use nuclear weapons on some battlefield.

There is much that is paradoxical and counterintuitive when it comes to the relationships between strategy, deterrence, and NC3, but a brief discussion of each of these concepts can set the stage for a deep dive into the factors that dominate contemporary discussions of NC3 and the US National Military Command System (NMCS), which is the focus of this volume. The following section sets off by discussing how deterrence is a type of strategy that creates a rather demanding set of command, control, and communications requirements, especially when deterrence involves nuclear weapons. The chapter then turns to a discussion of the key issues that animate both theoretical and practical discourse surrounding NC3. It then briefly explores why NC3 has recently risen to the top of policy agendas and the steps that have been taken to revitalize the US nuclear deterrent in general and NC3 in particular. The chapter then turns to a survey of the challenges and potential new roles NC3 will face in the immediate future. The chapter concludes with a few observations about the relationship between NC3, deterrence, and future challenges.

DETERRENCE STRATEGY: UNPACKING CONCEPTS

Strategy is the art of using all of the resources at one's disposal to alter the opponent's political objectives and perceptions in a way that suits our interests.[1] Although there is a tendency to focus immediately on kinetic effects when military or national security strategy is under discussion, just about anything and everything can be employed in an orchestrated manner to alter the political perceptions of the opponent (i.e., what it believes is in its interests). For instance, diplomacy, economic sanctions or inducements, information campaigns via social media or traditional outlets, references to scientific findings, or appeals to reason, history, or equity can all be mustered to shape opinions among friends and foes alike. By providing evidence of domestic political commitment to foreign audiences, strategy can also signal that interest in some issue or region is not a passing fancy but is instead a matter of important or vital national interest. Force plays a part in this mix, but the use of force should never be an end in itself. Force should always be used to influence politics. It also should be used only after all nonkinetic tools in the strategy basket have failed to produce a satisfactory political outcome. Force should be used only as a last resort.

Deterrence is an exquisite strategy because it threatens the use of force, while not actually using force, to achieve political objectives.[2] In essence, the purpose of deterrence is to create a perception in the mind of the opponent that it is not in its interest to use violence to achieve its objectives, usually by promising that the costs suffered in retaliation will outweigh the benefits gained by initiating hostilities. Although the strategies used to achieve deterrence can be highly nuanced, they usually attempt to achieve several goals: prevent the outbreak of war, prevent abrupt territorial change or some other form of fait accompli, and guarantee that international change is accomplished through diplomacy or accepted legal frameworks or democratically sanctioned actions. In other words, deterrence is intended to foster peaceful change in world politics and to prevent the use of violence to achieve political objectives. Deterrence is a war-prevention strategy, despite the fact that its effectiveness is enhanced if it actually incorporates a credible capability to follow through on deterrent threats—that is, to actually fight a war. This paradox of deterrence is captured by the famous Roman adage *Si vis pacem para bellum* (If you want peace, prepare for war).

The outbreak of war would thus mark the complete and catastrophic failure of deterrence as a strategy. The party issuing threats would confront a situation—namely, war—that it hoped to avoid by adopting a deterrence strategy in the first place. The motto of US Strategic Air Command (SAC)—"Peace Is Our Profession"—was not some sort of cruel joke but instead reflected its *deterrence* mission and its goal of preventing the outbreak of nuclear war. The fact that the essence of deterrence is about war preventing, not warfighting, is something that strikes officers today as somewhat odd, given the decades spent cultivating a warfighting culture in the US military. Deterrence is a concept that is alien to officers who have found themselves in almost continuous conventional combat or various "gray zone" activities since the end of the Cold War. By contrast, the officers who manned SAC's bombers and missile launch-control centers were not in the practice of referring to themselves as "nuclear warfighters."

To be effective, the opponent must believe that a deterrent threat is credible in the sense that the side making the threat will actually execute the threat in the event of a failure of deterrence. Possession of capability, the material capacity to execute the threat, bolsters deterrence credibility. Nevertheless, it is the capability that remains in place after a deterrence failure—the forces that will survive after a potential attack by the opponent—that ultimately backstops the credibility of deterrent threats. The importance of the ability to retaliate after being attacked, which is often described as a "second-strike" capability, can appear counterintuitive for those grounded in conventional, not nuclear, operations. Albert Wohlstetter's famous Project RAND study, *The Delicate Balance of Terror*, for instance, highlighted the vulnerability of SAC's forward bomber bases to attack. Wohlstetter made the point that only the bombers that survived a surprise attack could play a part in deterring an opponent.[3]

On balance, it is harder to degrade the destructive power of deterrent threats that are based on nuclear weapons, as opposed to conventional forces, because the survival of just a few hundred nuclear weapons could inflict catastrophic damage on an opponent. Thomas Schelling called this the diplomacy of violence—nuclear deterrence can remain credible despite the fact that a country or conventional military might lie in ruins and the opponent's military capabilities remain intact.[4] By contrast, threats based on conventional weapons might appear "contestable" to the target in the sense that the conventional forces needed to execute a deterrent threat might be destroyed in a preemptive attack or rendered ineffective in a long attritional campaign.[5] It makes a difference if nuclear or conventional weapons form the basis of deterrent threats, but with both types of weapons it is the forces that survive after deterrence failure that are important when the opponent assesses the capability and credibility behind deterrent threats.

The type of threat made as part of an overall deterrence strategy also influences the target's perception of capability and the credibility of threats.[6] Deterrence by denial strives to prevent the opponent from achieving its goals in the event of deterrence failure. It conjures up images of somehow stopping the opponent at some geographic point of attack and physically forcing a return to the status quo ante bellum. Deterrence by retaliation, on the other hand, seeks to inflict unacceptable costs should some infraction occur. The opponent might keep its ill-gotten gains, but retaliatory strikes will inflict costs out of proportion to the benefits of its initiative. Deterrence by punishment threatens to inflict pain at steady or escalating increments until the opponent abandons its objectives. In a sense, when executed, punishment threats actually turn into a form of compellence or coercion because they raise the costs of some unacceptable action until the opponent abandons its efforts.

Two types of situational awareness can also influence the effectiveness of deterrence strategies. First, those issuing deterrent threats usually want to make the target aware of so-called red lines—they need to make the opponent aware of the actions that are likely to cause a failure of deterrence, triggering the threatened retaliatory action. There is a spirited scholarly debate about drawing red lines clearly.[7] Distinct red lines can prompt the opponent to engage in "salami tactics"—taking initiatives that gradually move closer to achieving prohibited objectives without triggering deterrent threats. By contrast, a lack of clarity might result in inadvertent activation of deterrent threats, which is in no one's interest. Second, the side issuing deterrent threats needs to maintain sufficient situational awareness to monitor and assess potential behaviors that could possibly cross stated red lines. One might think that Information Age technologies make accomplishing this task a simple matter. Nevertheless, the deluge of data from myriad sources can make it difficult to ascertain the difference between facts on the ground and alternative realities that animate the virtual world.[8] During crises, when time is short and the stakes are high, policymakers can find that accurate situational awareness is in short supply. For deterrence to function, however, the party that is to be deterred needs to be aware of what activity is prohibited and the party that is making deterrent threats needs to be aware if its deterrence strategy has failed.

Embracing deterrence as a strategy thus involves a good deal more than just possessing a weapons system; it also involves developing and preserving accurate situational assessments in peacetime, during crisis, and during war itself. Deterrence strategies of denial, retaliation, and punishment also carry different implications for NC3. Denial strategies create a demand for keen situational awareness and flexible targeting so that the opponent's strategies, operations, and tactics, which are difficult to anticipate fully in advance, can be counteracted effectively once hostilities commence. Similarly, deterrence strategies based on punishment require an ability to assess ongoing events and to escalate the geographic scope or intensity of attacks, placing a premium on exquisite control of forces that themselves might be subject to nuclear attack. Deterrence also involves maintaining control of deterrent forces so they are not accidentally or inadvertently activated. So far, at least, NC3 has not allowed an accidental discharge, so to speak, of a nuclear weapon, although accidents involving nuclear weapons and associated delivery systems have occurred.[9] Most importantly, deterrence strategies dictate that the NMCS must be available if deterrence fails, even after NC3 systems have suffered a nuclear attack. Prudence dictates that plans for positive control—executing an order to actually employ a nuclear weapon and the execution of deterrent threats—must take place in a post-nuclear-attack environment.

NC3 is thus a critical enabler of deterrence because it provides the capability necessary to execute deterrence threats. Without effective NC3, deterrence lacks credibility for the simple reason that doubts would exist about *ex ante* threats to retaliate should deterrence fail. Those subjected to deterrence threats understand the importance of NC3. Decapitation attacks—preemptive strikes to incapacitate leadership and destroy critical sensor and communication networks—are always a possibility when opponents contemplate ways to sever nuclear forces from legitimate command authority. NC3 might just be the Achilles' heel of nuclear deterrence. It might not be possible to destroy all the weapons in a large nuclear arsenal to avoid nuclear retaliation, but it might be possible to destroy an opponent's ability to fire those weapons by disrupting or destroying its NC3.

KEY ISSUES OF NC3

Nuclear deterrence involves more than nuclear weapons and their associated delivery systems. Logistic and maintenance infrastructure, trained and motivated personnel, and especially NC3 bolster the credibility of deterrent threats because they provide evidence that deterrence is taken seriously and that deterrent forces will actually function if they are activated. NC3, however, is the element of a nuclear deterrent that is fully active in peacetime, in crises, and during nuclear war itself. Without the capability to control nuclear forces under all circumstances, the effectiveness of nuclear deterrence not only is diminished, but the very presence of a nuclear arsenal can also become a dangerous liability. Because NC3 contributes to the safety and surety of nuclear forces in peacetime and helps guarantee that they remain in their authorized status, there is never a moment when NC3 is not connected to the nuclear deterrent. NC3 guarantees that the nuclear force is safe and can be activated only by legitimate authority.

A basic function provided by NC3 is that it serves as a mechanism for national authorities to develop and maintain situational awareness, especially as normal conditions deteriorate into a crisis in which deterrence failure might be possible. To select an appropriate retaliatory response, policymakers will want to know about social, military, and political developments in areas of concern and to monitor deterrence red lines for evidence that the opponent has deliberately crossed them. This is no small matter. National authorities do not want to respond to a false alarm—the inevitable false positives produced by technical glitches, atmospheric phenomena, or human error in sensors or networks must be assessed and rectified before they produce tragic consequences. Similarly, physical accidents experienced by our own or opposing forces must be assessed quickly to prevent them from leading to inadvertent escalation, a problem that is enhanced during crises when forces might already be on alert and political tensions are high. If red lines are in fact crossed, national authorities also will want to know if the infraction is minor or if it signals a significant political-military initiative on the part of the opponent. Prompt attack assessment thus becomes crucial because it can signal the scope, nature, and potential strategic intent of an opponent's hostile action.

Ironically, creating accurate situational awareness for national authorities and maintaining it even if the United States suffers a nuclear attack is a function that is often taken for granted in discussions of NC3. The degradation of sensors and communications in both a conventional and a nuclear wartime environment often emerges as a major concern when it comes to keeping users of the NMCS informed about ongoing events. A lack of situational awareness could delay execution of deterrent threats and even facilitate the destruction of deterrent forces if national authorities do not recognize or understand that a full-scale attack is underway.[10] The data deluge produced by the information revolution also can lead to an adverse signal-to-noise ratio, especially given the need for rapid assessment during a crisis.[11] The need to sift through a data tsunami could overwhelm decision-makers, leaving them with poor situational awareness of fast-moving events. Poor situational awareness can lead to false positives, leading to overreactions to accidents, minor provocations, or spurious assessments.

A second critical function of NC3 is that it must guarantee that legitimate authority always exercises command and control of the nuclear force, even in the most daunting situations, such as following a nuclear attack. In all circumstances, NC3 must be able to transmit a legitimate order from national authority to employ the nuclear force—often referred to as "positive control." At the same time, NC3 must never allow the force to be employed accidentally or by unauthorized personnel. This guarantee that the force will not be severed from legitimate political authority and used in an unauthorized, inadvertent, or accidental manner is called "negative control."[12] Once again, maintaining positive control and maintaining negative control appear to be simple and clear objectives, but upon reflection scholars often note that in reality these objectives are complicated by the so-called always-never dilemma.[13] In other words, actions taken to strengthen positive control tend to diminish negative control because strengthening positive control tends to remove technical, administrative, and communication protocols and procedures that prevent the arsenal from going off accidentally or without authorization from proper authorities. By contrast, actions taken to strengthen negative control might make it difficult, if not impossible, to employ the arsenal quickly while under nuclear attack or to employ the arsenal at all after NC3 systems are damaged by an attack. The always-never dilemma, the trade-off between positive and negative control, cannot be eliminated. Policymakers, however, need to keep in mind how efforts to strengthen some aspects of NC3 can damage other desirable technical or procedural qualities in the system.

By acknowledging the always-never dilemma, policymakers can choose deliberately where NC3 is positioned along a continuum of capabilities and procedures. On the positive control side of the continuum, firing procedures are streamlined and simplified, leaving few checks and safeguards between a decision to fire and weapons employment. The negative control side of the continuum would create a demanding set of requirements before an employment order (positive control) can be issued. Where NC3 systems sit on this continuum reflects political and military decisions about the risks that must be run to guarantee deterrence. For instance, in periods of low threat, safety and surety concerns might rise to the forefront, leading to procedures that are biased toward negative control. In more perilous times, when opponents appear highly risk-acceptant or the threat of nuclear attack appears high, steps might have to be taken to bolster positive control to guarantee that NC3 can function quickly and efficiently upon warning, while under attack, or in a postattack environment.

Since the end of the Cold War, NC3 has placed greater emphasis on negative control, although at times during the Cold War greater emphasis was placed on positive control to such an extent some observers complained that nuclear forces were on a "hair-trigger" alert.[14] Nevertheless, NC3 for the US strategic nuclear force was never designed to "fail deadly"—there is no evidence to suggest that damage to the NC3 system would inevitably lead to nuclear use as a matter of deliberate policy or procedure. In other words, the system was not designed to fire in the event that the negative control capabilities of the NMCS were damaged by enemy action. Loss of negative control does not correspond to a positive directive to employ the nuclear arsenal; NC3 is not a sort of perverse "dead man's switch," whereby the command "do not fire" is continuously sent to operational forces. It is probably better to think of the nuclear force as being "deactivated" in its normal peacetime state. Observers have pointed out, however, that in the case of the eruption of high-intensity conventional combat, NC3 could be severed from nuclear forces, leading to inadvertent nuclear escalation as nuclear forces and NC3 are activated and degraded during hostilities.[15] This was in fact the scenario that formed the basis of the 1960s movie *The Bedford Incident*, which was discussed in the introduction to this volume. Additionally, it is impossible to eliminate the risk of "normal" accidents involving nuclear weapons, despite the fact that nuclear forces are in a peacetime status and that the NMCS emphasizes negative control of the nuclear arsenal.

A third critical function of NC3 is that it must be immune from environmental influences in general and the opponent's actions in particular. Environmental influences range from things as mundane as the weather, to unauthorized access to systems, to efforts to spoof or misdirect sensors, to deliberate efforts to degrade the performance of sensors and communication networks. "Ghosts in the system," glitches, or "out-of-spec" activities can reduce confidence in NC3, which can have a particularly dangerous impact during a crisis. The fact that the operators and operations of NC3 systems always must be held to the highest standards creates a set of extremely taxing demands on organizations and their managers. Additionally, steps have to be taken to prevent "ratcheting effects": interactions between competing NC3 systems that might produce feedback loops that raise political tensions and alert levels.[16] Because nuclear crises are mercifully rare and have become even rarer since the denouement of the Cold War, ratcheting effects might be novel to future officers and policy-makers, making the phenomenon itself difficult to recognize in its early stages. NC3 has to work as intended and anticipated both in peacetime and in the harshest wartime environments; extraneous internal and external influences that emerge in unanticipated ways will raise serious concerns about the integrity of positive and negative control of the nuclear arsenal.

Today threats to the integrity of the NC3 systems also appear to be moving further "left of launch," so to speak.[17] Preserving the integrity of NC3 now involves more than surviving in a post-nuclear-attack environment; cyberattacks against critical communication hubs or command centers now occur on an ongoing basis. Nuclear forces, infrastructure, and command and control systems from the analog era now operate in our digital age, a situation that is unanticipated, unprecedented, and potentially destabilizing. Nuclear weapons now exist in a "cyber context," which includes "the security implications of a more extensively digitized global nuclear order and a greater reliance on information technology throughout the nuclear weapons enterprise." Those mostly Cold War nuclear systems also face the threat of "cyber operations: measures designed to attack, compromise, destroy, disrupt, or exploit activities involving computers, networks, software, and hardware/infrastructure, and the people who engage with them."[18] When combined, cyber context and operations seem to open the door to everything from normal accidents to deliberate sabotage, undermining confidence in the security of the nuclear forces controlled by governments around the world. Opposing governments or even casual hackers continuously attempt to penetrate NC3 systems to do everything from creating a nuisance to laying the groundwork for a disabling cyberattack. Cyber penetration of NC3 systems, perpetrated by insider threats or remote-system compromise, would greatly reduce confidence in positive and negative control of the nuclear force, leading officials to make difficult decisions about undertaking partial or system-wide shutdowns to search for cyber intruders. Additionally, the impact of cyberattacks on NC3 systems might also be exacerbated by precision-guided conventional attacks against key sensors or communication hubs or electromagnetic pulse (EMP) strikes intended to degrade communication and electrical networks that interact with dedicated NC3 systems.

Admittedly, cyber and other exotic efforts to tamper with NC3 systems are extraordinarily risky endeavors, which could in fact be taken by the victim of tampering as signs of an impending nuclear attack or could lead to an inadvertent use of a nuclear weapon if the NC3 system responds to damage in unanticipated ways.[19] In other words, there is always a chance that if the NC3 system is damaged, a situation could be created that might be beyond the control of operators, leading to unanticipated or unwelcome outcomes. Similarly, if operators are unaware that the system is damaged, they might misinterpret glitches or anomalies as an indication of nefarious action or even impending attack. Even though the NC3 system is designed not to fail deadly, cyber and other exotic efforts to tamper with NC3 could create the conditions for a normal accident to occur. New concerns about the vulnerability of NC3 systems to tampering, hacking, or other forms of nonkinetic damage are just another reminder of the important role played by NC3 in adopting and executing deterrence strategies. No matter what new technology comes along, NC3 will suggest itself as a tempting target.

This brief survey highlights how nuclear deterrence depends on NC3. National authorities and military operators alike must have confidence in their ability to exercise positive and negative control of their nuclear forces at all times and under all conditions, regardless of what the opponent does. In the parlance of nuclear deterrence, NC3 must operate in a second-strike mode—positive and negative control of the nuclear arsenal has to be maintained even after the NC3 system has been subjected to a concerted nuclear attack. If the opponent has reason to doubt the integrity of NC3 following a preemptive attack, deterrent threats will lose credibility.

THE ORIGINS OF RENEWED INTEREST IN NC3

Current interest in renewal of the US NC3 system can be traced to several developments that reflect broad political and strategic trends that have unfolded over the last thirty years. With the end of the Cold War, the political and strategic motivation for maintaining a large nuclear arsenal diminished rapidly. Funding for nuclear force modernization evaporated, and both the United States and Russia eliminated force structure quickly. Figure 1.1 shows the scale and pace of the American strategic nuclear weapons reductions that occurred over the last several decades.

These reductions have been codified in a series of arms control treaties between the United States and Russia that have culminated in the so-called New START (Strategic Arms Reduction Treaty) Agreement that entered into force on February 5, 2011. Both parties reached the central limits specified by the treaty in February 2018. The treaty limits each side to a total of seven hundred intercontinental ballistic missiles (ICBMs), deployed submarine-launched ballistic missiles, and deployed nuclear-capable heavy bombers. Each party is limited to 1,550 nuclear warheads deployed on these delivery systems. (Each bomber is counted as carrying one nuclear warhead.) Verification and transparency of the treaty is accomplished by combining elements of the verification protocols from the 1991 START Treaty with a series of annual on-site inspections, data exchanges, and notifications related to force structure and facilities.

New START still allows the United States and Russia to deploy robust nuclear forces. Nevertheless, today's forces are only a fraction of the approximately ten thousand nuclear warheads atop over two thousand delivery vehicles that were each deployed by the United States and the Soviet Union in the mid-1980s.[20]

As this drawdown was occurring, a problem emerged related to the maintenance of the nuclear deterrent. The human capital necessary to support nuclear weapons and associated delivery systems began to shrink as Cold War scientists and technicians retired from the workforce and young people avoided what they saw as diminishing career prospects offered by the US nuclear complex. As one blue-ribbon commission noted in the 1990s, doubt had emerged within the nuclear workforce about the continuation of US deterrent capabilities and

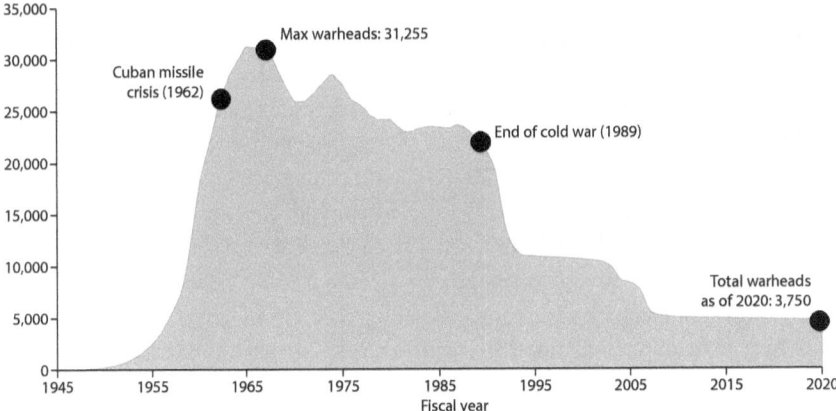

FIGURE 1.1. US Nuclear Weapons Stockpile, 1945–2020. Source: US Department of State, "Fact Sheet: Transparency in the US Nuclear Weapons Stockpile," October 5, 2021, https://www.state.gov/wp-content/uploads/2021/10/Fact-Sheet_Unclass_2021_final-v2-002.pdf.

policies: "In spite of public declarations by national leaders, we found a high degree of skepticism . . . about the nation's long-term commitment to nuclear weapons programs."[21] What the so-called Chiles Commission suggested was that nuclear scientific, technical, engineering, and operational expertise was a living art and that this art was in decline. Indeed, by 2005 John Harvey, then policy planning director of the National Nuclear Security Administration, summarized the state of US nuclear forces and policy as follows:

1. Nuclear forces, after the Cold War, have been rightly deemphasized under the [2001] Nuclear Posture Review.
2. They no longer compel the same attention from senior military or civilian DoD [Department of Defense] officials, or from Congress for that matter (despite the controversy over the Robust Nuclear Earth Penetrator warhead).
3. The military career path for the nuclear mission has serious shortfalls.
4. The bipartisan consensus we had during the Cold War has evaporated.
5. We have not designed or developed a new warhead in 20 years—as a result some key capabilities the nation has asked us to maintain are in jeopardy.
6. We stopped testing nukes in 1992.[22]

Harvey's points are critical because they reflect the impact of the nuclear test moratorium, the end of the Cold War, and the general loss of political or military urgency behind maintaining a highly robust nuclear capability. Avner Cohen, known for his histories of Israeli nuclear programs, summed up the situation within the US nuclear complex in more direct terms when he noted that "the sociology deteriorates before the hardware."[23]

This general decline in the nuclear enterprise soon began to manifest in operational glitches. On August 29, 2007, six cruise missiles armed with W80 nuclear warheads were mistakenly carried on a B-52H bomber from Minot Air Force Base in North Dakota to Barksdale Air Force Base in Louisiana. For thirty-six hours, the weapons remained unprotected by required security protocols, the resulting investigation revealing that many personnel had failed to follow proper nuclear handling procedures. Numerous personnel actions ensued, including the resignations of the Air Force secretary and chief of staff.[24] The turmoil from this incident was still ongoing when it was revealed that sometime in late 2006 the Defense Logistics Agency mistakenly shipped fuses used in the nose cones of Minuteman III intercontinental ballistic missiles to Taiwan. When the Taiwanese discovered the mistake in March 2008, the then secretary of defense Robert Gates ordered the Air Force and Navy secretaries "to conduct a comprehensive review of all policies, procedures, as well as a physical site inventory of all nuclear and nuclear-associated material equipment across their respective programs."[25]

In a report to Secretary Gates dated September 12, 2008, the Task Force on DOD Nuclear Weapons Management assessed the declining ability of the Air Force to accomplish its nuclear mission. It offered a concise summary of how the breakdown of the "sociology" in the nuclear enterprise was undermining its effectiveness. The post–Cold War environment, the implementation of arms control treaties, the attenuation of the nuclear alert posture, and the priority assigned to the conventional and space missions had led the Air Force to give markedly less attention and fewer resources to the nuclear enterprise. The result was five broad accelerating trends:

1. Nuclear missions became embedded in organizations whose primary focus is not nuclear;
2. Overwhelming emphasis was given to conventional operations;
3. The grade levels of personnel in line and staff appointments whose daily business involved nuclear weapons were lowered;
4. The nuclear mission and those who performed it were generally devalued; and
5. There was no single command to advocate for the resources required to support nuclear capabilities. Collectively this meant that no one Command in the Air Force had "ownership" of the nuclear mission.[26]

In response to these findings, the Air Force created Global Strike Command in August 2009, giving a single command responsibility for ICBM and bomber forces. Even though reviving the nuclear enterprise became a priority for the Air Force, overcoming decades of neglect could not occur overnight. In 2013 the commander of the ICBM enterprise was relieved of command after it was discovered that Air Force officers at Malmstrom Air Force Base, Montana, were cheating on tests gauging their mastery of ICBM operations.[27] The incident at Malmstrom did not reflect some fundamental dishonesty on the part of Air Force officers. Instead, it reflected their willingness to treat the ICBM test as just another routine and inconsequential training requirement.

Reorganization and reform of US NC3 followed the creation of Global Strike Command. Beginning in 2013, congressional attention turned to NC3, which was soon designated as a "weapons system" by the Air Force in an effort to better organize for the management of all of the personnel, processes, and equipment that combine to create the NMCS.[28] In 2015 the Air Force's Nuclear Oversight Board recommended that NC3 be placed under a single command, leading to the creation of the Air Force NC3 Center at Global Strike Command to take responsibility for the sixty-two different components that make up the NC3 weapons system. As Col. Mark Jablow, USAF, the first commander of the NC3 Center, noted upon taking charge in April 2017, "as the means by which national leadership have a secure, survivable and resilient communications path to issue nuclear orders to the warfighters, the Air Force is responsible for about 70 percent of the nation's NC3 systems, and now we have this center to serve as a focal point for maintenance, sustainment, and modernization of those systems."[29] The February 2018 Nuclear Posture Review identified the need for creating an even more cohesive organization to manage the NC3 weapons system. In response, the chairman of the Joint Chiefs of Staff in July 2018 appointed the commander of Strategic Command to be the NC3 enterprise lead with increased responsibility for operations, requirements, and systems engineering and integration. How Strategic Command consolidates its control over the NC3 weapons system and the role to be played by the NC3 Center continues to unfold.

The formation of Global Strike Command, the creation of the NC3 Center, the designation of NC3 as a weapons system, and naming Strategic Command as the lead for the entire NC3 enterprise highlight efforts to emphasize the nuclear deterrence mission in US national security strategy. These efforts also are intended to reconstitute human capital and to reinvigorate the esprit de corps of the men and women assigned to the nuclear enterprise. Much progress has been made in eliminating conditions that fostered past deterioration, but it will take time to reverse the effects of decades of neglect. As a list of the DOD's top management challenges in 2018 noted, "Despite efforts to sustain nuclear delivery platforms, nuclear support infrastructure, and NC3 systems... those systems are deteriorating at a faster rate than their scheduled replacement. Those in charge of the NC3 weapons system have their work cut out for them."[30]

CHALLENGES AND NEW ROLES FOR THE NC3 WEAPONS SYSTEM

The immediate agenda for the NC3 Center and Strategic Command is to continue to take steps to stop and reverse the material deterioration and personnel losses plaguing the NC3 enterprise. These efforts to reorganize and revitalize the NC3 weapons system are ongoing. Important efforts have already enhanced and empowered the NC3 workforce. These efforts have occurred none too soon. Observers have noted that the NC3 weapons system has to be updated to meet the requirements of the digital age, despite the fact that it consists of analog-age technologies and is based on analog-age philosophies. Important decisions have to be made about which systems are converted to digital technology, and assessments have to be made about how the overall digital context of the Information Age will interact with older analog systems.[31] NC3 also has to come to terms with nonkinetic threats—cyber, EMP, digital context, insider threats—that were not seen as a primary concern when the NC3 weapons system originally emerged in the 1950s. Similarly, new ideas about organizational pathologies—for instance, normal accidents and breakdowns in principle-agent relationships that lead to out-of-spec operations—should be factored into organizational and procedural reform efforts. These left-of-launch threats not only might undermine positive control of the nuclear force, but they also might create lingering doubts about the ability of legitimate authority to maintain negative control on an ongoing basis.

Despite the steps already taken to reorganize and reinvigorate the US nuclear enterprise, many observers prefer not to acknowledge the role nuclear deterrence plays in US national security strategy. Some observers believe that American conventional superiority in general and global surveillance and precision-strike capabilities in particular largely make nuclear deterrence irrelevant. For these observers, nuclear weapons and deterrence strategies are just a holdover from the Cold War, kept around by inertia and the prevalence of "oldthink." There also is a normative predisposition for eliminating nuclear weapons from arsenals everywhere. Indeed, many hold the mistaken impression that the US military readily embraces nuclear weapons and the deterrence mission, when in fact the opposite is true. Nuclear weapons are considered to be burdensome and potentially dangerous to one's career because they come with a series of demanding administrative and operational requirements that must be followed without any failure. Those missileers at Malmstrom who cut corners on what appeared to be meaningless paper drills found out the hard way that conducting nuclear operations out of spec or without proper documentation ends careers. In any event, many people simply want nuclear weapons to "go away" for a host of reasons; these individuals are loath to acknowledge the benefits provided by using nuclear forces as the basis for a credible deterrence strategy. Although attitudes within the services, among elected officials, and average citizens could become more favorable, for the time being political support for NC3 revitalization exists, but it does not run very deep. The need to cultivate support for the new NC3 enterprise is an ongoing requirement.

Another challenge faced by the NC3 community is that many observers, both in and out of the military, give short shrift to the strategic and political value of nuclear weapons, preferring to highlight US conventional forces as the locus of US military capability. Because US nuclear forces are generally intended for use as a deterrent and are not for use in the majority of realistic conflict scenarios that the United States faces today, many dismiss their relevance to strategy or to national defense because "they will never be used." Nevertheless, this judgment ignores the fact that potential opponents have to account for the existence of a highly capable US nuclear arsenal and that deliberately or inadvertently crossing red lines could prompt a nuclear response. Put somewhat differently, some observers fail to recognize that the strategic effect of a well-maintained NC3 weapons system and associated nuclear force can actually exceed strategic intent. Senior officers and elected officials do not plan to employ nuclear forces on a casual basis, but it is not too hard to imagine that potential opponents might think twice before they put that observation to a test.[32]

Deterring nuclear attack against the United States, its allies, and its military forces has long remained the primary mission of NC3. Nevertheless, the nuclear deterrent plays a variety of roles in US national security in general and in supporting specific types of military operations in particular. The impact of US nuclear forces is rarely acknowledged during the conduct of these operations, but it is easy to identify the role they play or the potential role they might play in operations or various aspects of US defense policy. As members of the NC3 enterprise think about the future, they should consider these various scenarios and how their efforts might contribute to successful deterrence.

The US nuclear deterrent creates escalation dominance. In other words, the ability to use nuclear weapons first or second in a conflict reduces the incentives for opponents to seek an advantage in a crisis by initiating or escalating conflict. Escalation dominance allows the United States to utilize its conventional forces while minimizing the incentives for opponents to engage in horizontal escalation, by undertaking hostilities in additional geographic regions or by attacking the United States itself, or in vertical escalation, by using chemical, biological, or nuclear weapons. Escalation dominance is especially important in counterproliferation operations because it creates an incentive for the opponent to "lose rather than use" their weapons—because using them could invite retaliation. Escalation dominance tends to "fix" the target, helping to create a set of circumstances that permits its destruction with conventional weapons.[33] Ironically, the fact that a robust nuclear deterrent provides the United States with escalation dominance is an advantage that is often simply "pocketed" by defense planners—their plans exploit this capability without acknowledging the important role it plays. Members of the NC3 enterprise, however, must understand the important role they actually play in providing US forces with escalation dominance and how they backstop conventional military operations.

The US nuclear deterrent also helps protect against the risk of opportunism and catastrophic failure of US conventional forces, threats that are rarely acknowledged by elected officials or senior officers. Opportunism occurs when opponents or third parties decide to exploit the fact that the bulk of US conventional forces are engaged in a specific theater or ongoing conflict by initiating hostilities at another location. "Every decision to wage war," according to historian Geoffrey Blainey, "is influenced by predictions of how outside nations will affect the course of the war."[34] In an extreme emergency produced by horizontal escalation or opportunistic action by third parties, US nuclear weapons could be used as part of a denial strategy to prevent significant damage to US interests. Catastrophic failure of conventional forces might occur if the exquisite "system of systems" that gives US commanders superior situational awareness and precision-targeting capability fails, leaving US forces outgunned and outmanned at the end of a precarious "just-in-time" logistics chain. The possibility that cyber or EMP attacks that target communication networks, military computer systems, or even the US electrical grid might be used to hamstring US conventional military capabilities is an ongoing concern.[35] Once again, the NC3 enterprise needs to consider its role in these disaster scenarios in which US conventional capabilities are not available to respond to critical threats to national security and the operating environment has been affected by the ability of the opponent to cripple key military and civilian systems.

The NC3 enterprise also plays a role in slowing nuclear proliferation by helping to extend deterrence to US allies. Because allies benefit from the so-called nuclear umbrella provided by the United States, it reduces their incentives to acquire their own nuclear deterrent, which in turn might set off a regional arms race. NC3 also plays a part in raising the bar when it comes to potential peer competitors because it creates capabilities (outstanding situational awareness and early-warning, rapid-response, and resilient networks under all circumstances) that enhance US capabilities without increasing the size of US nuclear forces. US extended-deterrence policies highlight that a resilient and highly effective NC3 weapons system can serve as an important force multiplier by fulfilling a demanding global mission to deter nuclear attacks on the United States and its allies. In other words, a highly effective NMCS can reassure allies that a growing nuclear arsenal is not necessary to deter an expanding list of potential opponents. US nuclear forces do not have to match opponents "weapon for weapon" in a theater because US NC3 can bring the nuclear force to bear *tous azimuts*, to borrow an idea from French nuclear doctrine.[36] In other words, nuclear targeting can adapt to counter rapidly emerging threats.

By maintaining second-strike capabilities, NC3 also supports US missile defenses. US missile defenses are not intended to replace US nuclear forces and deterrence policies. Instead, they provide a form of insurance against accidental missile launches or limited strikes undertaken by what are commonly referred to as "rogue regimes." Sound NC3, however, can help create a situation in which missile defenses are never tested in the first place because even a limited strike would not endanger positive or negative control of the US nuclear force. The role of the NC3 weapons system in missile defense scenarios, however, never seems to receive much attention, despite the fact that potential interactions between missile defense and robust NC3 can produce synergistic effects that can bolster national security.

The proliferation of nuclear, biological, chemical, and radiological weapons, so-called weapons of mass destruction (WMD), highlights another disturbing scenario. If an opponent initiates a campaign to use these weapons against US or allied forces or civilian targets, officials will be under time pressure to end WMD hostilities as quickly as possible to prevent massive military and civilian losses. War termination will take precedence over other political and strategic objectives.[37] Under these circumstances, officials might not be willing to wait days or even weeks for conventional forces to terminate WMD use; the decision might be made to make it stop quickly by using nuclear weapons in a concerted counterforce attack. Once again, this scenario highlights the complex set of demands placed on the NC3 weapons system to respond to novel scenarios or strategic surprises by bringing US nuclear forces to bear in a constructive manner to eliminate threats quickly.

CONCLUSION

Without a highly capable and resilient NC3 weapons system, the United States could not credibly embrace a nuclear deterrent strategy. No one disputes this proposition. The relationship between NC3 and deterrence is widely recognized and accepted. Less well understood, however, is the need to arrest the deterioration of the NC3 weapons system, which has generally proceeded apace with the reduction of funding and interest in the overall US nuclear enterprise. Within the last five years, action has been taken to revitalize the organizations and support the individuals who work to make NC3 a reality. Designation of NC3 as a weapons system and the centralization of responsibility for NC3 at the NC3 Center and at Strategic Command have already done much to turn things around, creating an atmosphere of renewed professionalism and responsibility throughout the NMCS. With growing concern about the rise of great-power competition and the possibility that nuclear forces might play a greater role in US defense strategy, it is probably safe to assume that NC3 modernization will continue to receive funding and high-level attention in the years ahead.

The world has changed significantly since the NC3 system reached its maturity over forty years ago, and the pace of change is accelerating. As Moore's law affects virtually every aspect of social, political, economic, and military affairs, the pace of significant innovations increases, making it difficult for states, organizations, and individuals to adapt. Today most analysts recognize a short list of contemporary challenges confronting the NC3 weapons system produced by this acceleration: cyberthreats and cyber context, insider threats, principle-agent problems created by a breakdown of organizational routines and individual discipline, and information overload that undermines the development and maintenance of accurate situational awareness. Nevertheless, there are even newer technologies—for instance, artificial intelligence, data analytics, continuous global surveillance, and quantum computing—that have not been fully evaluated in the NC3 context. In other words, simply refurbishing old systems and reinforcing adherence to existing procedures and protocols might not be the best way forward given this changing strategic and technological environment.

The ultimate challenge facing those responsible for NC3 might in fact be the need to adapt the system continuously to a world of accelerating change, while preserving the stability and predictability of the NC3 weapons system itself. There might be another looming trade-off to add to the always-never dilemma. In other words, a continuum also exists between adaptability and predictability. Will decision-makers want an NC3 system that can adapt rapidly to new strategic and technological threats and opportunities, knowing that they must sacrifice the predictability of tried-and-true procedures? Or do they gravitate toward the tried and true and hope that existing systems will not be affected by new technologies or new strategic challenges? The effort to come to terms with these sorts of trade-offs will preoccupy those responsible for maintaining the NMCS for years to come.

NOTES

1. Colin Gray, *The Strategy Bridge: Theory for Practice* (Oxford: Oxford University Press, 2010), 238–39.

2. It is exquisite because, as Sun Tzu noted, "to subdue the enemy without fighting is the acme of skill." Sun Tzu, *The Art of War*, trans. Samuel B. Griffith (New York: Oxford University Press, 1971), 77.
3. Albert Wohlstetter, *The Delicate Balance of Terror* (Santa Monica, CA: RAND Corp., 1958), https://www.rand.org.pubs/papers/P1472.html.
4. Thomas C. Schelling, *Arms and Influence* (New Haven, CT: Yale University Press, 1966), 64–65.
5. Richard J. Harknett, "State Preferences, Systemic Constraints, and the Absolute Weapon," in *The Absolute Weapon Revisited: Nuclear Arms and the Emerging International Order*, ed. T. V. Paul, Richard Harknett, and James J. Wirtz (Ann Arbor: University of Michigan Press, 1996), 52–53.
6. James J. Wirtz, "How Does Nuclear Deterrence Differ from Conventional Deterrence?," *Strategic Studies Quarterly* 12, no. 4 (Winter 2018): 58–75.
7. Bruno Tertrais, "Drawing Red Lines Right," *Washington Quarterly* 37, no. 3 (Fall 2014): 7–24.
8. Robert Mandel, *Global Data Shock: Strategic Ambiguity, Deception, and Surprise in an Age of Information Overload* (Stanford, CA: Stanford University Press, 2019).
9. Eric Schlosser, *Command and Control: Nuclear Weapons, the Damascus Accident, and the Illusion of Safety* (New York: Penguin, 2014).
10. Bruce G. Blair, *Strategic Command and Control* (Washington, DC: Brookings Institution, 1985).
11. Mandel, *Global Data Shock*.
12. Scott D. Sagan, *The Limits of Safety: Organizations, Accidents, and Nuclear Weapons* (Princeton, NJ: Princeton University Press, 1993), 278–79.
13. Peter D. Feaver, "Command and Control in Emerging Nuclear Nations," *International Security* 17, no. 3 (Winter 1992–93): 160–87.
14. Bruce G. Blair, Harold A. Feiveson, and Frank N. von Hippel, "Taking Nuclear Weapons off Hair-Trigger Alert," *Scientific American* 277, no. 5 (November 1997): 74–81.
15. Barry R. Posen, *Inadvertent Escalation: Conventional War and Nuclear Risks* (Ithaca, NY: Cornell University Press, 1991).
16. Paul Bracken, *The Command and Control of Nuclear Forces* (New Haven, CT: Yale University Press, 1983).
17. Left-of-launch attacks occur before the eruption of hostilities and are intended to damage or compromise surreptitiously an opponent's systems before they are employed.
18. Andrew Futter, *Hacking the Bomb: Cyber Threats and Nuclear Weapons* (Washington, DC: Georgetown University Press, 2018), 4.
19. Complex systems operated out of spec are likely to produce unanticipated human-machine interactions that can lead to unanticipated results. See Charles Perrow, *Normal Accidents: Living with High-Risk Technologies* (Princeton, NJ: Princeton University Press, 1999).
20. Robert S. Norris and Hans M. Kristensen, "Global Nuclear Weapons Inventories, 1945–2010," *Bulletin of the Atomic Scientists* 66, no. 4 (2010): 77–83.
21. *Report of the Commission on Maintaining United States Nuclear Weapons Expertise*, March 1, 1999, https://www.breckenridgeinstitute.com/1999-CHILES-COMMISSION-REPORT.pdf.

22. John R. Harvey, "Moving the Nuclear Weapons Program to DoD?" address to the Federation of American Scientists' Sixtieth Anniversary Celebration, National Press Club, Washington, DC, November 30, 2005.
23. Avner Cohen, "Strategy after 9/11: Monterey Strategy Seminar," presentation at the Naval Postgraduate School, Monterey, CA, September 20–22, 2005.
24. Michael Spencer, Aadina Ludin, and Heather Nelson, *The Unauthorized Movement of Nuclear Weapons and Mistaken Shipment of Classified Missile Components: An Assessment* (Maxwell Air Force Base, AL: USAF Counterproliferation Center, Air University, January 2012), https://media.defense.gov/2019/Apr/11/2002115520/-1/-1/0/56UNAUTHMOVEMENTNUCLEAR.PDF.
25. Thomas Shanker, "Missile Parts Sent to Taiwan in Error," *New York Times*, March 26, 2008, https://www.nytimes.com/2008/03/26/world/asia/25cnd-military.html.
26. *Report of the Secretary of Defense Task Force on DoD Nuclear Weapons Management: Phase I; The Air Force's Nuclear Mission* (Arlington, VA: DOD, 2008) 2, https://dod.defense.gov/Portals/1/Documents/pubs/Phase_I_Report_Sept_10.pdf.
27. Bud Fuji-Takamoto, "Organizational Dysfunction in the US Air Force: Lessons from the ICBM Community" (master's thesis, School of Advanced Air and Space Studies, Air University, 2016), 38–41, https://apps.dtic.mil/dtic/tr/fulltext/u2/1030376.pdf.
28. Government Accountability Office, "Nuclear Command, Control, and Communications: Update on Air Force Oversight Effort and Selected Acquisition Programs," GAO-17-641R, August 15, 2017, https://www.gao.gov/products/GAO-17-641R.
29. Carla Pampa, "AFGSC Stands Up Air Force NC3 Center," Air Force Global Strike Command AFSTRAT-AIR, April 3, 2017, https://www.afgsc.af.mil/News/Article-Display/Article/1139359/afgsc-stands-up-air-force-nc3-center/.
30. Department of Defense, Office of Inspector General, "Top DoD Management Challenges: Fiscal Year 2018," https://www.dodig.mil/reports.html/Article/1377306/top-dod-management-challenges-fiscal-year-2018/.
31. Futter, *Hacking the Bomb*.
32. Paul C. Avey, *Tempting Fate: Why Nonnuclear States Confront Nuclear Powers* (Ithaca, NY: Cornell University Press, 2019).
33. James J. Wirtz, "Counterproliferation, Conventional Counterforce, and Nuclear War," *Journal of Strategic Studies* 23, no. 1 (2000): 5–24.
34. Geoffrey Blainey, *The Causes of War* (New York: Free Press, 1973), 57.
35. James J. Wirtz, "The Cyber Pearl Harbor," *Intelligence and National Security* 32, no. 6 (March 2017): 758–67; Kenneth Geers, "The Cyber Threat to National Critical Infrastructures: Beyond Theory," *Information Security Journal: A Global Perspective* 18, no. 1 (2009): 1–7; Ernest Allan Rockwell, ed., *Electromagnetic Defense Task Force 2018 Report*, LeMay Paper 2 (Maxwell AFB, AL: Air University Press, 2018).
36. Therese Delpech, "French Nuclear Policy: More Continuity than Change," in *Nuclear Disarmament in the Twenty-first Century*, ed. Wade L. Huntley, Kazumi Mizumoto, and Mitsuru Kurosawa (Hiroshima: Hiroshima Peace Institute, 2004), 132. In French nuclear doctrine, the term *tous azimuts* is meant to indicate that French nuclear forces can respond to threats from any direction. The phrase suggests that French nuclear doctrine "can take on all comers."
37. Jeffrey A. Larsen and Kerry M. Kartchner, eds., *On Limited Nuclear War in the 21st Century* (Stanford, CA: Stanford University Press, 2014).

TWO

NC3 DURING THE BOMBER AGE
1945-57

James Clay Moltz

The nuclear command, control, and communications (NC3) complex that the United States operates today can be traced back to 1945. Although the first use of nuclear weapons was aimed at the defeat of Imperial Japan, the bomb soon became a critical tool in the Cold War against the Soviet Union. The original NC3 system responsible for warning, decision-making, and the communication and execution of nuclear orders was rudimentary. It emerged slowly in the late 1940s and early 1950s, when nuclear weapons were few and the delivery of these bombs remained tethered to relatively slow, manned aircraft. The NC3 system then evolved considerably from the mid-1950s onward, when nuclear numbers increased dramatically, destructive capabilities expanded exponentially with the deployment of massive hydrogen bombs, and warning time decreased significantly with the advent of intercontinental-range ballistic missiles.

Challenges to the successful operation of this system included both technological and functional obstacles (such as the initial lack of ability to store ready-to-use weapons) as well as policy-related hurdles and constraints (such as periodic funding cuts for the NC3 mission). As a result, the NC3 system faced many difficulties and underwent considerable changes over time. Shifts in the nature of the Soviet threat also affected NC3 operational challenges, requiring sometimes disruptive countermeasures.

The purpose of this chapter is to explore the history of the operational and political factors affecting the NC3 system during the bomber age, from 1945 to 1957. The chapter that follows will examine the missile age of the Cold War, from 1957 to 1991.

Before jumping into this complex history, it is worth briefly mentioning certain continuities and themes that extend throughout the Cold War period.

The "tasks" of NC3, for example, have remained essentially the same. NC3 operators have always been responsible for trying to provide adequate early warning of nuclear attack to allow national decision-makers (particularly the president) to reach an informed decision on whether and how to retaliate. Unfortunately, the Soviet threat changed over time, from slow, propeller-driven bombers armed with fission weapons to much-faster long-range missiles with vastly more destructive hydrogen bombs and later to missiles carrying multiple nuclear warheads. Complexities imposed by adversary weapons targeting individual components of the US NC3 system, including Soviet antisatellite weapons, raised other concerns, such as the viability of US early warning, targeting, and communications before and during a crisis. In addition, NC3 operators have been responsible for transmitting the orders of the president (or a replacement national-level authority, if the president were dead or disabled) to US military units armed with nuclear weapons and others tasked with responding to a nuclear attack. Survival of the chain of command and the viability of communications links in the midst of a nuclear war raised serious challenges. The NC3 system also faced the difficult task of trying to conduct battle-damage assessment in the midst of a conflict before transmitting new orders to the forces that remained. The fact that there is no way to simulate fully a nuclear war made all of these functions of the NC3 system difficult to undertake and assess and raised frequent concerns about the network's readiness, operational effectiveness, and sustainability in a conflict.

Other enduring themes emerge from the experience of NC3 operators in the *policy* realm during the Cold War. Throughout the Cold War, US interservice rivalries plagued the NC3 system as each branch tried to assert the requirement to maintain its own authorities and systems and to reject efforts to create a unified nuclear command. In addition, the high cost of NC3 technologies, which often required long lead times for construction of new transmission equipment, radars, and other facilities, meant that budgets for needed upgrades often proved inadequate or were spread out over many years. In some cases, the systems were obsolete before they could be completed, thus starting another cycle of attempted catch-up to newly emerging threats. The "targets" of the NC3 system also changed over time, at least in terms of the urgency of specific threats. While the Soviet Union remained the central focus of NC3 efforts throughout this period, changing technologies moved the concerns at various times from bombers to missiles to submarines and raised or lowered the perceived likelihood of war. For example, tensions increased during the Cuban Missile Crisis, lowered during the détente era (1970–75), and rose again in the early 1980s. Changes in US nuclear strategy over time—from massive retaliation to flexible response to mutual assured destruction—also affected both the arsenal and the NC3 system and process. Finally, the role of US allies in Europe and, to a lesser extent, in Asia in possible nuclear conflicts affected planning and increased the need for consultations during a crisis.

These factors highlight that the US NC3 system has always stood at the intersection of the changing foreign nuclear threat, the evolving US nuclear arsenal, and the makeup and policy preferences of US political leaders at any given time. During the Cold War, these determinants were in constant flux, even as NC3 operators struggled to keep the US nuclear arsenal safe, ready, and responsive.

BUILDING AND USING THE ATOMIC BOMB

The initial processes used for NC3 emerged in an ad hoc manner from the command and control structures established during World War II for conventional warfare in the Pacific theater. The original motivation for developing the atomic bomb had come largely from fears of Nazi acquisition of such a device, which American scientists (along with recent émigré scientists from Europe) believed Germany's scientists might well develop first, given their status as the world's leading academics in physics.[1] President Franklin D. Roosevelt began a small project in 1939 under the name of the Advisory Committee on Uranium, which was moved in 1940 to the newly formed National Defense Research Council.[2] After Pearl Harbor the program burgeoned into the secret Manhattan Project (named for the location of the engineering district where its funding was channeled) from January 1942 to August 1945. President Roosevelt named Brig. Gen. Leslie Groves, the project manager for the construction of the Pentagon, to oversee the complicated and highly secretive effort. General Groves selected University of California physicist Dr. J. Robert Oppenheimer as chief scientist to run the program, choosing to focus on his brilliant intellect and to overlook his socialist leanings, communist friends, and lack of any prior management experience. Later historians marveled at how this unlikely partnership succeeded in creating the most destructive weapon ever built and in a period of only some two-and-a-half years.[3] Work for this effort took place at dozens of facilities around the country but focused especially on three main locations: Hanford, Washington (where reactors were built to irradiate uranium to create plutonium, which then had to be painstakingly separated from batches of highly radioactive spent fuel); Oak Ridge, Tennessee (where a huge plant sought to "enrich" uranium by separating out the rare bomb-grade isotope U-235 from natural material with 99.3 percent U-238, first through gaseous diffusion and later by electromagnetic separation); and Los Alamos, New Mexico (where scientists under Oppenheimer were trying to design and build an atomic bomb using both plutonium and uranium as possible fuels).

The atomic bomb effort proved costly and time-consuming, at least in the context of the ongoing war. Oppenheimer and his team of some of the world's top scientists struggled with the complex conceptual and engineering problems of building a bomb from fickle materials that could fail to go off or, alternatively, spontaneously ignite but whose controlled detonation would produce unprecedented heat, radiation, and blast effects that surpassed the largest conventional explosives by several thousand times. After trying and rejecting various designs, two bomb types advanced in the spring of 1945: a plutonium implosion device (which required a symmetrical explosion using shaped charges to crush a sphere of plutonium and cause a chain reaction and massive explosion) and a uranium gun-type device (which involved smashing two shaped slugs of highly enriched uranium into one another to create a chain reaction and massive explosion).[4] President Roosevelt, who had kept the bomb program a close-held secret among only his highest military advisers, which had excluded even Vice President Harry Truman, died in April 1945. After being briefed on the bomb, the now president Truman decided to continue the Manhattan Project, and work continued toward testing and eventual use, despite the fact that Nazi Germany—whose scientific might had originally stimulated the US nuclear program, out of fear Hitler might acquire a weapon first—surrendered in May before any bomb was even ready to test.

A lack of adequate fissile material had plagued both implosion and gun-type design efforts. But adequate plutonium was available by June 1945 for the so-called Trinity test outside Alamogordo, New Mexico. Scientists gingerly drove the two specially cast, nickel-plated plutonium spheres, which were warm from their steady emission of alpha particles, to the test site for assembly.[5] Despite a dangerous thunder and lightning storm that had earlier threatened to ignite the bomb, the weather cleared and scientists detonated "the gadget" in the predawn hours of July 16, creating a tremendous flash of light across the dark valley and an earth-shaking 18.6 kiloton blast, "nearly four times what Los Alamos expected"[6] and over three thousand times the yield of the largest conventional bomb in the US arsenal.[7] Witnesses reported that an eerie purple cloud of radioactive particles hung in the sky above the smoky plume of the explosion and reported finding carcasses of wild animals eviscerated by the blast. Farm animals farther from ground zero died later from radiation poisoning.[8] The large, spherical "Fat Man" implosion bomb with its plutonium core had worked.

By early August, as the war in the Pacific dragged on, a combat version of the Fat Man bomb and an untested, cylinder-shaped uranium weapon ("Little Boy")—both with tail fins to aid in their delivery from a B-29 bomber—had been readied at Tinian Island for use against Imperial Japan. A one-page bombing order was issued by the War Department. Consistent with practices in conventional bombing missions, it had predelegated authority for the use of both bombs on a series of possible targets picked by a committee in Washington but to be individually selected by field commanders based on weather and the ability to visually sight the target. Prior proposals by scientists for a "demonstration shot" had been overruled as impractical,[9] given the limited quantities of material, the risk of a dud, and the possibility that detonation over a deserted area would fail to impress the Japanese.

A B-29 aircraft piloted by Maj. Paul Tibbets dropped the world's first uranium bomb on the city of Hiroshima on August 6, 1945, generating an explosive force of thirteen kilotons and killing sixty-five thousand Japanese (and thousands more later) from the blast, burns, and radiation poisoning. Three days later, Maj. Charles W. Sweeney dropped the world's second plutonium bomb on his secondary target of Nagasaki, creating an explosive force of twenty-two kilotons, destroying the city's factories, and killing some forty thousand people immediately, plus thousands more in the following months. These nuclear strikes were accompanied by the Soviet Union's entry into the war in the Pacific on August 8, which together demonstrated to Tokyo the futility of continuing to fight.

The authority and control reflected in this initial use of nuclear weapons was simply an extension of the wartime procedures employed to direct the use of conventional weapons, albeit in sometimes massively destructive operations. Although commanders' authorities to employ their weapons were limited to designated targets, the fact that these weapons were turned over to field commanders without formal safeguards or monitoring by higher authorities is unique in the history of NC3. No effort was made to separate authority to act from access to the weapon itself, while issues such as the "always-never" dilemma (that a weapon should always be available but never detonated by mistake) were subsumed by worries that the new weapon would either fail to detonate or accidentally explode on takeoff from the airbase on Tinian. Concerns about positive and negative control had yet to be voiced within the emerging US nuclear enterprise.

INITIAL POSTWAR NC3 UNDER PRESIDENT TRUMAN: 1945–48

With peace achieved in 1945, the United States began to grapple with the challenges posed by its newfound power and world influence. After the defeat and occupation of Nazi Germany and Imperial Japan and the relative decline of the other two Western powers, the United Kingdom and France, the United States found itself in a new role as leader of the noncommunist world. The Soviet Union's gradual extension of control over the countries of Eastern Europe by the early 1950s created a sharp political division among the wartime allies, establishing the roots of the Cold War. But the role of nuclear weapons in the postwar environment remained unclear. President Truman had been sobered by the effects of the bomb in Japan and sought to portray nuclear weapons as suitable only for use in a "last resort," such as to end a major existential threat to the nation. Nevertheless, in the atmosphere of peacetime and with a major reduction in US conventional forces following the end of hostilities, the US government did not establish any special guidelines or procedures for future use of nuclear weapons. In fact, not foreseeing any near-term conflict, it had built relatively few nuclear weapons. By 1946 the US "arsenal" consisted of only one Mark 3 Fat Man weapon, with a shelf life of just a few weeks.[10] New weapons had to be assembled from parts, a process that required thirty-nine specialists two days to complete.[11]

The United States set up a commission in 1946 to consider the future of the atomic bomb. The so-called Acheson-Lilienthal Committee issued a report, written largely by Oppenheimer, calling for the extension of control by the newly formed United Nations over the entire fuel cycle—from mining, to fuel fabrication, to enrichment, to reactors—in all countries to prevent an international arms race.[12] President Truman named Bernard Baruch, an elderly financier and former US government adviser during both world wars, to introduce the plan at the United Nations. But critics of the effort (including Leslie Groves) altered Oppenheimer's original proposal (later known as the Baruch Plan) to require swift and strict enforcement of its provisions and sanctions against violators, something the original committee believed would lead to its rejection. The Acheson-Lilienthal Committee suggested that it might be better to devise enforcement mechanisms by participating states after the plan's approval.[13] In the end, Soviet opposition to the proposal—due to its distrust of American intentions and desire for equal military power—caused the Baruch Plan to be formally rejected by the end of 1946.

The Truman administration also moved quickly on the domestic front to set up a legal structure for governing the secret nuclear complex it had built under Army auspices during the war. The Atomic Energy Act of 1946 overrode objections from the US military, which wanted to maintain control of the nuclear program in general and nuclear weapons in particular, and instead turned over all of the production facilities and materials to a civilian-led Atomic Energy Commission (AEC).[14] The Atomic Energy Act of 1946 established both a military and a scientific committee to advise the AEC on technical matters but stipulated that civilians would make the key decisions on the direction of the nuclear weapons program. The act also gave the president of the United States the sole authority to make decisions on any future use of the bomb in wartime. The act specified that "the President from time to time may direct the [Atomic Energy] Commission . . . to deliver such quantities of fissionable material or weapons to the armed forces for such use as he deems necessary in the interest of national defense."[15] Statements by President Truman later specified, however, that only the president was empowered to authorize the use of the atomic bomb.[16]

The US military also was quick to take steps to make room for nuclear weapons in its existing force structure. By the end of 1946, the Army Air Forces had established Strategic Air Command (SAC) under Gen. George Kenney to organize the future delivery of nuclear weapons. However, given the strong desire for peace after the sacrifices of World War II and the perceived lack of near-term threats (with the devastated condition of the Soviet Union, its distance from the United States, and its lack of nuclear arms), the priority of the mission seemed less than urgent. Indeed, by November 1946 there were only approximately twenty nuclear-capable bombers in the US force (all modified B-29s) with only ten nuclear-trained combat crews. The stockpile itself consisted of only nine "weapons" or, in actuality, nine sets of nuclear components in a disassembled condition.[17]

The Berlin Crisis in the fall of 1948, however, changed the almost casual US attitude and readiness regarding nuclear weapons, exposing the need for an improved and fully operational NC3 system. With the Soviet Union's cutoff of the allies' access to Berlin (then jointly occupied by the four victorious Allied powers), the United States faced possible war for the first time since 1945. President Truman shuffled his military leadership to move Maj. Gen. William H. Tunner, who had commanded the airlift from Burma to Nationalist forces in China during World War II, from his postwar job as head of the new Military Air Transport Service in Massachusetts to command of the Berlin Airlift. Meanwhile, Lt. Gen. Curtis LeMay, who had racked up extensive experience in carrying out strategic bombing missions against both Germany and Japan and had been running the airlift as commander of US Air Forces in Europe, now replaced General Kenney as head of SAC.[18] LeMay's task was to ready SAC for potential war with the Soviet Union.

Due to both political and technical reasons, a ready-to-use nuclear arsenal would not emerge until the 1950s. No real command and control structures had yet been developed because the bombs themselves remained in the custody of the AEC, not the military, and commanders lacked information on how many weapons even existed and might be available for use in a conflict. Early plans expected that it would take between thirty and forty-five days to generate US nuclear forces, based on the knowledge that the AEC had only two bomb-assembly teams and still needed twenty-four hours to assemble each weapon.[19]

SAC'S REORGANIZATION AND CHANGES IN THE NUCLEAR THREAT

While by August 1948 Kenney had already ferried sixty B-29 aircraft to England in preparation for possible conflict, the Berlin Crisis eventually ended peacefully, with the Soviets standing down in the face of the successful US airlift of supplies to relieve the besieged Berliners. In the late fall of 1948, newly arrived General LeMay decided to test his SAC forces with an exercise that required a mock bombing of Dayton, Ohio. As author Jim Baggott notes, the exercise revealed many issues that called into question SAC's ability to execute its mission:

> Crews were issued photographs of the target that were ten years old, on the basis that reconnaissance photographs of Soviet cities were of a similar vintage. Neither the crews nor the aircraft were used to flying at high altitude. The crews were insufficiently trained to target using radar. And the weather was bad. Of the 150 crews that flew the mission, none completed it as directed. Few crews even managed to find Dayton, let alone target the city accurately. LeMay called it the "darkest night in American military aviation history."[20]

Particularly noteworthy is the fact that the exercise did not even consider issues of command, control, and communication between the bomber crews and higher authorities, suggesting that once the order was given and the attack was underway, the crews would be largely on their own.

Through LeMay's vigorous training, reorganization, and resupplying of SAC forces, however, the United States developed nuclear war readiness for the first time. In the 1949 Off Tackle war plan, SAC would have ferried bombers and weapon components to the United Kingdom, where they would have been assembled and delivered. This would have occurred regardless of the fact that there was no official agreement with the British government to construct and deploy nuclear weapons on its soil.[21] The Soviet Union's first test of a nuclear weapon in August 1949 brought a new urgency to the question of nuclear delivery. SAC expanded its overseas bases, including building permanent facilities in Morocco, and began to exercise simulated overseas deployments.[22]

In the fall of 1949 the AEC tasked the civilian General Advisory Committee, led by Oppenheimer, to make recommendations on priorities for the US nuclear arsenal in the context of the Soviet acquisition of the bomb, including the issue of whether the United States should pursue the vastly more powerful (but still only theoretical) hydrogen bomb. The General Advisory Committee report, a highly classified study completed in October 1949, recommended that the United States take several specific steps to increase its nuclear capabilities: (1) expand its production of fissile material (plutonium and U-235) for weapons, (2) develop low-yield tactical nuclear weapons for the purposes of both deterrence and possible battlefield use, and (3) pursue development of so-called boosted fission bombs, whose more efficient fissioning of nuclear material could increase yields to several hundred kilotons.[23] Nevertheless, the report declined to endorse development of the much more powerful multi-megaton hydrogen bomb, stating that its capacity for infinitely higher yields meant that it would not serve military purposes but would instead be useful only for killing vast numbers of people. As an alternative to developing a more powerful weapon, the General Advisory Committee suggested that a proposal be made to the Soviet Union to "renounce" the hydrogen bomb.[24] This bomb's concept—using a fission explosion to compress another bomb that would then explode with a far greater yield—was strongly supported by émigré Hungarian scientist Edward Teller, influential University of California scientist Ernest Lawrence, and several other leading scientists.[25] In January 1950 President Truman decided to move forward with the first three recommendations of the General Advisory Committee and also to back Teller's push for the hydrogen bomb, based on recommendations from several top officials that the United States could not trust the Soviets to restrain themselves.[26] Yet the complex hydrogen bomb still remained merely a concept for the next two years.

By 1950 SAC had begun forward basing of nonnuclear components for existing fission weapons. But the AEC still continued to control the fissile material cores until wartime. Only in 1951 did SAC receive its first full set of bomb components and then only nine (a figure that remained unchanged until 1954).[27] LeMay would serve as SAC commander from 1948 to 1957 and would therefore be responsible for most of the progress in the area of nuclear delivery readiness made in the 1950s in regard to bombers. During his tenure, SAC went from possessing a largely "notional" nuclear delivery capability to an ability to launch a comprehensive and devastating strike across the entire Warsaw Pact.

To counter the rising Soviet threat, the AEC's research and development program began to make more fissile material and construct new nuclear weapons. In the fall of 1952, the AEC tested a boosted fission weapon with a yield of five hundred kilotons (code-named King).[28] The first test of a hydrogen device involved a bus-sized structure that used supercooled liquid deuterium in its secondary stage due to the lack of a facility to produce solid lithium deuteride. The so-called Mike test conducted in the South Pacific in November 1952 yielded a massive force of ten megatons and vaporized the island of Elugelab.[29] The nuclear arms race had now entered a new phase, with weapons capable of destroying large swaths of territory and their inhabitants. But US policy continued to focus mainly on deterring, not starting, a third world war. The communications portion of the NC3 complex evolved with improving delivery capabilities, albeit at a slower pace. In general, however, the multiple actors and limited technology involved in NC3 at this time made operations slow and difficult to perform. The individual services controlled the main radio systems and frequently relied on commercial telephone connections for other communications. A SAC command post exercise in 1950, using existing radio communications, revealed an average transmission time of four hours and forty-four minutes simply to alert units of their wartime assignments.[30] With bombers still serving as the only delivery system for nuclear weapons, these slow communications were worrisome but not viewed as catastrophic. It would take at least ten hours for any Soviet aircraft to reach the continental United States from Russia.

Yet world events continued to put pressure on the US nuclear complex and raised fears that nuclear weapons might soon be required for warfare. The fall of China to communist forces under Mao Zedong in October 1949 began to boost concerns about the global expansion of communism. The subsequent North Korean invasion of South Korea in June 1950 and the start of the Korean War brought US forces into direct conflict with communist troops in Asia, where China's decision to support North Korean forces in the fall of 1950 meant—to Gen. Douglas MacArthur and others—that nuclear weapons might need to be employed on the peninsula. By the early 1950s, nuclear war was no longer a Eurocentric issue but also became a possibility in Asia, placing further demands on US nuclear basing and NC3.

At the same time, the fear of a Soviet air attack on the continental United States with nuclear-equipped bombers also began to focus the minds of US defense planners. The US military was woefully unprepared to provide adequate early warning of an impending Soviet strike because the threat of war before 1949 had not seemed either imminent or highly consequential, given the Soviet Union's relatively small and short-range bomber force and conventional arsenal. But the prospect of technological developments and even one-way Soviet bombing missions with nuclear weapons after 1949 suddenly created existential fears of possibly devastating Soviet attacks. In 1951 only five radars had been deployed in southern Canada, just across the US border, along with two ships operated by the Navy in the Pacific. To provide increased warning of Soviet actions, the Department of Defense (DOD) began constructing the Pinetree Line radar network, an expanded series of installations that would provide at least two hours notice of a significant bomber attack on the United States. This work, involving twenty-two radar stations, would not be completed until 1957, and facilities on the Aleutian Islands and on Greenland would not be operational until 1958.[31]

IKE AND CHALLENGES OF NC3 UNDER THE "NEW LOOK" NUCLEAR EXPANSION

President (and former General of the Army) Dwight D. Eisenhower assumed the presidency in January 1953 with the aim of reducing the defense budget and making more effective use of the US nuclear deterrent. In October 1953 his administration approved a new strategy in National Security Council document 162/2 (NSC 162/2), which called for enhancing deterrence by threatening the early use of nuclear weapons in a conflict and the possible rapid escalation of a conventional conflict. By the spring of 1954, the Eisenhower administration had issued its New Look nuclear strategy.[32] Secretary of State John Foster Dulles emphasized in a major speech that the Soviets now faced the imminent threat of "massive retaliation" in response to tests of US resolve. The Eisenhower administration sought to reduce ground forces by stressing that nuclear weapons would be available, as the president stated in a press conference, "exactly as you would use a bullet or anything else."[33]

To meet the demands of the New Look strategy and to ensure that his branch would not be bypassed in firepower by the others, each of the service chiefs sought to acquire large numbers of nuclear weapons during the mid-1950s.[34] During Eisenhower's two terms as president, the US nuclear arsenal would increase from 841 weapons to 25,540 bombs and warheads.[35] The Air Force engaged in a massive buildup of its bomber force, while continuing to develop intermediate- and long-range missiles. The Navy deployed nuclear-armed Regulus cruise missiles aboard diesel submarines, nuclear-armed bombers aboard its then conventionally powered aircraft carriers, and a growing array of nuclear depth charges, short-range missiles, and torpedoes. The Army deployed short-range Corporal and Honest John nuclear-armed missiles and began to develop smaller battlefield weapons for use from artillery pieces and even bazookas.

The expanding arsenal posed new challenges for command and control. Each of the services continued to defend its right to develop separate target sets and its own lines of communication. SAC continued to operate the bulk of the strategic force and developed capabilities for air refueling of its bomber force using KB-50 and KC-97 tankers.

Following the first Soviet hydrogen bomb test in 1953, the US military became more concerned about the fragility of its NC3 system and its vulnerability to attack. Fears about the survivability of the Pentagon itself caused the DOD to designate Fort Ritchie, Maryland, as an alternative command post. In seeking to improve transmission times for orders to nuclear units, SAC created its own single-side band (SSB), high-frequency, point-to-point radio system, which supplemented other communications, including radio teletype, submarine cables, landline teletype, and landline telephones. In terms of warning, the DOD funded a major northward expansion of the Pinetree Line to more numerous sites along the Canadian and Alaskan coastlines facing the Soviet Union in the Distant Early Warning (DEW) Line, with the aim of providing an additional two to three hours of warning of Soviet bomber attacks. (The DEW Line became the North Warning System, which is still in use.)[36]

Meanwhile, facing gaps in its ability to provide early warning of attacks coming from over the Atlantic Ocean against major East Coast cities, the US government built radars on "Texas Towers" (their design based on offshore oil rigs) along the Atlantic coast.[37] Staffing these facilities in difficult weather conditions and ensuring reliable communication with them remained serious challenges. These radars were supplemented by thousands of volunteers in the Ground Observer Corps, who continued a tradition started in World War II of civilian sky watchers.[38] By 1957 the US military had stood up North American Air Defense (NORAD) Command to bring together these information sources into a single warning system. But it remained a work in progress. Still, SAC now boasted a capability of being able to reach any wing commander via its nineteen worldwide SSB stations within thirty seconds of the issuing of an order, a major improvement from 1950.[39]

CONCLUSION

The period from 1945 to 1957 witnessed dramatic changes in the US NC3 system. From an initial procedure during World War II based on the theater structure of wartime command of conventional forces, the NC3 structure had evolved into a more sophisticated system that centralized control of the nuclear force even as it increased in size and was deployed globally. But the process had taken time to develop. In the late 1940s, as civilian control over the bomb and its production was established, the US military had precious little access or even knowledge of nuclear weapons, making targeting and planning difficult. The time-consuming process of bomb assembly meant that forces would be generated and used only slowly. The expected limited reach and decisiveness of nuclear weapons affected nuclear planning as well, meaning that these forces were not believed to be necessarily decisive in a conflict, given the huge expanse of the Soviet Union and the possibility of robust air defense, especially for targets hundreds of miles within Soviet borders. Communications also remained relatively slow and vulnerable, meaning that command problems could be expected. Initial early warning of Soviet attack lagged as well, even against relatively slow Soviet bombers. Budgets in the late 1940s remained in a postwar decline, exacerbating the technical problems and strategic shortcoming inherent in existing NC3 systems and procedures.

But various crises—from Berlin in 1948, to the Soviet acquisition of nuclear weapons in 1949, to the communist invasion of South Korea in 1950—elevated the importance of more effective NC3. Major reforms sped the communication of orders, and radars began to expand warning time, offering prospects for robust counterattacks, thus strengthening deterrence. But the limits of technology hampered the kind of control over nuclear weapons use below the strategic level that would later emerge, due to the likely pace of warfare along the inter-German border, leading to the delegation of authority. Similarly, problems in initial coordination of target sets meant that fratricide among the weapons controlled by each of the three services was likely as each service attempted to attack the same target simultaneously. Finally, gaps in US intelligence created by the vulnerabilities of manned aircraft over Soviet territory meant that knowledge of the quantity and quality of the Soviet nuclear arsenal remained rudimentary, creating frequent overestimation of the threat, thus accelerating service demands for increasing numbers of weapons. The vast expansion of the US arsenal under Eisenhower in many ways exacerbated NC3 challenges, given the rapidly increasing variation in the size of weapons, their delivery systems, and the units that operated them. The armed forces were shifting from a conventional to a nuclear focus, further increasing NC3 demands. Nevertheless, the US military lacked a clear road map to deconflict the tactical, theater, and strategic nuclear delivery systems that were being fielded by the services. This impasse, however, did not last for long. It was broken when a major innovation in Soviet delivery technology created a new set of NC3 requirements, putting "bomber-age" assumptions about the conduct of nuclear war in question.

NOTES

1. Vince Houghton, *The Nuclear Spies: America's Atomic Intelligence Operation against Hitler and Stalin* (Ithaca, NY: Cornell University Press, 2019).
2. John Newhouse, *War and Peace in the Nuclear Age* (New York: Knopf, 1989), 22.
3. See, e.g., James Kunetka, *The General and the Genius: Groves and Oppenheimer—the Unlikely Partnership That Built the Atom Bomb* (New York: Perseus, 2015), xii.
4. Kunetka, 230–32.
5. Richard Rhodes, *The Making of the Atomic Bomb* (New York: Simon & Schuster, 1986), 659.
6. Rhodes, 677.
7. The US Army's "Grand Slam" conventional bomb used during World War II yielded the equivalent of 6.5 tons of TNT, while the Trinity bomb yielded 18,600 tons. (Calculated by author.)
8. Rhodes, *Making of the Atomic Bomb*, 677.
9. Lawrence Freedman, *The Evolution of Nuclear Strategy*, 3rd ed. (New York: Palgrave Macmillan, 2003), 18.
10. L. Douglas Keeney, *15 Minutes: General Curtis LeMay and the Countdown to Nuclear Annihilation* (New York: St. Martin's, 2011), 34.
11. Keeney, 34.
12. McGeorge Bundy, *Danger and Survival: Choices about the Bomb in the First Fifty Years* (New York: Random House, 1988), 158–61.
13. Gregg Herken, *Brotherhood of the Bomb: The Tangled Lives and Loyalties of Robert Oppenheimer, Ernest Lawrence, and Edward Teller* (New York: Henry Holt, 2002), 165–66.

14. Jim Baggott, *The First War of Physics: The Secret History of the Atom Bomb, 1939–1949* (New York: Pegasus, 2010), 412.
15. Atomic Energy Act, as quoted in L. Wainstein, C. D. Cremeans, J. K. Moriarty, and J. Ponturo, *The Evolution of U.S. Strategic Command and Control and Warning* (Arlington, VA: Institute for Defense Analyses, 1975) (declassified September 15, 1992), 37.
16. Atomic Energy Act, 37.
17. David Alan Rosenberg, "U.S. Nuclear Stockpile, 1945 to 1950," *Bulletin of the Atomic Scientists*, May 1982, 26.
18. General Kenney moved to serve as the head of the Air Force's Air University. On these changes, see Keeney, *15 Minutes*, 48; and Warren Kozak, *LeMay: The Life and Wars of General Curtis LeMay* (Washington, DC: Regnery, 2009), 276–79.
19. Wainstein et al., *Evolution of U.S. Strategic*, 17.
20. Baggott, *First War of Physics*, 441.
21. Wainstein et al., *Evolution of U.S. Strategic*, 20.
22. Keeney, *15 Minutes*, 73.
23. Herbert F. York, *The Advisors: Oppenheimer, Teller, and the Superbomb* (Stanford, CA: Stanford University Press, 1976), 46–53.
24. Cited in York, 52.
25. Herken, *Brotherhood of the Bomb*, 201.
26. York, *Advisors*, 66.
27. Wainstein et al., *Evolution of U.S. Strategic*, 34.
28. York, *Advisors*, 83–84.
29. York, 82–83.
30. York, 78.
31. York, 196.
32. On the new strategy, see Herman S. Wolk, "The 'New Look,'" *Air Force Magazine*, August 2003.
33. Eisenhower quoted in Freedman, *Evolution of Nuclear Strategy*, 73.
34. In congressional hearings, for example, Army lieutenant general James M. Gavin stated that the Army would need a total of 151,000 nuclear weapons, including 106,000 tactical weapons for use in close-in combat, 25,000 for air defense, and 20,000 for support of allies. On this point, see Robert S. Norris, "The History of the U.S. Nuclear Stockpile: 1945–2013," Federation of American Scientists, August 15, 2013, https://fas.org/pir-pubs/the-history-of-the-u-s-nuclear-stockpile-1945-2013/.
35. Robert S. Norris and Hans M. Kristensen, "Global Nuclear Weapons Inventories, 1945–2010," *Bulletin of the Atomic Scientists*, July/August 2010, 81.
36. Wainstein et al., *Evolution of U.S. Strategic*, 207.
37. Keeney, *15 Minutes*, 102–3.
38. Wainstein et al., *Evolution of U.S. Strategic*, 96–97.
39. Wainstein et al., 163.

THREE

NC3 DURING THE MISSILE AGE
1957-91

James Clay Moltz

Dramatic increases in the destructive capability of nuclear weapons, the speed of their delivery, and the resultant vulnerability of US nuclear forces required significant changes in US nuclear command, control, and communications (NC3) beginning in the late 1950s. While the essential tasks of NC3 remained the same, the vastly more powerful hydrogen bombs and a sharp decline in nuclear warning time meant that surprise attacks might not only be more likely but also more effective, possibly even catching most US forces on the ground. This, at least, was the threat that nuclear planners—in the absence of definitive intelligence on Soviet missile forces—believed they confronted. Unlike with bombers, however, no defense against ballistic missiles existed, and for a number of years the United States lacked any system to detect Soviet launches until the missiles had gotten dangerously close to the US mainland. These concerns raised the importance of maintaining as many US nuclear forces on constant alert as possible, putting additional stress on the NC3 system. Nevertheless, as films such as *Dr. Strangelove* and *Fail-Safe* from the 1960s emphasized, keeping human decision-makers in the loop needed to remain a top priority. Advances in automated communications, computing, and launch detection increased the capabilities, while introducing complexities, glitches, and "ghosts" within the NC3 system.

The period from 1957 to 1991 witnessed dramatic NC3 changes as early warning evolved from ground-based radars to space-based infrared satellites and communications moved from land lines and simple radio links to computer signals and satellites. The Soviet threat also shifted from a combination of slow bombers and relatively inaccurate intercontinental ballistic missiles (ICBMs) to a modern triad force combining much more capable bombers, dozens of nuclear-powered submarines, and increasingly accurate ICBMs carrying multiple nuclear weapons. Such conditions would cause some US military thinkers in the late 1970s and early 1980s to mirror claims of the 1950s that the Soviet Union might be capable of a "disarming" first strike against US nuclear forces.[1] While others criticized this viewpoint, noting in particular the inevitable retaliation possible from stealthy and survivable US nuclear submarines, faith in the concept of "mutual assured destruction" and the stability of nuclear deterrence that had emerged in the late 1960s now seemed at risk.

This chapter examines how the advent of ballistic missiles posed new challenges to the US NC3 system, requiring new responses. Throughout the period from 1957 to 1991, the NC3 network struggled to meet new technological demands to operate effectively against an ever-increasing Soviet nuclear arsenal, often with an inadequate budget. While the détente era in the early to mid-1970s and the first US-Soviet arms control agreements provided a brief respite from the steady arms racing of the 1950s and 1960s, the Soviet deployment of its first multiple independently targetable reentry vehicles (MIRVs)—following earlier US deployments—marked a particular new threat, allowing Moscow to pass the United States in overall warhead numbers for the first time. The decision under President Ronald Reagan to expand the US nuclear arsenal and to research a radical new approach to security (the Strategic Defense Initiative, or SDI) pushed fears of a new nuclear crisis to a peak not seen since the 1962 Cuban Missile Crisis. By the late 1980s, however, reforms under Soviet general secretary Mikhail Gorbachev and the resumption of arms control created conditions that reduced threats to their lowest levels since the beginning of the Cold War. The Soviet breakup in 1991 finally ended the Cold War and ushered in a decade of unprecedented arms reductions and cooperative security approaches, including US-Soviet military-to-military and laboratory-to-laboratory collaboration in the dismantlement of Soviet nuclear delivery systems and the safeguarding of nuclear materials.

Technological innovations such as electronic miniaturization, the shrinking size and increasing power of computers, and ongoing advances in satellite technologies interacted synergistically to allow considerable improvements in America's NC3 system over the decades. These were critical upgrades given the diversification of the US nuclear force structure and the increasingly complex war plans in the missile age. All these changes placed new and more challenging requirements on NC3 in terms of situation monitoring, early warning, message trafficking to and from national security leaders, and tracking and coordinating strike forces.

EFFECTS OF THE MISSILE REVOLUTION

The Soviet Union's test of its first long-range ballistic missile (the R-7) in August 1957, followed by its launch of the Sputnik satellite in October, created a wholly new and more dangerous threat than that posed previously by slow, long-range Soviet bombers. US military planners now had to deal with the prospect that a Soviet ballistic missile would soon be able to deliver a powerful hydrogen bomb against any major US city or military installation within twenty to thirty minutes of launch. Moreover, the existing US early-warning system would be useless against such high and fast-moving objects.

The evolved Soviet threat forced the United States to redouble its efforts to improve readiness, reduce vulnerabilities, and build survivable communications and command posts. The speed of the attack shortened the time to relocate people, and the power of the hydrogen bomb reduced the confidence that burying facilities underground would save them, thus putting a new emphasis on possible mobile command posts to prevent a decapitating attack. This meant pursuing both airborne and seaborne command and control systems. By the early 1960s, these efforts would lead to the fielding of the first National Emergency Airborne Command Post on EC-135 aircraft and the National Emergency Command Post Afloat on USS *Northampton* and USS *Wright*.[2] The Army's entry into the mobility competition—a rail-based nuclear command post—was rejected by the Dwight Eisenhower administration.[3]

The Soviet missile threat also spurred US efforts to diversify its nuclear weapons delivery systems beyond bombers. In 1957 the Air Force began tests of the liquid-fueled Atlas missile, eventually deploying the intercontinental-range Atlas D in vertical gantry launchers in 1959. Later versions were stored horizontally in aboveground coffin shelters. However, both deployment configurations were highly vulnerable to attack, even with conventional weapons. The Atlas also utilized highly flammable liquid fuels, which had to be loaded just before launch. Under Maj. Gen. Bernard Schriever, commander of the Western Development Division of the Air Research Development Command, the Air Force continued research on solid-fuel missiles (the planned Minuteman); the Titan missile, which could be stored with a full load of liquid fuel; and underground-silo launch facilities that would reduce the vulnerabilities associated with storing missiles out in the open. The US military also began deploying nuclear-armed intermediate-range Thor missiles in the United Kingdom and Jupiter missiles in southern Europe, all pointed at the Soviet Union. Finally, Strategic Air Command (SAC) began to experiment in 1958 with continuous airborne alert of elements of its B-52 bomber force. Keeping a portion of the B-52 fleet airborne and fully armed at all times became a standing SAC policy in 1960. The level of effort associated with this type of operation was staggering. By 1960 SAC had grown to two hundred and fifty thousand personnel and thousands of aircraft.[4]

Thanks to the hard-driving efforts of Adm. Hyman Rickover, the Navy also worked to create a survivable sea-based nuclear deterrent. The Navy put to sea its first nuclear-powered submarine (USS *Nautilus*) in 1954. After a difficult process of research and development of missiles and launch mechanisms, the Navy deployed its first nuclear-powered ballistic missile submarine (SSBN) in 1960, USS *George Washington*, equipped with sixteen single-warhead Polaris missiles.[5] The United States now had a nuclear triad force (bombers, intercontinental ballistic missiles [ICBMs], and submarine-launched ballistic missiles [SLBMs]), which could help guarantee against a possibly debilitating attack against any individual leg of its strategic deterrent. The submarine force, particularly given its nuclear propulsion (which ended the need to surface to charge batteries, as with prior diesel boats), promised to provide stealth and survivability. Nevertheless, the early Polaris missiles lacked both intercontinental range and accuracy, forcing their deployment close to Soviet shores and making their weapons useful mostly as retaliatory or countercity weapons. SAC, however, failed in its effort to convince the Navy to put the SSBN fleet under a new, unified command. Instead, the Navy successfully argued for its own control over its ballistic missile submarines, leading to continued frictions and coordination problems with the Air Force that lasted through the end of the Cold War. The Army also retained separate command over its battlefield weapons, causing other difficulties.

The vast expansion of the nuclear arsenal, which by 1960 surpassed twenty thousand warheads under three services, created major problems in terms of target duplication. To combat this nuclear overkill and to prevent potential fratricide of incoming US weapons, the Eisenhower administration ordered the creation of the Single Integrated Operational Plan (SIOP). In order to facilitate this coordinated effort, the Joint Chiefs of Staff created the Joint Strategic Target Planning Staff at SAC in 1960 to help integrate Army and Navy nuclear operations with those of the Air Force.[6] The first SIOP it created, however, only consolidated the various targets sets; it did not eliminate duplication or provide limited attack options to the president. Part of the problem encountered in building flexibility into the SIOP was the difficulty of ensuring NC3 in the midst of a nuclear war. As a result, the initial SIOP envisioned a rolling set of attacks that would be generated by various nuclear delivery vehicles as they became available, with all units being used in the attack, and no forces being held back once the initial order had been issued.[7]

KENNEDY AND THE CHALLENGES OF "FLEXIBLE RESPONSE"

The John F. Kennedy administration entered office with the aim of more actively combating Soviet aggression around the world by opposing Soviet premier Nikita Khrushchev's support for so-called wars of national liberation. Regarding nuclear weapons, President Kennedy set aside information from his intelligence community indicating that the Soviets possessed a relatively small nuclear force and went ahead with a US nuclear buildup. At the same time, he tasked his secretary of defense, Robert McNamara, to examine US nuclear planning and provide the administration with "flexible response" options against the Soviets, preferring to fight limited wars whenever possible. But McNamara's initial discussions with SAC planners yielded shock and frustration, as the existing nuclear plan provided for only a "one-shot" war, meaning that all nuclear weapons would be used once the war began.[8] A core obstacle to providing options, according to his top military advisers, was that the United States only had a one-shot NC3 system. In other words, the military had no confidence that it would be able to continue to transmit orders once a nuclear conflict had begun, due to the vulnerability of existing communications to physical destruction of the largely aboveground command and control facilities, degradation of communications from electromagnetic pulse (EMP) effects from nuclear explosions, and doubts about the ability of the top civilian leadership to survive the opening nuclear attacks. For these reasons, nuclear war meant firing everything at once and hoping for the best.

US NC3 upgrades continued to advance as projects begun under President Eisenhower began to come to fruition. The Worldwide Military Command and Control System established more reliable communication links in 1962, tying the National Command Authority (the president and other national leaders authorized to make decisions on the use of military force) to both unified and specified commands and their individual communication systems.[9] In addition, the various mobile command facilities had now begun to function under both Air Force and Navy auspices. New computer technology allowed the stand-up of the Semi-Automatic Ground Environment network, which linked air defense radars from multiple sites along the northern, eastern, and western borders of the United States, but these aboveground facilities remained highly vulnerable to attack and of limited use in tracking incoming Soviet missiles (versus aircraft), now deemed to be the most significant threat. By 1963 the US military began to decommission stations along the Distant Early Warning Line as it moved to replace them with more advanced antimissile radars in Thule (Greenland), Fylingdales Moor (United Kingdom), and Clear (Alaska), which were to form the new Ballistic Missile Early Warning System. Nevertheless, serious doubts remained about providing US military and civilian leaders with stable communications once nuclear weapons were used, due to the outright destruction of critical facilities and likely disruptions to remaining links caused by EMP effects generated by nuclear detonations.

In terms of nuclear strategy, the Kennedy administration sought to move beyond what it believed to be an unrealistic policy of "massive retaliation" toward a more credible policy of "flexible response," whether by nuclear or conventional means. Early in the administration, it also sought to reduce the potential for escalation by declaring a "no cities" policy, meaning that it would seek to attack only Soviet *military* targets early in a conflict and call upon the Soviet Union to do the same.[10] President Kennedy argued that this would reduce incentives for escalation and might keep future wars limited. Nevertheless, such a policy—from the view of the armed services—was tantamount to a counterforce doctrine, meaning that the objective of early attacks would be to render the Soviet military incapable of attacking the United States. As a result, each of the services requested increases in its nuclear forces in order to accomplish this counterforce mission. SAC's leader, Gen. Thomas Power, stated that he would need ten thousand Minuteman missiles to carry out the new doctrine.[11] (Congress eventually supported a figure of one thousand missiles.) To the Soviet Union, the policy appeared to be geared to the development of a US first-strike capability. Given an approximately ten-to-one US advantage in nuclear weapons and the presence of significant forward-deployed US nuclear forces in Europe and Asia, the Soviets saw themselves at a major disadvantage and responded negatively to the new doctrine.

Although a serious US-Soviet crisis over the status of Berlin in the summer of 1961 nearly led to conventional hostilities, the Soviet decision the following summer to begin stationing nuclear-tipped ballistic missiles in Cuba created the world's first (and most serious) nuclear crisis. After US intelligence detected the facilities, the Kennedy administration demanded that they be dismantled, using a naval blockade to enforce its demands. In the face of local US conventional superiority and strategic nuclear advantages, Soviet leader Nikita Khrushchev eventually backed down. But events during the crisis highlighted a number of troubling gaps in the US NC3 system as well as more general concerns about crisis stability. A US U-2 aircraft doing air sampling to detect possible nuclear tests inadvertently strayed into Soviet airspace over the Chukotka Peninsula, causing Soviet aircraft to scramble and leaving Soviet officials to ponder whether the intrusion might be part of a US attack.[12] Crews at Vandenberg Air Force Base conducted a routine test launch of an ICBM in the midst of this hair-trigger crisis, despite the fact that some units at the site had been armed with nuclear weapons and that such a test might appear to the Soviets to be an attack.[13] In addition, General Powers, at SAC, decided on his own to broadcast via an open channel an order to bomber, tanker, and missile forces to raise the threat level to defense condition 2 (the second-highest level), in order to warn the Soviets that the United States meant business.[14] President Kennedy had no knowledge that SAC had ordered such a message to be sent in the clear, assuming instead that General Powers's order to raise the threat level was being done via secure channels. In addition, the Atomic Energy Commission conducted a number of nuclear weapons tests in the atmosphere and in space during the crisis, any one of which could have been mistaken for a nuclear attack.[15] Finally, analyst Scott Sagan raises the possibility that senior military leaders might have taken "matters into their own hands" under the assumption of the earlier predelegation authority granted by Eisenhower in especially threatening circumstances.[16] This could not help but raise concerns in the Kennedy White House. As nuclear historian Eric Schlosser summarizes, "the SIOP was centralized, inflexible, and mechanistic. The pre-delegation order was exactly the opposite."[17]

On the Soviet side, a Soviet surface-to-air missile crew in Cuba defied Moscow's orders and shot down a U-2 taking photos of nuclear installations under construction on the island.[18] A Soviet submarine captain, whose boat was being challenged with percussion charges as it neared the US blockade of Cuba, nearly launched a nuclear-tipped torpedo at the US vessel dropping the explosives. His action was blocked only by the opposition of another senior officer, whose consent was required to authorize a nuclear launch.[19] In sum, the Cuban Missile Crisis exposed gaps in both nations' command and control capabilities and highlighted the risks of possible accidental nuclear war.

Following the crisis, the two sides made progress over the next year on a range of issues aimed at stabilizing the nuclear arms race: (1) signing the Partial Nuclear Test Ban Treaty (1963), prohibiting nuclear weapons testing in the oceans, air, and space (but not underground); (2) establishing a hotline between Moscow and Washington to speed communication between the two capitals in any future crisis; and (3) resolving at the United Nations to ban the stationing of any weapons of mass destruction in space. These measures promised to improve future crisis stability and reduce certain NC3 challenges.

JOHNSON AND MAD

Following the assassination of President Kennedy in November 1963 and Vice President Lyndon Johnson's assumption of the presidency, the United States continued to seek ways to stabilize the arms race and to ensure survivability of the US NC3 system in a crisis. The rhetoric emanating from the Pentagon began to highlight the importance of *preventing* rather than winning a nuclear war. With the US nuclear arsenal nearing its peak of 31,255 deployed weapons in 1967,[20] the Department of Defense (DOD) had begun implementing a series of measures aimed at improving both positive control (ensuring reliable ability to use) and negative control (prevention of unauthorized use) within the arsenal. Serious concerns about the reliability of US control over weapons at various overseas sites was receiving growing attention. At some bases in Western Europe, a single enlisted soldier armed with "an old-fashioned, bolt-action rifle" was the only thing standing between a "fully assembled Mark 7 bomb" and its possible seizure by infiltrators or its unauthorized use by allied forces.[21] As a result, the Pentagon issued new requirements, including the two-man rule for nuclear handling and special codes for arming weapons, called Permissive Action Links.[22] The Navy established its Take Charge and Move Out aircraft command system, which used low-frequency communications to reach US nuclear-armed submarines around the globe. The Air Force's airborne command centers also developed the capability to directly launch nuclear weapons from silos within line-of-sight of the aircraft.[23] Another system developed during this time was the Emergency Rocket Communications System, which placed a radio transmitter atop a Minuteman ICBM. The purpose of the rocket was to ensure the delivery of orders to ground units in cases where land-based communication links had been destroyed.[24] The system remained in use from 1967 to 1991, when satellite communications made it obsolete.

Despite these developments, the rising costs of the Vietnam War and McNamara's skepticism about "arming our way" out of conflict with the Soviet Union led to a gradual move toward the acceptance of the emerging situation of mutual assured destruction. In essence, the DOD was coming to terms with the likelihood that the Soviet Union would eventually achieve parity with the United States and that more weapons alone would not improve US security. Instead, McNamara moved to begin talks with the Soviet Union on limiting anti–ballistic missile defenses (just then being developed by both sides) in order to prevent the escalation of the arms race into defensive systems and, by implication, a need for more offensive weapons to overcome them. But the talks made only limited progress under President Johnson's tenure and had to be resumed by his successor, Richard Nixon.

NC3 AND DÉTENTE

The security strategy developed by National Security Adviser Henry Kissinger for President Nixon focused on great-power management of the international system and US-Soviet détente, with a major reliance on arms control to reduce US defense expenditures, which were escalating because of the ever-increasing costs of conducting the war in Vietnam. Nixon's nuclear policy came to be known as "sufficiency," and the administration accepted the notion of nuclear parity with Moscow, at least in abstract terms. Nevertheless, secretly it continued to develop new MIRVs for its long-range ICBMs and SLBMs. The first major US-Soviet arms control treaty—the 1972 Strategic Arms Limitation Treaty (SALT)—focused on freezing the number of launch vehicles on both sides. The United States accepted limits of 1,054 ICBM launchers and 656 SLBM launchers, levels that remained almost unchanged through the end of the Cold War. Bombers—where the United States had an advantage—were not included in the first SALT agreement (due to the complexity of counting loaded bombs), for which the United States compensated the Soviets by allowing them higher missile launcher numbers. The US side also aimed to continue deploying MIRVed ICBMs (the Minuteman III) and SLBMs (such as the ten-warhead Poseidon missile), thus increasing its arsenal of strategic warheads while remaining compliant with the SALT limits on launchers. But US defense planners failed to think through fully the implications of eventual Soviet development of MIRV technology, which was all but inevitable.[25]

In the Anti–Ballistic Missile Treaty, also signed in 1972, both sides agreed to forgo national missile defenses in order to prevent the escalation of the arms race, as each side recognized it would have to build even more offensive forces to counter the other side's defenses. The treaty allowed site defenses of one hundred interceptors at two locations—to protect either the national capital or an ICBM base. In 1974 the two sides altered the treaty to allow just one site. The Soviets had built an anti–ballistic missile facility with nuclear-tipped interceptors near Moscow, and the United States had deployed nuclear-tipped Spartan and Sprint interceptors at the ICBM base at Grand Forks, North Dakota. By 1976 high operational costs, fears of EMP effects if the system were ever used, and the perceived ineffectiveness of the interceptors against Soviet MIRVed missiles led US officials to dismantle the Grand Forks facility, although a tracking radar remained at the base.

A critical capability underlying the Nixon administration's confidence in the ability to engage in arms control and still defend the United States lay in the strengthening of the US missile early-warning network: specifically, the deployment of the first-generation Defense Support Program infrared-detection satellites in geostationary orbit in 1971. The Defense Support Program satellites, able to detect the hot exhaust of Soviet ballistic missiles soon after launch, increased US warning time from twenty minutes to some thirty minutes, thereby modestly increasing the president's decision-making time in a nuclear crisis. The Defense Support Program satellites, located 22,300 miles above the earth, faced no threat of attack and could be counted on—unlike ground-based radars—to survive even an extended nuclear war, providing valuable warning and locational information about the origins of each salvo during an ongoing conflict. In addition, US deployment of advanced reconnaissance satellites offered the first near-real-time images of Soviet territory, with their ability to transmit images directly to ground stations electronically rather than having to wait for film capsules to be deorbited, recovered, and processed, as with the old Corona system. This capability greatly increased US confidence in its knowledge of the Soviet order of battle, particularly Soviet strategic missile sites.

As the 1970s wore on, however, the Soviet Union confounded US predictions of the speed with which they would develop MIRVed ICBMs. By 1974 the Soviets began deploying their first multiple-warhead missiles, eventually building large numbers of "heavy" SS-18 ICBMs carrying ten warheads apiece. Soviet work on improving missile accuracy and in hardening their silos caused growing concerns about the US ability to survive a Soviet first strike and target remaining Soviet missiles. The increasing number of Soviet warheads also raised new concerns about the survivability of US NC3 systems. One classified study conducted in the 1970s concluded that a focused nuclear strike by just 1 percent of the Soviet arsenal on US NC3 nodes could take out 80 percent of the US political-military nuclear command structure.[26] Communications among remaining nodes would be further degraded by EMP effects, likely worsened by command uncertainties in case of the death of the US president and other senior civilian and military leaders.

With President Nixon's resignation in 1974 over the Watergate scandal and with continuing Soviet adventurism in support of Third World communist movements, the foundations of US-Soviet détente began to crumble. Growing nuclear arsenals on both sides showed that arms control did not necessarily lead to a reduction of tensions or even of nuclear threats. New US president Gerald Ford, however, continued the focus on arms control, agreeing to a new set of launcher ceilings in the SALT II agreement, signed in Vladivostok in November 1974. But the US Senate did not ratify the new deal, believing that its terms favored the Soviet Union. Perhaps in response, the Soviets halted their previous moratorium on antisatellite weapons tests and began a series of trials using a new infrared (instead of radar) seeker, threatening to put US NC3 assets in low earth orbit, such as reconnaissance satellites, at risk.[27] Such threats might "blind" US leaders in the midst of a conflict, raising fears that critical decisions on nuclear weapons use might have to be made with severely limited information.

SOVIET MIRVS AND CARTER'S "COUNTERVAILING" STRATEGY IN EXTENDED CONFLICT

Former nuclear submariner and Georgia governor Jimmy Carter assumed the presidency in early 1977 amid growing concerns about Soviet mobile intermediate-range ballistic missiles in Eastern Europe, which targeted US allies in the North Atlantic Treaty Organization (NATO). These transporter-erector-launcher SS-20 missiles eventually carried three warheads and were hard to locate and destroy before launch, thus increasing NATO vulnerabilities. Moreover, these intermediate-range systems were not counted (or limited) under the SALT agreements. Under President Carter, who briefly attempted to convince the Pentagon to consider a much smaller all-SLBM nuclear deterrent, steps were taken to strengthen NATO resolve and capability. One misstep in this area was a proposal announced in January 1978 that the United States would deploy an enhanced-radiation nuclear weapon in Europe (publicly dubbed the "neutron bomb"), with the aim of increasing deterrence by minimizing blast damage, saving cities, and allegedly making the Soviets believe that it was more plausible that it might be used early in a conflict, compared to a larger-blast weapon. The effort backfired, however, when European populations objected to a weapon that seemed more suited to killing people rather than destroying cities, which few found reassuring.[28]

At the strategic level, the Carter administration got off on the wrong foot with Soviet general secretary Leonid Brezhnev by calling for changes in the SALT II agreement (already agreed to by President Ford). These talks dragged on for nearly the whole Carter presidency. In the meantime, the Soviet military continued to add MIRVed weapons of various sorts to its arsenal. While the United States continued to lead the Soviets in overall strategic weapons, when added to the Soviets' robust force of tactical nuclear weapons, total deployed Soviet nuclear warheads moved past the US nuclear arsenal for the first time in 1978 with 25,393 weapons.[29] Still, despite the decommissioning of many tactical weapons, the US strategic arsenal also continued to grow, especially MIRVed SLBMs, but at a slower rate overall than Soviet forces. President Carter also canceled certain high-cost weapon systems, such as the nuclear-capable B-1 bomber, which he deemed a waste of scarce US defense resources. On the other hand, extensive research continued to address feared US missile vulnerability to increasing Soviet warhead numbers and accuracy. The US Missile Experimental (MX) system planned to address these threats through a mobile basing mode that would have created thousands of miles of special roadways and some forty-six hundred shelters in Utah and Nevada to mask the exact locations of these proposed mobile missiles.[30] Nevertheless, high costs and environmental concerns eventually nixed this deployment option, leading to more conventional basing plans in existing silos.

US nuclear strategists also began to worry that in contrast to prior assumptions that the Soviet Union would quickly expend its entire nuclear arsenal in a future war, it might instead opt for a series of limited attacks, possibly linked to the seizure of West European territory with conventional forces. The result might be a protracted nuclear war in which attacks might take place over weeks or months and effective NC3 would become even more of a premium. In this context, the Carter administration developed the concept of a "countervailing" strategy that might help guide nuclear operations in an extended nuclear conflict started by Moscow, most likely in Europe.[31] In December 1979 NATO approved a plan to deploy US Pershing II intermediate-range missiles and ground-launched cruise missiles to Europe to address fears of "decoupling" the alliance in the face of the growing Soviet threat. The deployments worried Moscow because the flight time of the Pershing missile, in particular, was mere minutes to reach the Soviet capital. This raised concerns that Soviet leaders might be forced into a difficult "use them or lose them" scenario, leading to full-scale nuclear retaliation against both Western Europe and the United States, even in the case of a limited Pershing attack. Many NATO leaders hoped the missile might be negotiated away before the deployments started.

In an eerie realization of the growing tension with the Soviet Union, the North American Air Defense Command suffered a real-life nuclear scare when a training tape simulating a nuclear attack was inadvertently put into its computer system in early November 1979. For several minutes, nuclear watch officers and personnel believed that the Soviets had launched a full-scale attack, even waking up National Security Adviser Zbigniew Brzezinski in the middle of the night in case President Carter needed to be roused quickly for a possibly critical decision. Fortunately, the exercise tape was discovered a few minutes later, ending this dangerous minicrisis. But it exposed the serious NC3 risks posed by the increasing US reliance on computers and the possible human mishandling of incoming data in conditions of uncertainty.

After the Iranian seizure of the US embassy in Tehran in late November 1979, the Carter administration took a hardline turn against the Soviets, as National Security Council Director Brzezinski moved increasingly to the forefront of decision-making, eventually causing Secretary of State Cyrus Vance to resign. But the worsening global oil crisis and Moscow's continued nuclear buildup led to US feelings of impotence and growing fears of nuclear war. Carter's renegotiation of the SALT II agreement reduced the number of allowed strategic nuclear delivery vehicles on each side from the earlier 2,400 level to 2,250 and included sublevel caps for heavy MIRVed ICBMs. Nevertheless, the Soviet invasion of Afghanistan in December 1979 caused him to pull the treaty from Senate consideration in January 1980. In July the Carter administration issued Presidential Directive 59, which outlined a range of problems for US command and control in a nuclear war environment, including threats posed by EMP effects on communications and to leadership survival in the National Emergency Airborne Command Post. Under the leadership of Secretary of Defense Harold Brown, the administration laid out requirements for fighting a possibly "protracted nuclear war."[32] The trends in nuclear policy had clearly turned more ominous than during the prior détente era.

Republican presidential candidate Ronald Reagan went a step further, using fears of a "window of vulnerability" to rally support for his campaign to confront the Soviet Union and restore what he perceived as the nuclear advantage turning away from the United States.

REAGAN AND NC3 WORRIES—HOW TO "PREVAIL" IN A NUCLEAR WAR?

Ronald Reagan's victory in the 1980 US presidential election led to a major increase in US defense spending, including funding for a revived B-1 bomber program; the MX missile (originally conceived as a mobile missile but eventually deployed in a MIRVed configuration in Minuteman silos); the new, highly accurate Trident SLBM; and new NC3 systems. The Reagan administration halted efforts to pass SALT II and rebuffed Soviet proposals for space arms control, charging that Moscow was attempting to lock in its antisatellite system advantages. The White House tasked the Pentagon with publishing a yearly report, Soviet Military Power, showing the vast array of its conventional forces and tracking the current and possible future expansion of the Soviet nuclear arsenal, including the nuclear throw weight of its large missiles, its continuing progress in accuracy, and evidence of an expanding program to harden silos. Later evidence, however, revealed that neither of the latter two Soviet efforts had actually achieved as much success as the US report claimed.[33]

The new nuclear strategy of the Reagan team came out in National Security Decision Document (NSDD)-13 in November 1981 and became known as the "prevailing" concept.[34] In other words, the new administration accepted that a future nuclear war might be protracted. Accordingly, it made major investments in new ultrahardened (or buried) continuity-of-government facilities near Washington, DC. The Reagan administration insisted, however, that the United States would ultimately *prevail* in nuclear conflict by doing more than just firing back after a Soviet nuclear strike. One senior Reagan official gave comments to the media suggesting that Americans could successfully survive a nuclear war by digging a trench, covering it with a few doors, and then shoveling three feet of dirt on top.[35] The prevalence of this kind of unrealistic rhetoric led many Americans to believe that nuclear war was coming closer to reality than at any time since the Cuban Missile Crisis.

Tensions in Europe rose dramatically in 1981 as the Reagan administration began to move forward with deployment of 108 Pershing II missiles and 464 ground-launched cruise missiles in NATO countries bordering the Warsaw Pact. In the West German capital, a quarter of a million people protested this move in one of the largest public demonstrations of the postdétente era. To assuage these sentiments, President Reagan offered the Soviets a "zero option" deal: the United States would withdraw its new missiles if the Soviets agreed to withdraw their already deployed SS-20s. On their part, the Soviets attempted to win over NATO populations by adopting a "no-first-use" pledge in 1982, promising not to be the first to use nuclear weapons, implicitly putting the onus on the United States. In New York, one million people marched to the United Nations to protest rising superpower tensions. They supported calls for a "nuclear freeze" on all new systems and on further testing of nuclear weapons.

One response by President Reagan to increasing domestic pressures for a nuclear freeze with the Soviet Union was his announcement of SDI in March 1983. The stated goal of this effort was to create a space-based defensive shield to protect the United States against a Soviet nuclear attack by queuing a massive fleet of orbital interceptors stationed in low earth orbit to destroy over two thousand Soviet missiles in their boost phase, before their multiple MIRVed weapons could be released. Nevertheless, several elements of the proposed system violated the 1972 Anti–Ballistic Missile Treaty, causing conflict with the Soviet Union—whose officials viewed SDI as part of a US first-strike strategy (since, if it worked, it could potentially stop any Soviet missiles not destroyed in an initial US attack). The Democratic-controlled Congress also rejected the Reagan administration's argument that SDI did not violate the Anti–Ballistic Missile Treaty since it relied on new physical principles. They noted that the treaty actually required bilateral consultations to deal with any such new systems. SDI continued throughout the Reagan years, but none of the technologies—space-based interceptors, lasers, and rail guns—ever reached maturity or showed prospects of handling more than a fraction of the Soviet ballistic missile force that could be launched in a concerted attack.

In the NC3 arena, changes in US strategy already underway since the Carter administration to support operations in a protracted nuclear war continued to move communications into geostationary orbit, including the joint Navy–Air Force Fleet Satellite constellation. These trends marked a major positive shift in the survivability of US communications from the prior era. By the end of the 1980s, advanced sensors such as the first Lacrosse radar-imaging satellite had joined the Defense Support Program early-warning satellites in geostationary orbit, making them virtually invulnerable to Soviet attack. On the offensive side, the Air Force tested a kinetic-kill, antisatellite missile launched from an F-15 aircraft in 1985 to match Soviet capabilities against satellites in low earth orbit.

Despite these developments, concerns about nuclear crisis stability continued to worry US military leaders throughout the 1980s. Two near-crises occurred in 1983 that could have spilled over into nuclear war. In the first event, a Soviet military aircraft shot down a Korean Air Lines passenger plane with 169 people aboard, which had strayed into Soviet airspace over Sakhalin Island on the Pacific coast. Soviet military pilots apparently feared that—despite its profile—it was a US intelligence-gathering aircraft. The second involved a Soviet misinterpretation of NATO's Able Archer military exercise in November 1983 of a simulated nuclear attack in Europe as an actual offensive, which Soviet officials only later realized was just a drill. These superpower crises highlighted the dangers of overreaction in a world of increasing nuclear mistrust.

Frustrated by US actions and wanting to send a signal to both Washington and West European populations, the Yuri Andropov–led government in Moscow began a boycott of talks on European nuclear forces. The move raised superpower tensions further and, for NATO countries, meant that no progress would be made toward halting the ongoing deployments of new US nuclear forces on their soil. Soon the Soviets announced that they were walking out of the strategic nuclear arms control talks as well.

Over the course of Reagan's two terms in office, the emphasis on nuclear warfighting led to a vast expansion of the target list in the Soviet Union, the Warsaw Pact countries, and China. Perhaps not surprisingly, the 1982 Nuclear Weapons Employment Policy's emphasis on "prevailing" caused the military services to expand their target sets in order to ensure adequate destruction of Soviet and allied targets in order to guarantee victory. But the effect, according to one senior DOD official, was that SIOP targeting had gotten "out of control."[36] As a result, during Reagan's second term, Secretary of Defense Caspar Weinberger initiated specific revisions of his guidelines to rein in excessive targeting practices. These new procedures were finally established by the time of the 1987 version of the US Nuclear Weapons Employment Policy.[37]

Soviet nuclear policies also had begun to undergo major changes. Following Brezhnev's death in 1983 and the quick succession of two elderly, ailing, and ineffective Soviet leaders (Andropov and Konstantin Chernenko), the Politburo elected the reformer Mikhail Gorbachev in March 1985 to serve as general secretary of the Communist Party. Although hardliners in the Reagan administration initially rejected the notion that any substantive policy change would occur, Gorbachev's offer to accept the zero option and withdraw all Soviet SS-20s from Eastern Europe (in return for a reversal of US Pershing and ground-launched cruise missile deployments) began to change some Americans' minds. Indeed, at the 1986 Reykjavík summit, Gorbachev's offer to engage in deep cuts in nuclear forces leading to zero shocked Reagan officials. It was only President Reagan's refusal to bargain away SDI that prevented the two leaders from signing a deal pledging the two superpowers to a ten-year course toward eventual total elimination of their nuclear arsenals. But Reagan eagerly endorsed an Intermediate-Range Nuclear Forces Treaty in 1987, which eliminated all missiles with ranges of between five hundred and fifty-five hundred kilometers, and talks toward halving deployed strategic nuclear arsenals continued through the end of Reagan's second term. Suddenly, the nearly constant nuclear arms race that had been a hallmark of the Cold War had begun to reverse itself, thus reducing the stress on the US NC3 system.

BUSH I, ARMS CONTROL, AND FURTHER REDUCTION OF THE SOVIET THREAT

In the late 1980s, tensions in the US-Soviet nuclear relationship dropped further when Soviet leader Gorbachev failed to intervene in a series of dramatic protests and prodemocratic regime changes that swept Eastern Europe in the fall of 1989, effectively ending the Soviet Union's forty-year domination of its neighbors, followed by the collapse of the Warsaw Treaty Organization shortly thereafter. As Soviet domestic political reforms continued—with the opening of the press, economic liberalization, and the first free elections since 1917—conflicts with the United States receded, as did the threat of nuclear war. These conditions allowed President George H. W. Bush to reach a historic arms control agreement in the summer of 1991 with Gorbachev in the Strategic Arms Reduction Treaty (START) to cut deployed strategic forces from around 12,000 warheads on each side to 6,000 weapons. The sublimits of the treaty included ceilings of 1,600 for strategic delivery systems, 4,900 for ICBM warheads, and 154 for heavy ICBM launchers. For the first time, the treaty included intrusive, on-site verification of the destruction of delivery systems on both sides.

To further reduce the threat of nuclear war and its likely consequences, the two presidents announced parallel unilateral statements in the fall of 1991, which removed all nuclear weapons from surface ships, eliminated additional short-range nuclear forces (including artillery shells) from army units in Europe, and withdrew short-range missiles from East Asia. These withdrawals and the eastward movement of Soviet-controlled borders created a feeling of security in Europe not enjoyed since the end of World War II.

Nevertheless, the very processes of reform begun by Gorbachev had begun to spin out of control by late 1991. The fifteen constituent national republics—now free to elect their own leaders—began to declare their independence from the Soviet Union, beginning with the Baltic states and culminating in December 1991 with the simultaneous withdrawal of Russia, Kazakhstan, Ukraine, and Belarus (all of them with Soviet strategic nuclear weapons), effectively ending the existence of the Union of Soviet Socialist Republics. The Russian Federation, under Boris Yeltsin, inherited the bulk of the Soviet nuclear arsenal, although with the challenge of retrieving weapons from the remaining three nuclear-inheriting states.

For the United States, the unexpected end of the Cold War brought new concerns. Although US nuclear planners had remained prepared for nuclear war against the Soviet Union right until its end, the country's breakup into fifteen separate governments, four of which (including Russia) had nuclear weapons under questionable conditions of security, created wholly new fears: the theft of nuclear weapons or fissile material and inadvertent or even accidental nuclear war. In anticipation of these problems, legislation that came to be known for its two Senate cosponsors (Sam Nunn and Richard Lugar) initiated a revolutionary new program to assist the Soviet Union and, after December 1991, the four newly independent states (Belarus, Kazakhstan, Russia, and Ukraine) with strategic nuclear weapons on their soil to dismantle their delivery systems and remove the warheads to safe storage to ensure their compliance with the START I Treaty. As a result of the Nunn-Lugar legislation, DOD began the Cooperative Threat Reduction Program, which successfully dismantled thousands of nuclear delivery systems during the course of the 1990s, with the remarkable cooperation of the Russian military and nuclear laboratories as well as their counterparts in Belarus, Kazakhstan, and Ukraine. A corresponding initiative under the US Department of Energy, the Material Protection, Control, and Accounting Program, helped secure sensitive nuclear facilities throughout the former Soviet Union where fissile material had been left in unsecured laboratories, reactors, and other sites.[38]

A process of winding down the Cold War nuclear buildup also began in the United States. Congressional passage of the 1990 Base Reduction and Closure Act led to the gradual shuttering of dozens of nuclear-related facilities, including missile bases, air bases, and submarine facilities, as the United States removed thousands of nuclear weapons and their associated delivery systems from its arsenal. While the process caused economic hardship in a number of areas of the country, Congress also provided defense conversion funds to help these communities recover from their Cold War dependence on military expenditures and create new sources of local employment.

By contrast, in the former Soviet Union, the process of reversing the Cold War, disassembling weapons, and destroying delivery vehicles proved time-consuming, costly, and in some cases very risky. The once strong Soviet Union now featured many weak states incapable of providing physical security at many sites. Gates and fences fell into disrepair, guards abandoned their jobs due to lack of salaries, and storage facilities never meant to house large numbers of retired weapons overflowed, with nuclear armaments sometimes literally left outside to rot. Without the Nunn-Lugar program, the end of the Cold War could have been far worse and led to dangerous proliferation or even actual nuclear use.

In the United States, the process of coming into compliance with START I and reducing the vast arsenal that had built up during the Cold War proved safer and more orderly. Nevertheless, the three main US nuclear laboratories—Los Alamos, Sandia, and Lawrence Livermore—all took on new responsibilities for assisting in this process while also sending experts to help supervise assistance programs performing the same mission in the former Soviet states.

Regarding NC3, the Bush administration initiated a process that envisioned a new, unified command to replace SAC, the Joint Strategic Targeting Planning Staff, and the Navy command which together had controlled US strategic nuclear operations since the 1960s. In 1992 the Bush administration stood up US Strategic Command (STRATCOM), finally bringing all US nuclear forces under one authority. But although STRATCOM created a more centralized system, it did not eliminate the inherent challenges of communicating with and directing widely dispersed US strategic forces in the midst of a nuclear conflict, particularly one that might be extended over days, weeks, or months.

The 1990s would pose new challenges to US security, especially in regard to the proliferation of nuclear and missile capabilities. In the US-Russian context, Moscow cooperated in reducing its strategic nuclear weapons even further. Nuclear testing in both countries also halted during the Bush administration and, with the signing of the Comprehensive Nuclear Test Ban Treaty in 1996, would not resume (although the Senate failed to ratify the agreement in a vote held in 1999). But continued tensions on the Korean Peninsula, in the Persian Gulf, and in South Asia—where India and then Pakistan tested a series of nuclear weapons in 1998—meant that nuclear deterrence and NC3 remained key tasks for the US military, despite the end of the Cold War. Missile proliferation by North Korea and Iran, combined with troubling nuclear programs in both countries, presaged a future environment fraught with uncertainty.

CONCLUSION

The evolution of the US NC3 system during the Cold War closely followed changes in US nuclear capabilities and the evolving foreign (especially Soviet) threat. As the US nuclear force structure diversified, new types of delivery systems presented their own operational requirements and conflicting time constraints on NC3 systems and procedures. Increasingly complex war plans, including a variety of target "withholds" and enduring attack options, also placed new and challenging requirements on NC3, which now had to retain significant functionality deeper into an ongoing nuclear exchange. Factors internal to the US political system (including budget limitations) and the US military (such as interservice rivalries) also affected NC3 structures and policies. Operators struggled throughout the period to try to protect the nation amid often uncertain early warning, questions about the viability of NC3 assets under conditions of nuclear war, and changes in US strategy. Fortunately, the end result was peaceful, although various crises—both externally and internally generated—tested the NC3 system in specific periods, sometimes leading to reforms.

The fact that NC3 systems often lagged rather than led nuclear technology changes and alterations in the US and Soviet force structures should give one pause. The notion that a nuclear war might have been fought under poorly controlled conditions rendered reasonable predictions about the outcome and the prospects for US victory (however defined) dubious. Of course, the same or worse could have been said about the Soviet NC3 system. At the same time, just as uncertainties and understandable fears about the effects of nuclear explosions on each nation led to caution, the very unpredictability of the NC3 system may have caused at least some US (and possibly Soviet) leaders to exercise greater restraint in crises. This may not give great comfort but should spur the US military to be cognizant of what factors might well remain beyond its control in a future nuclear conflict.

Advances in technology have now mitigated several concerns that NC3 faced during the Cold War. At the same time, vulnerabilities introduced by the Internet and cyber warfare techniques on the part of US adversaries have created new threats. Thus, as during the Cold War, NC3 challenges remain, and the target is a moving one. These points should be sobering, and tasks in the NC3 sector should be undertaken both with a sense of humility and with the utmost seriousness. The nuclear weapons enterprise and ideas about the possible resort to nuclear war must only be considered in full recognition of the multiple risks entailed by any nuclear action, particularly when multiple uses of weapons over an extended period of time are being considered. As shown in the past, the importance of training, exercises, and an appreciation for what could go wrong should be guiding themes for the education of the NC3 workforce and its employment for its most important mission: effective *deterrence* of nuclear warfare.

NOTES

1. On the analysis of such groups as the Committee on the Present Danger, see John Newhouse, *War and Peace in the Nuclear Age* (New York: Knopf, 1989), 296.
2. L. Wainstein, C. D. Cremeans, J. K. Moriarty, and J. Ponturo, *The Evolution of U.S. Strategic Command and Control and Warning* (Arlington, VA: Institute for Defense Analyses, June 1975; declassified September 15, 1992), 234.
3. Wainstein et al., 235.
4. Wainstein et al., 169.
5. Lisle A. Rose, *Power at Sea: A Violent Peace, 1946–2006* (Columbia: University of Missouri Press, 2007), 58.
6. Sandia National Laboratories, "U.S. Strategic Nuclear Policy: A Video History, 1945–2005," disk 2: 1954–64, National Security Archive, George Washington University, http://www.gwu.edu/~nsarchiv/nukevault/ebb361/index.htm.
7. Sandia National Laboratories, disk 2.
8. Sandia National Laboratories, disk 2.
9. Wainstein et al., *Evolution of U.S. Strategic*, 392–405.
10. Lawrence Freedman, *The Evolution of Nuclear Strategy*, 3rd ed. (New York: Palgrave Macmillan, 2003), 224–26.

11. Robert S. Norris, Steven M. Kosiak, and Stephen I. Schwartz, "Deploying the Bomb," in *Atomic Audit: The Costs and Consequences of U.S. Nuclear Weapons since 1940*, ed. Stephen I. Schwartz (Washington, DC: Brookings Institution Press, 1998), 189.
12. Scott D. Sagan, *The Limits of Safety: Organizations, Accidents, and Nuclear Weapons* (Princeton, NJ: Princeton University Press, 1993), 136–37.
13. Sagan, 79.
14. Sagan, 68–69.
15. James Clay Moltz, *The Politics of Space Security: Strategic Restraint and the Pursuit of National Interests*, 3rd ed. (Stanford, CA: Stanford University Press, 2019), 134–35.
16. Sagan, *Limits of Safety*, 149–50.
17. Eric Schlosser, *Command and Control: Nuclear Weapons, the Damascus Incident, and the Illusion of Safety* (New York: Penguin, 2013), 207.
18. Newhouse, *War and Peace in the Nuclear Age*, 184.
19. William Burr and Thomas S. Blanton, eds., "The Submarines of October: U.S. and Soviet Naval Encounters during the Cuban Missile Crisis," National Security Archive Electronic Briefing Book 75, October 31, 2002.
20. Robert S. Norris and Hans M. Kristensen, "Global Nuclear Weapons Inventories, 1945–2010," *Bulletin of the Atomic Scientists*, July/August 2010, 81.
21. Schlosser, *Command and Control*, 258.
22. Sagan, *Limits of Safety*, 106.
23. Wainstein et al., *Evolution of U.S. Strategic*, 335.
24. Wainstein et al., 336.
25. Newhouse, *War and Peace in the Nuclear Age*, 203.
26. DOD report from 1972, cited in Wainstein et al., *Evolution of U.S. Strategic*, 414.
27. Nicholas L. Johnson, *Soviet Military Strategy in Space* (New York: Jane's, 1987), 150.
28. Newhouse, *War and Peace in the Nuclear Age*, 310–11.
29. Norris and Kristensen, "Global Nuclear Weapons Inventories," 81.
30. Norris, Kosiak, and Schwartz, "Deploying the Bomb," 186.
31. Freedman, *Evolution of Nuclear Strategy*, 387.
32. Sandia National Laboratories, "U.S. Strategic Nuclear Policy: A Video History, 1945–2005," disk 3: 1965–83, National Security Archive, George Washington University, http://www.gwu.edu/~nsarchiv/nukevault/ebb361/index.htm.
33. On this evidence, see Pavel Podvig, "The Window of Vulnerability That Wasn't: Soviet Military Buildup in the 1970s," *International Security* 33, no. 1 (Summer 2008): 118–38.
34. Freedman, *Evolution of Nuclear Strategy*, 388.
35. Undersecretary of Defense Thomas K. Jones, cited in Schlosser, *Command and Control*, 445.
36. Sandia National Laboratories, "U.S. Strategic Nuclear Policy: A Video History, 1945–2005," disk 4: 1984–2003, National Security Archive, George Washington University, http://www.gwu.edu/~nsarchiv/nukevault/ebb361/index.htm.
37. Sandia National Laboratories, disk 4.
38. On these programs, see Jason Ellis, *Defense by Other Means: The Politics of US-NIS Threat Reduction and Nuclear Security Cooperation* (Westport, CT: Praeger, 2001).

PART II

FOUR

US NUCLEAR COMMAND, CONTROL, AND COMMUNICATIONS
AN OVERVIEW

Jeffrey A. Larsen

On October 25, 1962, at the height of the Cuban Missile Crisis, a bear climbed over a fence at a military base near Duluth, Minnesota. Sensors activated warnings of a potential Soviet incursion at airfields in the region, causing pilots at Volk Field, Wisconsin, to rush to their nuclear-armed fighters in preparation for an alert launch. Fortunately, the base commander at Volk contacted Duluth to confirm the alert prior to launching his fighters and discovered it was a false alarm.[1]

On June 6, 1980, four nuclear-armed B-52 Stratofortresses, ten KC-135 Stratotankers, and a pair of F-106 Delta Dart interceptors were on nuclear alert at Loring Air Force Base in northern Maine. The klaxons sounded, and crews abandoned their softball game to rush to their aircraft. As the engines were being started, the message from Strategic Air Command (SAC) was decrypted as a "survival launch"—meaning the crews were ordered to get their planes in the air and figure out what was happening later. This same message was received at all four SAC bases in the northeastern United States because North American Air Defense Command (NORAD) computer screens at Cheyenne Mountain, Colorado, showed inbound Soviet intercontinental ballistic missiles (ICBMs) heading for that part of the country. Because this was the third such warning in less than a year, common sense prevailed and none of the nearly sixty aircraft on alert launched from any of the bases, including B-52s and FB-111s loaded with multiple nuclear weapons. It was later determined that a software glitch in the NORAD computers was the cause of the alert message.[2]

On September 26, 1983, at a time of increased tensions between the Soviet Union and the West, including the Soviet shootdown of a Korean Air Lines passenger plane and the ongoing Able Archer exercise of the North Atlantic Treaty Organization (NATO), a Soviet command post computer suddenly warned that multiple ICBMs were coming over the North Pole from the United States. Fortunately, the Soviet commander of the post decided to wait to see if it was a real attack rather than suggest to his superiors that they launch an immediate retaliatory strike based solely on electronic warning. It turned out he was right to do so because the Soviet early-warning satellites had been spoofed by sunlight reflecting off cloud cover.[3]

On January 13, 2018, alarms were sounded across Hawaii announcing an impending nuclear missile strike, clearly stating that "this is not a drill." Panic ensued, but it turned out to be a false alarm. An employee of Hawaii's Emergency Management Agency had accidentally pushed the wrong button at his computer station.[4]

In each of these cases, a false warning led policymakers, military personnel, and members of the public alike to question what appeared to be legitimate alert messages of an impending attack. This highlights the vital importance of a nation's nuclear command, control, and communications (NC3) network. Such a system must be accurate, timely, and redundant; it cannot afford to fail, even (and especially) when under stress. The fact that these four scenarios took place across six decades implies that while the United States relies on its NC3 system for early warning and communications and as the backbone of its deterrence strategy, problems remain within the complex systems that control nuclear forces.

The nuclear deterrence forces of the United States have been developed over the past seventy-five years to deter any adversary from attacking the US homeland, its forces deployed abroad, its allies and partners, and its other vital national interests around the globe. In this mission, many would argue, American nuclear forces and policies have been successful. There has been no major great-power conflict since World War II, and the United States has retained its position as a leading superpower.

Deterrence requires both the capability to threaten what potential adversaries hold most dear and the capability to demonstrate convincingly to them that one has the willingness to carry out that threat. The combination of these two elements will theoretically dissuade a rational actor from taking any first step toward war, for fear of the consequences if they do. US deterrence strategy since the late 1940s has relied on the credible threat of nuclear weapons use. The ultimate authority for the release of American nuclear weapons rests in the hands of the president. Deterrence requires America's political leadership to be aware of the pertinent details surrounding any situation, to make timely decisions, and to be able to communicate those decisions with the appropriate forces. The command and control (C2) of nuclear forces is a vital piece of the

US deterrence mission, and communications is the necessary link to ensure C2 over those weapons under all conditions.

NC3 thus provides the links between nuclear forces and presidential authority. It enables nuclear command and control (NC2) through a system of early-warning satellites, radars, and sensors; facilities to collect and interpret early-warning information; fixed and mobile networked command posts; and a communications infrastructure that includes land lines, satellite links, radars, radios, and receiving terminals in ground stations and aboard strike vehicles; and the shooters themselves, the nuclear triad of delivery vehicles. On paper, NC3 is a simple concept; in reality, it is a huge and diverse set of systems that must serve a single customer and a single purpose. It must not fail.

Despite this responsibility and the centrality to US national security that this would imply, NC3 systems today face multiple challenges after more than two decades of neglect of America's nuclear forces and NC3 infrastructure. However, the United States is beginning a major modernization effort of all three legs of the nuclear triad as well as the underlying and critical NC3 systems.[5] Indeed, some analysts call NC3 the "fifth pillar" of the US nuclear deterrent, after the three legs of the triad and nuclear weapons themselves.

This chapter reviews the legacy NC3 system of the United States as it developed since the early Cold War but with greater emphasis on the past three decades since the end of that conflict. The system that unfolded over the past three generations is in the midst of a sea change. In late 2018 the secretary of defense appointed the commander of US Strategic Command as the enterprise lead for NC3 and its next-generation architecture. The need to ensure robust existing capabilities for the current system, plus the desire to create a new system that is more than a simple modernization of existing capabilities, in a world facing more diverse threats, all while harnessing the value added by new technologies, means that the NC3 system twenty years hence may bear little resemblance to its current arrangement.

NC3: LEGACY OF THE ANALOG AGE

America's NC3 system was last updated in the 1980s.[6] It is a vintage system created in a predigital world and in an ad hoc manner that had no master plan or deliberate design. In fact, NC3 is a collection of parts that were basically cobbled together as they came online, reflecting new systems that were created to address new needs as they arose, rather than an organized and efficient system of systems. As a recent government study explained, "There is no one NC3 system. The NC3 system as it exists today is a patchwork of disparate systems, each with its own characteristics. There is no one operating system or coding language."[7] This is the antiquated system on which American security rests today.

From the beginning of the nuclear age, several elements of what we today call the NC3 system were well recognized. Decision-makers needed as much information about an attack as possible, as early as possible, in order to decide on an appropriate course of action and to get the retaliatory forces safely away before being destroyed along with their bases. This was the essence of deterrence: the need to maintain a secure second-strike capability. In order to meet this requirement, the United States began developing and deploying networks of early-warning radars to warn of a Soviet air (and eventually missile) attack; created planning and targeting organizations to develop response options in order to save time in a crisis; procured cutting-edge aircraft, missiles, submarines, and land- and sea-based forces to carry out retaliatory strikes; and established duplicative communication systems (radios in multiple frequencies and, later, digital information), including building terrestrial transmission and receiving stations, designing secure coding and emergency action message systems, and training operators in their use. All of this effort was meant to ensure that no matter what happened, at least one form of communication could be maintained with US forces (the so-called thin line). The final element was the management and logistic capacity to maintain all these elements of the nuclear deterrent mission. It was a massive undertaking.

The ultimate purpose of NC3 was to identify an attack, provide that information to the president, and then relay his instructions back to the forces in the field. As a recent Air Force Doctrine pamphlet put it, "Because only the President can authorize the employment of US nuclear weapons, nuclear operations require NC3 systems to provide national leaders with situational awareness, advance warning, and command and control capabilities. Deterrence, stability, and escalation control require that these capabilities endure during and after nuclear attack so that no adversary is capable of a disarming first strike."[8]

The NC3 System in Action: A Scenario

As an example of how the system was designed to operate, consider a scenario from Cold War years in which a radar in northern Canada spots a squadron of Soviet bombers coming across the Arctic, heading south. It would relay this information to the command center in Cheyenne Mountain, Colorado. Once the information was validated by another source (so-called dual phenomenology), the warning would be transmitted to SAC headquarters in Nebraska, to the National Military Command Center in the Pentagon, and to the president, wherever he might be. The president and his senior advisers would then hold a telephone conference to determine their response, and the coded response message would go out to the bombers, submarines, ICBMs, and other forces on alert around the globe. This would be accomplished in part by using the special communications link and codes carried by a military officer near the president at all times (the so-called nuclear football). The orders to launch some portion or the entirety of the alert force would go from the president through SAC headquarters and then via dedicated communication systems to the crews, who would use their own codes to validate the message before launching their aircraft or firing their missiles. The ensuing fight would be coordinated (to the extent that would have been possible in a nuclear environment) through various communication channels and follow-on orders from the national command authority.

Such was the plan for managing deterrence and nuclear war. And as missile capabilities improved throughout the Cold War, the time available to do all these steps continued to shrink. In the beginning, however, few of the necessary elements to make this concept workable were even in place.

The Evolution of the NC3 System of Systems

In the early 1950s, as the Cold War began, the United States faced intelligence gaps due to a shortage of early-warning systems. The first portion of the NC3 system to be put in place, therefore, was the series of Distant Early Warning (DEW) radars begun in 1955 by the United States and Canada to warn of an incoming Soviet bomber attack. A network of fifty-seven separate radar stations stretched from the Aleutian Islands across northern Canada to Greenland. Development efforts accelerated after the Soviet Sputnik launch in 1957, but a rudimentary C2 system was not in place until the late 1950s, more than a decade after the development of the first atomic bomb. Prior to that point, the plan was to use commercial telephone networks and long-range radios to notify bases hosting nuclear armed bombers of their orders. President Dwight Eisenhower created a Minimum Essential Emergency Communications Network in the 1958 National Defense Reorganization Act. The necessity for such a communication system was obvious as the number of US nuclear weapons grew from a handful at the beginning of the 1950s to some twenty-five thousand operational warheads by 1959, with more joining the inventory every year. Despite presidential direction, the Air Force and the Navy developed incompatible systems and infrastructure that could communicate solely with their own forces.[9] Each of the military services jealously guarded their particular communication systems and targeting priorities, rather than coordinating with one another. SAC, despite its central role in providing deterrence for the country, was an Air Force command and was unable to convince the Navy to pursue unified C2 or targeting.

The system developed its modern appearance during the 1960s with the addition of a National Military Command System (NMCS), a Worldwide Military Command and Control System, and a more responsive architecture capable of ensuring C2 over a growing triad of forces: ICBMs, submarine-launched ballistic missiles (SLBMs), and strategic bombers. This C2 network, the NMCS, was in place by 1962. Tying all this together between the three nuclear services was the Joint Strategic Target Planning Staff and its primary product, the Single Integrated Operational Plan. This plan, first introduced in 1961, was put in place by the secretary of defense in order to coordinate Air Force, Navy, and Army tactical targeting and C2. It continued to inform nuclear planners with regularly updated versions for the next thirty years. The United States also began developing more survivable C2 systems and centers, including the Alternative National Military Command System Command Post at Fort Ritchie, Maryland; the Cheyenne Mountain Complex in Colorado Springs, Colorado; and airborne command posts for the president and for military leaders from SAC and the Navy.

The United States and Canada established NORAD in 1957 and began enhancing their early-warning systems in the far North. These included the DEW line radars and the establishment of "Texas Tower" radar stations in the North Atlantic Ocean. Improved over-the-horizon radars called the Ballistic Missile Early Warning System were also built in Thule, Greenland; Clear, Alaska; and Fylingdales Moor, United Kingdom. And NORAD created the Semi-Automatic Ground Environment (SAGE) system as a centralized C2 network that would link data from early-warning satellites and the DEW line to air defense systems across North America. The twenty-four SAGE centers were provided with the first IBM mainframe computers, the fastest and most capable computers of the day.[10] SAC was soon linked into the SAGE notifications as well. SAC also built a large underground command post at its headquarters in Omaha, Nebraska, albeit one that realistically would have provided little protection from a direct nuclear attack.

Many of the systems and concepts introduced in the 1960s are still being used today. The first Defense Support Program satellite for ballistic missile launch warning was launched in 1971; that system also remains a primary element of American early-warning efforts. In addition, new satellite systems were being placed in orbit that could provide enhanced intelligence, surveillance, and reconnaissance information. These would eventually include the Space-Based Infrared Radar System. Yet, even in 1970, there were noticeable deficiencies in US early-warning systems. Undersecretary of Defense William Perry argued at the time that NC3 was "perhaps the weakest link in our strategic forces today."[11] These concerns were enhanced by the growth of Soviet missile stockpiles, many with multiple independently targetable reentry vehicle warheads, and antisatellite capabilities that threatened the survivability of the US strategic arsenal and associated NC3 systems.

In response, the United States again recognized a need to modernize its NC3 and early-warning capabilities. Major upgrades to NC3 took place in the

Ronald Reagan administration nuclear buildup of the early 1980s. Improvements included renovated and modernized underground command posts at SAC headquarters and the alternate NMCS site for continuity of operations and continuity of government, the initial deployment of the Global Positioning System satellite constellation, and better hardening against electromagnetic pulse (EMP) effects in sensors and receivers.[12] The United States also added three radars of the Precision Acquisition Vehicle Entry Phased Array Warning System (PAVE PAWS) along America's coasts (in California, Massachusetts, and Florida) to the nation's early-warning system. The objectives of NC3 modernization during this period were threefold: to improve the capability and redundancy of the NC3 system in case of a surprise attack, to provide a more thorough and detailed assessment of an attack to policymakers, and to improve the endurance and survivability of the NC3 system in order to be better prepared to fight a longer nuclear war—a result of thinking in the Jimmy Carter administration that was codified in Presidential Directive 59 on nuclear doctrine and policy.[13]

Such dire predictions and the need for enhanced NC3 capabilities led the Reagan administration to pursue measures to deal with shortfalls in the system. It added redundant and survivable early-warning and communication systems, including global positioning satellites, EMP hardening, upgrades to the NMCS, extremely low frequency communications antennas for reaching submerged nuclear submarines, and mobile command posts in trucks as backups to the airborne command posts. All these efforts addressed the objectives for a modernized system but at the cost of greater complexity and yet more systems that needed to work together without a master plan describing the best way to do so.

Following the end of the Cold War, NC3 systems faced the same twenty years of neglect as did nuclear forces and deterrence thinking in general. SAC was disestablished in 1992, replaced by US Strategic Command. The new command quickly found itself nearly overwhelmed with major missions in addition to deterrence, and nuclear forces and NC3 systems soon found themselves at the bottom of the priority list. The world was breathing a sigh of relief at the end of the Cold War, and the dramatically reduced emphasis on nuclear weapons, deterrence, and related matters seemed to much of the world to be a well-deserved "peace dividend" following forty years of expense, worry, and danger. Nevertheless, this neglect had consequences. For example, the US Air Force had to deal with a series of embarrassing mistakes involving the movement of nuclear weapons in 2006 and 2007. Investigative reports that followed recommended a national commitment to keeping deterrence and nuclear understanding alive, including the need for a renewed look at NC3.[14] The Air Force created Global Strike Command, headquartered at Barksdale Air Force

Base, Louisiana, as a way of restoring an organization with a singular focus on these matters, with the new command expected to carry on a role similar to the central role played by SAC during the Cold War.

The terrorist attacks on the United States on September 11, 2001, gave further credence to the need for modern early-warning and C2 systems that could operate in the modern world, even in situations not involving nuclear attack. Concerns grew over the possibility of further attacks by rogue states or violent nonstate actors that could undermine America's deterrent capabilities. One result of these concerns was the US decision to withdraw from the Anti–Ballistic Missile Treaty in 2002. Chinese and Russian military modernization and behavior in the years that followed caused further concern and raised the stakes for US homeland security and its ability to carry out global military operations when necessary.

Given the time since the last major upgrades and the return of great-power competition, the need for a major reconsideration of how best to organize US NC3 is obvious. Many of its systems are outdated and require modernization or replacement. Senior leadership in the US government and the Pentagon have recognized this deficiency for more than a decade, based on studies such as the 2002 Scowcroft Commission Nuclear Command and Control System End-to-End Review and the 2009 Federal Advisory Committee Nuclear Command and Control System Comprehensive Review.[15] It was not until 2014, however, that a Council on Oversight of the National Leadership Command, Control, and Communications System was established by Congress. This committee effort was a step in the right direction but not enough to satisfy the secretary of defense, leading to the 2018 decision to designate the commander of US Strategic Command as the go-to individual responsible for NC3 operations and modernization. The 2018 Nuclear Posture Review called for a major upgrade of aging American NC3 systems over the coming years.[16] The commander of US Strategic Command summed up the situation he faced in 2014: "Assured and reliable NC3 is critical to the credibility of our nuclear deterrent. The aging NC3 system continues to meet its intended purpose, but risk to mission success is increasing. Our challenges include operating aging legacy systems and addressing risks associated with today's digital security environment. Many NC3 systems require modernization, but it is not enough to simply build a new version of the old system."[17]

DEFINITIONS

According to the Congressional Research Service, the Nuclear Command and Control System "collects information on threats to the United Sates, communicates that information through the chain of command to the President, advises the President on options for a response, communicates the President's chosen response to the forces in the field, and controls the targeting and application of those forces."[18] In order to accomplish these missions, according to the Pentagon's *Nuclear Matters Handbook*, NC2 represents a complex concept with numerous critical functions:

- Situation monitoring—including the ability to collect intelligence, assess a threat, provide tactical warning and attack assessment to decision-makers, and give them updates on the readiness levels of US forces. This includes gathering and sharing information on friendly forces, adversary forces, and potential targets as well as global events of interest. The hardware requirements to do all of this are broad and demanding.
- Planning—developing war plans, including the use of nuclear weapons, so as to minimize decision time in a crisis or conflict. This may also entail adaptively planning responses during a crisis.
- Decision-making—senior military and political leaders assessing the situation, consulting through communications conferences, and considering the use of nuclear weapons in certain scenarios.
- Force management—assigning, maintaining, training, and supporting nuclear weapons, nuclear delivery vehicles, and support forces; maintaining force readiness; and ordering the dispersal or deployment of nuclear forces.
- Force direction—NC3 enables NC2 by ensuring the accurate transmission of messages executing lawful strike orders with US strategic nuclear forces or terminating operations at the end of a conflict.[19]

The disparate elements of NC3 support the NC2 mission and boil down to three things: *understanding* the situation, *deciding* what to do, and then *doing* it.

NC3 has three major capability requirements that enable it to accomplish its mission of support to national C2. First, it must provide assurance and security. This means the capability to operate with certainty to ensure information availability, integrity, authentication, confidentiality, and repudiation.

Second, the system must be reliable. It must have the capability to perform its intended functions at required levels for a specified interval, under stated conditions.

Finally, it must show resilience. This is the capability to withstand, operate through, or recover quickly from difficult and unpredictable or adverse situations, conditions, or environments—the most stressful of all being thermonuclear conflict.

In 2016 the Air Force decided to identify its NC3 system as a weapons system, labeled AN/USQ-225. According to Joint Publication 3-0, a weapon system is "a combination of one or more weapons with all related equipment, materials, services, personnel, and means of delivery and deployment required for self-sufficiency."[20] The Air Force recognized that such a designation was not a perfect fit for a large, complex system of systems like NC3, but it was the best they could come up with to highlight NC3's importance and address the multitude of issues and lines of effort necessary to ensure it meets the rigid specifications enumerated above. Depending on whom you ask and how they count, the US NC3 system consists of as many as 160 different systems: satellites, aircraft, command posts, communication networks, land stations, radio receivers, and so on—a system of systems perhaps too complex for any one person to totally understand. The Air Force NC3 Center alone is responsible for sixty-two distinct subsystems. US Strategic Command wants a simpler and more flexible system to come out of the ongoing modernization effort.

TECHNOLOGICAL ELEMENTS OF NC3

Given its size, complexity, redundancy, and criticality to the nation's survival, it is no surprise that the NC3 system has multiple parts. It may be easiest to envision it as the systems and connections shown in the simplified graphic in figure 4.1.

Warning systems include space-based satellites and ground radars that provide early warning of an adversary missile launch or potential attack. These include the legacy Defense Support Program satellite constellation, the newer Space-Based Infrared System, the Nuclear Detonation Detection System and sensors, and the future Third Generation Infrared Sensors. They also include terrestrial systems such as the Ballistic Missile Early Warning System, over-the-horizon backscatter radars on the three coasts of the mainland United States (now retired), PAVE PAWS radars on the US coasts and in Alaska (now mostly retired), the Cobra Dane phased-array radar installation in Alaska, the Perimeter Acquisition Radar Attack Characterization System in North Dakota, possibly the radar elements of the European Phased Adaptive Approach missile-defense system being deployed by NATO, and the radars of the Terminal High Altitude Area Defense, Aegis, and Patriot missile-defense batteries now deployed widely. New systems such as the Long-Range Discriminating Radar and the Army/Navy Transportable Radar Surveillance and Control Model 2 (AN/TPY-2) are in the developmental stage, and the Missile Defense Agency is designing a global Command, Control, Battle Management, and Communications (C2BMC) network to enable greater communications for missile defense and battle management.[21] Together, these provide an overlapping set of networks that can quickly identify and attribute any missile launch directed at North America as well as identify the intended target and possibly even the makeup of the delivery package.

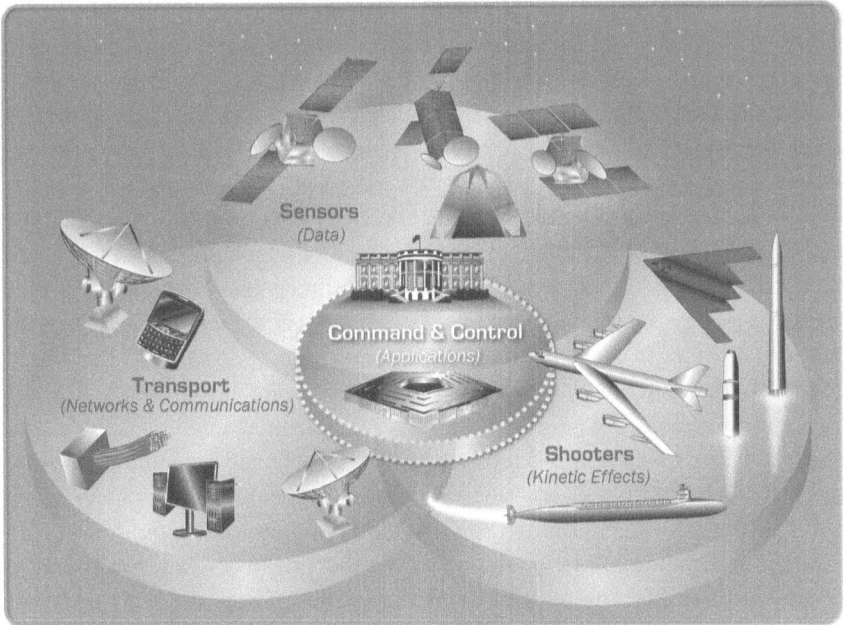

FIGURE 4.1. The US Nuclear Command and Control System. *Source: Nuclear Matters Handbook: 2016* (Washington, DC: Office of the Deputy Secretary of Defense for Nuclear Matters, 2016), 78, available at https://www.lasg.org/Nuclear-Matters-2016.pdf.

Terrestrial and transport systems are land-based receiving stations for the data provided by satellite networks, the physical and electromagnetic means of delivering that data to the appropriate centers for analysis, and the command posts that provide political decision-makers with recommendations and advice. If necessary, they also provide a secure conduit for orders to US strike forces. These are connected by communications transmitters and receivers that operate across the entire electromagnetic spectrum, from extremely low frequency to ultra-high frequency. Each frequency band has characteristics that make it more or less suitable in different environments. Some bandwidths are easier to jam or spoof; some work (or fail to work) following an EMP or in an atmospheric scintillation environment; some offer greater fidelity or quantity of real-time data.[22] As a result, the Air Force and Navy have over the decades developed multiple means of receiving data and sending transmissions to their forces so that they can reach the bomber crews, missile crews, and submarines in any scenario. This requires a multitude of satellite constellations, each designed and deployed to take advantage of a particular capability. It also requires several different terrestrial antennas of varying sizes, including massive extremely low frequency arrays for communicating with submerged submarines. Each frequency requires the proper communications equipment for both transmission and reception. Size and weight limits often constrain how many types of systems a strike vehicle can carry. In the case of submarines, the underwater environment limits which of these will be most effective in reaching the crew.

Warfighting systems constitute the three legs of the triad: bombers, ICBMs, and SLBMs. These three distinct systems, each of which provides the United States with a guaranteed second-strike capability against any adversary, buttress deterrence and preclude a rational actor from attacking the United States in the first place. They also reduce the risk of technological surprise that might otherwise threaten any one of the legs of the triad. For the United States, the current triad consists of approximately sixty-six manned, nuclear-capable strategic bombers (B-2s and B-52s) with gravity bombs and air-launched cruise missiles, four hundred Minuteman III single-warhead ICBMs, and fourteen *Ohio*-class fleet ballistic submarines, each carrying up to twenty SLBMs with multiple independently targetable reentry vehicles.[23] The US Department of Energy ensures that the military services providing these delivery platforms are equipped with nuclear warheads for delivery on the orders of the president. These weapons systems form the backbone of US deterrence—but they cannot be used without a secure NC3 system in place to get launch orders to them. All three legs of the triad are scheduled to be replaced with modernized systems in the next fifteen to twenty years, requiring new communication links and possibly new NC3 systems to support them and their missions.

ORGANIZATIONAL STRUCTURE

The NMCS (sometimes also called the National Command and Control System) connects all the functions of NC2, using a multitude of systems that capture intelligence, provide early warning, transmit the information to the decision-makers, control strike forces, and relay decisions back to those forces as necessary.

The NMCS includes several core platforms and nodes. Ground stations to gather the information from space-based assets are located across the globe, including the National Military Command Center in Washington, DC; the Alternate National Military Command Center in Maryland; the Global Operations Center at US Strategic Command, Offutt Air Force Base, Nebraska; Headquarters North American Aerospace Defense Command (as renamed in 1981) and the Cheyenne Mountain Complex in Colorado Springs; and the large early-warning radars located across North America and Europe. It also includes airborne platforms, which are primarily dedicated to C2 of strike forces, such as the Air Force E-4 National Airborne Operations Center (a modified Boeing 747) and the Navy's E-6 Mercury Take Charge and Move Out (TACAMO) fleet of Boeing 707s.[24] There are also several types of land-based mobile backup centers.

The current responsibility for NC3 missions, equipment, personnel, training, acquisition, and maintenance is dispersed across numerous Department of Defense (DOD), Navy, and Air Force agencies and commands. The complexity and challenge of handling all of those elements was one reason for the recurring demand in official reports over the past decade that the DOD needed to reform the governance of the NC3 system. This process began several years ago, after similar recognition by the Air Force—which has been the lead authority for some 70 percent of all NC3 systems—that the system was basically a mess of parallel, overlapping, and complex parts that had little oversight or common vision. Over the years, the Air Force had simply added new capabilities whenever a requirement was identified, resulting in a large set of early-warning and communication networks that often worked independently of one another. The rationale for every system was legitimate and fulfilled an identified operational need, but the resulting spaghetti bowl of systems was not one any rational analyst would have created.

The US Navy is considerably more tight-lipped about all things nuclear than the Air Force. The Navy has designated the chief of naval operations as the responsible authority for the Navy nuclear deterrence mission, with the director of Strategic Systems Programs responsible for providing direction and guidance on the safety and security of Navy nuclear weapons and systems as well as the broader deterrence mission. NC3 operations fall under the deputy chief of naval operations for information warfare and the associated Navy NC3 Executive Steering Committee.[25] The Navy's TACAMO aircraft are now equipped with the airborne launch-control system so that they could serve as a backup to the Air Force National Airborne Operations Center if a situation required one of them to launch Minutemen ICBMs. They are equipped to communicate with US Strategic Command, the president, strategic bombers, and submerged ballistic missile submarines.[26]

In an effort to rationalize its organization regarding NC3, the Air Force has been tasked with modernizing the program for more than a decade. The 2010 Nuclear Posture Review called for modernizing legacy NC3 capabilities.[27] In 2012 the Senate Armed Services Committee questioned the piecemeal approach to NC3 being taken by the DOD. This was backed by a 2013 RAND Corporation study that pointed out the lack of coherent oversight of NC3.[28] As a result, in 2014 the National Defense Authorization Act required the DOD to establish a national oversight council for NC3. This council would sit at a much higher level than the Air Force. Nevertheless, criticism and recommendations continued: in 2013 and 2014 reports by the Government

Accountability Office (GAO) pointed out problems within the NC3 community.[29] In congressional testimony in 2014, the commander of US Strategic Command and an Air Force Scientific Advisory Board study both highlighted NC3 challenges and modernization requirements and made recommendations for improvement.[30]

As a result of this flurry of studies and recommendations, in 2014 the Air Force chief of staff issued new instructions for the NC3 enterprise.[31] This top-down direction resulted in numerous organizational changes over the following three years. First, NC3 was designated as a weapons system, with Global Strike Command, headquartered at Barksdale Air Force Base, assigned as the mission area lead command. Air Force Materiel Command established an NC3 Integration Directorate in the Air Force Nuclear Weapons Center at Kirtland Air Force Base, New Mexico, supported by the NC3 Analysis Directorate, also located at Kirtland. Training and education of new members of the NC3 team is handled by the NC3 Center at Barksdale.[32] All of this NC3 activity, spread across the nation and involving all eight Air Force commands, was to be coordinated by the NC3 Integration Directorate, located at Hanscom Air Force Base, Massachusetts.[33]

In 2016 and 2017 new national defense authorization acts provided additional direction to the Air Force on nuclear weapons and NC3. The Air Force was more invested in modernizing its NC3 systems than it had been in decades, but it still faced outside scrutiny. In 2017, for example, a GAO report claimed that most US Air Force efforts were focused on current systems vice future needs, patching existing systems rather than thinking about future requirements and new ways of doing business.[34] In 2018 the National Defense Authorization Act required US Strategic Command and the DOD to focus on NC3-related issues, resulting in direction by Secretary of Defense James N. Mattis to Gen. John E. Hyten, commander of US Strategic Command, to tackle this problem as the sole officer responsible for US NC3 systems effective October 2018.[35] This same decision named the deputy secretary of defense and the chairman of the Joint Chiefs of Staff as points of contact overseeing the NC3 enterprise, with US Strategic Command as the lead agency for making changes.

The future relationship between US Strategic Command and the Air Force in these matters is still being determined, but one must assume it will be much like the existing ties in the realm of other weapons systems, such as nuclear delivery platforms provided by the Air Force (ICBMs and strategic bombers). The Air Force is the service provider, ensuring that the combatant commander has the necessary matériel and trained personnel to do the job. It is the Air Force's responsibility and mission to train, organize, and equip aerospace forces for sustained combat operations. NC3 would likely become one more weapon that the Air Force will continue to provide—and one that it is already managing. The US Navy has a parallel mission to provide fleet ballistic missile submarines and SLBMs in the event of war.

CHALLENGES TO THE US NC3 SYSTEM

As highlighted in various US policy documents, the international setting is much changed since the Cold War and the interregnum that followed the end of that long faceoff. Today the United States faces a world of great-power competition and potential conflict, one that is more complex than the Cold War, with multiple nuclear powers and a growing number of pathways that might lead to war between nuclear-armed states. The NC3 system reflects the effects of neglect since the end of the Cold War, including the significant loss of expertise in all matters nuclear within the personnel system of the armed services. Furthermore, there is an inefficient diffusion of authority and responsibility for NC3 governance within the DOD. Fortunately, a consensus has developed since the Barack Obama administration's call for nuclear modernization as part of the Prague agenda he announced in 2009. The DOD, US Strategic Command, and the Air Force are now working diligently to overcome years of neglect.

Operationally, NC3 faces a number of significant challenges, all of them difficult and most of them inherent to nuclear weapons more broadly. First, the NC3 system must meet the "always-never" criteria. Just as nuclear weapons must always work when ordered to by legitimate authority and never go off accidentally or without proper authorization, so too must the NC3 system comply with this fundamental law of nuclear operations. NC3 must *always* be able to execute a legitimate order to employ nuclear force, under all circumstances. This is known as positive control. At the same time, NC3 must under all circumstances *never* allow the nuclear force to be used accidentally or by an illegitimate authority. This is known as negative control. Both are critical to deterrence.

NC3 must also be capable of operating in a second-strike mode—in other words, after the nation has absorbed a first strike, possibly without prior warning, and potentially one including nuclear weapons. This is clearly the most demanding scenario, with all the attendant characteristics of a nuclear environment in play. The system must also be able to deal with the blurred lines between conventional and nuclear command, control, and communication systems. For example, the NC3 weapons system must be able to distinguish between an adversary attack on different parts of the system during a conventional conflict and recognize whether that was part of the conventional campaign or the beginning of escalation to nuclear use. This problem is magnified when NC3 systems are dual-use. This raises questions of potential miscalculation and accidental escalation due to problems of entanglement. It may be quite difficult to determine an adversary's intentions when it strikes a dual-use system that knocks out a portion of America's nuclear NC3 capabilities. Was that a prelude to a nuclear strike or an attempt to blind conventional forces in a regional scenario?

NC3 must also be able to survive "left-of-launch" efforts to degrade its capabilities. These preconflict operations may include cyberattack, EMP effects generated by a high-altitude nuclear burst, or even direct kinetic attack on ground-based or space-based elements of the network by hypersonic weapons, precision-guided conventional weapons, or antisatellite weapons. The system must also be resilient enough to withstand possible insider threats, such as espionage or sabotage by disaffected individuals.

The current NC3 system is also reliant on the US civil infrastructure that provides electricity, water, and other logistic requirements to terrestrial bases that host NC3 receiving stations and command posts. This makes that element of NC3 subject to any break in service on the civilian side. The system is not completely autonomous.[36] Reliance on civilian infrastructure also places the NC3 weapons system within a "cyber context" that in theory subjects NC3 to threats that did not exist during the analog age.

The current age of the American NC3 system requires nearly across-the-board modernization. The world has transitioned from analog systems to a new digital reality, yet the US NC3 system remains primarily analog since it was designed prior to the age of personal computers, networked systems, and the Internet. Ironically, this means that the legacy system is actually *less* prone to cyberattack and thus more secure than many more modern systems. Nevertheless, it is outdated. Decision-makers today demand ever-increasing amounts of information, including real-time photographic and video downloads from NC3 systems, thus requiring ever-increasing bandwidth capabilities. There will be a need to mate the NC3 systems necessary in the cockpits and command capsules of the future, as the United States fields new delivery platforms across the triad over the next ten to twenty years. As the triad is modernized, delivery systems will rely on digital command and communication systems; it is difficult to imagine creating a smooth interface between the NC3 weapons systems and nuclear delivery systems without eliminating most legacy analog systems. And there is a need to replace lost expertise within the workforce that designs, builds, deploys, maintains, and operates NC3 systems, despite being able to draw on an increasingly sophisticated civil research, development, and manufacturing base for modern digital platforms.

The 2018 Nuclear Posture Review highlighted several initiatives required to modernize the US NC3 system and maintain its capabilities into the future. These recommendations, listed below, are valid and necessary. The challenge will be to create and maintain congressional interest in the project so that funding is available to finish the job. Absent a clear and present danger to the nation, Congress is notoriously fickle when it comes to funding long-term, multiyear national security programs. This may be particularly true today when Congress has already committed to replacing all three legs of the strategic triad, a trillion-dollar exercise over the coming decade. Despite the emphasis on the need to modernize NC3 in the face of new challenges and to ensure the best possible C2 of the new strategic forces in a more complex world, one can expect some pushback from legislators. NC3 modernization will not be inexpensive. Nevertheless, it will cost less than replacing any of the legs of the strategic nuclear triad, and none of those will work as planned without modernized NC3.

RECOGNIZING THE NEED FOR MODERNIZATION

While the world has become a more complex and diverse place since the end of the Cold War, the US NC3 system has not changed much to adapt to these new realities. Given the increasing number of potential threats, the challenge to American space-based assets, the rise in cybersecurity challenges, increased vulnerability to network attack in newer NC3 systems, and the requirement to meet the NC3 needs of an entirely new triad of nuclear forces, it is clear that the NC3 system of the 2030s will be very different from today. This adds yet another layer of demands on planners as they think about what might work best in the future vice simply improving the system in place—which was originally designed, after all, for a more straightforward 1960s missile and bomber threat from a country that no longer exists.

Efforts to modernize America's NC3 system began in earnest in the latter part of the first decade of the 2000s, to a large extent in response to the embarrassing incidents involving loss of control over nuclear weapons and nuclear-related materials by the US Air Force.[37] From 2010 to 2014 there were numerous reports by Congress and outside agencies that identified multiple problems within the US nuclear complex in general and the NC3 system in particular, which led to a bipartisan commitment to fixing those issues.

The 2017 National Security Strategy of the United States highlighted the need to "maintain the credible deterrence and assurance capabilities provided by its nuclear triad and US theater nuclear capabilities deployed abroad."[38] This meant that significant investment would be needed to maintain the nuclear arsenal and its supporting infrastructure and to modernize the nuclear enterprise. This also meant that "modernization and sustainment require investing in the aging command and control system."

Many of the requirements for a next-generation NC3 system were enumerated in the 2018 Nuclear Posture Review.[39] According to the report, the initiatives required to modernize the NC3 system include the following:

- strengthening protection against space-based threats by increasing the agility and resilience of US NC3-related space-based assets
- strengthening protection against cyberthreats
- enhancing integrated tactical warning and attack assessment by upgrading sensors and satellites that provide this information
- improving command posts and communications links by upgrading mobile command posts, ground command centers, and transmitters and terminals
- advancing design-support technologies to support better and faster decision-making
- integrating planning and operations at the regional combatant commander level
- reforming governance of the NC3 system.

The secretary of defense and the chairman of the Joint Chiefs of Staff took on the last item right away by designating the commander of US Strategic Command as the NC3 enterprise lead and giving the undersecretary of defense for acquisition increased responsibilities for NC3 systems engineering and integration. Strategic Command's NC3 Governance Improvement Implementation Plan was approved in October 2018. This plan focuses on NC3 and its modernization as an "enterprise of enterprises," encompassing the military services and other stakeholders in NC3 in an organized, holistic approach to determining and fielding the NC3 system of the future. As is already the case in the US Air Force, this approach will consider NC3 as a weapons system on par with the other parts of the nuclear triad. The two primary imperatives of the enterprise are to continue operating the current NC3 enterprise within established performance parameters, including the five critical mission functions and the "always-never" requirement and, second, to prepare and deliver a more rational and better-designed next-generation NC3 system. One danger in pursuing such a large modernization effort is the requirement to continue using and updating the "as-is" architecture while simultaneously building the "to-be" system. In the near term, this must be the requirement of any modernization program: to sustain existing capabilities until the new architecture is in place. Another danger is that modernization may mean increased complexity, which in turn may actually reduce America's security.[40]

CONCLUSION

America's NC3 system faces a number of operational and policy challenges. Operationally, there have been persistent challenges to mission fulfillment, including inadequate warning and response time, evolving threats, survival of the chain of command, timely delivery of orders, bomb-damage assessment, and communicating with follow-on forces during a conflict. From a policy perspective, the NC3 system has faced the impact of interservice rivalries and suspicions, the high cost of survivable NC3 systems, the long lead times for deployment of new systems, changes in the nature of America's adversaries (and even in who those adversaries are), uneven federal budgets, typically low and diminishing interest in national security affairs by the nation's leaders, changes in US strategies, and political relations with allies. Many of these challenges interacted in the three decades since the end of the Cold War to create a reduced level of interest, or sense of priority, in fixing the legacy system on which US security rests. Once state-of-the-art, the NC3 system today is subject to challenges from aging system components and new, growing twenty-first-century threats. In the past several years, fortunately, there appears to be an awareness across government that this danger must be addressed.

Sustainment of America's existing critical capabilities and acquisition of modernized systems are core requirements to maintaining the nation's strategic deterrence mission. The credibility of the US nuclear deterrent relies on its ability to be "believably resilient" to any attempt to disrupt US NC3 by an adversary. There is a national consensus today that the US NC3 enterprise needs to be modernized, and the DOD has made US Strategic Command responsible for the enterprise and its future. The US Air Force, as the preponderant force provider for the national military C2 system and its NC3 system, will be the military service most responsible for those modernization efforts. The US Navy will have equivalent responsibilities for its smaller but equally critical NC3 system connecting decision-makers with America's nuclear ballistic missile submarine fleet.

Some big questions that were looming over this effort have recently been answered in the affirmative. It is clear that beyond short-term sustainment, the United States needs a better version of the NC3 system than that which has been in place for the past sixty years. With congressional support, all involved agencies are now pursuing newer and better ways to accomplish the NC3 mission and enable it to support American security well into the future. There is consensus that the system is too big to continue patching while hoping for the best and too critical to the nation's survival to get wrong.

NOTES

This chapter is based on a revised version of a paper presented at a workshop at Stanford University on January 22–23, 2019, sponsored by Technology for Global Security, the Nautilus Institute, and Stanford's Preventive Defense Project, on "NC3 Systems and Strategic Stability: A Global Overview." The paper was posted as "Nuclear Command, Control, and Communications: U.S. Country Profile," NAPSNet Special Report, August 22, 2019, at https://nautilus.org/napsnet/napsnet-special-reports/nuclear-command-control-and-communications-us-country-profile/.

1. Recounted in Scott Sagan, *The Limits of Safety: Organizations, Accidents, and Nuclear Weapons* (Princeton, NJ: Princeton University Press, 1993), 3.
2. Author's recollections as a KC-135 pilot in SAC on alert at Loring Air Force Base that day. Also covered by Sagan, *Limits of Safety*, in the section titled "NORAD's 1979 and 1980 False Warnings," 225–46.
3. See Greg Myre, "Stanislav Petrov, 'The Man Who Saved the World,' Dies at 77," National Public Radio, September 18, 2017, https://www.npr.org/sections/thetwo-way/2017/09/18/551792129/stanislav-petrov-the-man-who-saved-the-world-dies-at-77.
4. See Emily Stewart, "Hawaii's Missile Scare 'Reminds Us How Precarious the Nuclear Age Is,'" Vox, January 14, 2018, https://www.vox.com/policy-and-politics/2018/1/14/16890148/hawaii-missile-false-alarm.
5. Amy F. Wolf, *U.S. Strategic Nuclear Forces: Background, Developments, and Issues*," CRS Report RL33640 (Washington, DC: Congressional Research Service, January 3, 2020).
6. For more in-depth consideration of the development of NC3 and its impact on US nuclear policy and forces more generally, see Clay Moltz's history in chapters 2 and 3 of this volume. A good short overview of the history of the US NC3 system can be found in David A. Deptula and William A. LaPlante, *Modernizing US Nuclear Command, Control, and Communications* (Arlington, VA: Mitchell Institute for Aerospace Studies and MITRE Corp., 2019), http://docs.wixstatic.com/ugd/a2dd91_ed45cfd71de2457eba3bcce4d0657196.pdf. A more comprehensive and critical history can be found in numerous books, including Bruce Blair, *Strategic Command and Control: Redefining the Nuclear Threat* (Washington, DC: Brookings Institution, 1985); Sagan, *Limits of Safety*; and Eric Schlosser, *Command and Control: Nuclear Weapons, the Damascus Incident, and the Illusion of Safety* (New York: Penguin, 2013).
7. "Nuclear Command, Control, and Communications System Operational Assessment Program Solicitation, number HC10471DR4009," Defense Information Systems Agency, Procurement Directorate, August 4, 2010.
8. "Nuclear Command, Control, and Communications," in *Air Force Doctrine Publication 3-72: Nuclear Operations* (Maxwell Air Force Base, AL: Curtis E. LeMay Center for Doctrine Development and Education, Air University, updated December 18, 2020), https://www.doctrine.af.mil/Doctrine-Publications/AFDP-3-72-Nuclear-Ops/.
9. Kristin Goodwin, "Nuclear Command, Control, and Communications (NC3): Strengthening a Neglected, but Critical, Component of the US Deterrent," unpublished paper, 2015, 11.
10. Deptula and LaPlante, *Modernizing US Nuclear*, 15.
11. Quoted in Deptula and LaPlante, 18.
12. Deptula and LaPlante, 19.
13. Deptula and LaPlante, 18–19.
14. See *Report of the Secretary of Defense Task Force on DOD Nuclear Weapons Management: Phase I; The Air Force's Nuclear Mission* (Arlington, VA: Secretary of Defense Task Force on DOD Nuclear Weapons Management, September 2008),

https://dod.defense.gov/Portals/1/Documents/pubs/Phase_I_Report_Sept_10.pdf.
15. As is often the case in NC3 studies, neither of these commissions released a public report.
16. For details on US modernization plans for NC3, see chapter 9 in this volume by Michael S. Malley.
17. Adm. Cecil Haney, "Fiscal Year 2015 National Defense Authorization Budge Requests from US Forces Korea and US Strategic Command," US House of Representatives, Committee on Armed Forces, 113th Cong., 2nd sess., April 2, 2014, https://www.hsdl.org/?view&did=754624.
18. Amy Woolf, "Defense Primer: Command and Control of Nuclear Forces," Congressional Research Service, December 11, 2018, 1, https://fas.org/sgp/crs/natsec/IF10521.pdf.
19. *Nuclear Matters Handbook: 2016* (Washington, DC: Office of the Deputy Secretary of Defense for Nuclear Matters, 2016), 73–81, available at https://www.lasg.org/Nuclear-Matters-2016.pdf.
20. *Joint Operations*, Joint Publication 3-0 (Washington, DC: DOD, January 17, 2017).
21. *Missile Defense: Delivery Delays Provide Opportunity for Increased Testing to Better Understand Capability*, GAO report 19-387 (Washington, DC: Government Accountability Office, June 2019), https://www.gao.gov/assets/700/699546.pdf.
22. This really is rocket science, so I refer the reader to the excellent chapter 5 in this volume on space technologies by Matthew R. Crook.
23. The missiles on a Trident submarine can carry up to eight warheads on each missile, though it is believed that their payloads are normally smaller than that.
24. To supplement the E-6 fleet, the Navy will procure specialized C-130s as a supplement to the TACAMO mission, possibly for use from austere bases. See Gareth Jennings, "U.S. Navy to Field C-130J-30 in Nuclear Communications Role," Janes, December 21, 2020, https://www.janes.com/defence-news/news-detail/us-navy-to-field-c-130j-30-in-nuclear-communications-role.
25. "Navy Nuclear Deterrence Mission Responsibilities and Authorities," OPNAV Instruction 8120.1A, January 10, 2018, https://fas.org/irp/doddir/navy/opnavinst/8120_1a.pdf.
26. Deptula and LaPlante, *Modernizing US Nuclear*, 22.
27. *Nuclear Posture Review* (Washington, DC: White House, 2010).
28. Don Snyder, Sarah Nowak, Mayhar Amouzegar, Julie Kim, and Richard Mesic, *Sustaining the US Air Force Nuclear Mission* (Santa Monica, CA: RAND Corp., 2013), https://www.rand.org/pubs/technical_reports/TR1240.html.
29. *Nuclear Command, Control, and Communications: DOD Actions Needed to Better Assess Overall System Performance and Address Operational Gaps*, GAO Report 14-88C (Washington, DC: February 28, 2014); *Nuclear Command, Control and Communications: Review of DOD's Current Modernization Efforts*, GAO Report 14-414R (Washington, DC: March 18, 2014).
30. "Nuclear Command, Control, and Communications," US Air Force Scientific Advisory Board study, 2014, abstract at https://www.scientificadvisoryboard.af.mil/Portals/73/documents/AFD-140728-028.pdf.
31. "Air Force Nuclear Command, Control, and Communications," Air Force Instruction 13-550, October 2, 2014, https://static.e-publishing.af.mil/production/1/af_a10/publication/afi13-550/afi13-550.pdf.

32. Barksdale also hosts Global Strike Command and the Eighth Air Force with its B-52 bombers. Global Strike Command would provide bombers and ICBMs to STRATCOM in the event of conflict.
33. Author interviews at Barksdale Air Force Base and Hanscom Air Force Base, May–June 2019.
34. *Defense Nuclear Enterprise: DOD Continues to Address Challenges but Needs to Better Define Roles and Responsibilities and Approaches to Collaboration*, GAO-19-29 (Washington, DC: Government Accountability Office, November 2018), https://www.gao.gov/assets/700/695197.pdf.
35. Sandra Erwin, "U.S. STRATCOM to Take Over Responsibility for Nuclear Command, Control and Communications," *Space News*, July 23, 2018; Justin Doubleday, "STRATCOM Establishes NC3 Enterprise Center," *Inside Defense*, February 14, 2019, https://insidedefense.com/daily-news/stratcom-establishes-nc3-enterprise-center.
36. Deptula and LaPlante, *Modernizing US Nuclear*.
37. See *Report of the Secretary of Defense Task Force: Phase I*; and *Report of the Secretary of Defense Task Force on DOD Nuclear Weapons Management: Phase II; Review of the DOD Nuclear Mission* (Arlington, VA: Secretary of Defense Task Force on DOD Nuclear Weapons Management, December 2008), https://archive.defense.gov/npr/docs/DOD%20NW%20Management%20Phase%20II%20Schlesinger.pdf.
38. *National Security Strategy of the United States of America* (Washington, DC: White House, December 2017), https://www.whitehouse.gov/wp-content/uploads/2017/12/NSS-Final-12-18-2017-0905.pdf.
39. *Nuclear Posture Review* (Washington, DC: DOD, February 2018), 36–38, https://media.defense.gov/2018/Feb/02/2001872886/-1/-1/1/2018-NUCLEAR-POSTURE-REVIEW-FINAL-REPORT.PDF.
40. Deptula and LaPlante, *Modernizing US Nuclear*.

FIVE

SPACE ARCHITECTURE FOR NC3
SYSTEMS AND TECHNOLOGIES

Matthew R. Crook

On August 2, 1939, Albert Einstein and Leo Szilard penned their famous letter to US president Franklin D. Roosevelt warning that it might be possible to develop a fission weapon and that the Germans had the scientific know-how to start their own nuclear program. Both scientists described the potential destructive capability of nuclear weapons in clear terms: "A single bomb of this type, carried by boat and exploded in a port, might very well destroy the whole port together with some of the surrounding territory."[1] It also is apparent from their letter that Einstein and Szilard thought nuclear weapons would be rather large, so large that only ships would be capable of delivering them and then only to coastal targets. No one had yet suggested that nuclear weapons could be miniaturized to the point where they could be delivered by aircraft. Even more unimaginable was the notion that the as yet to be developed nuclear weapon might be placed atop a missile and flown through space to its target.

By the time the United States launched nuclear attacks against the Japanese cities of Hiroshima and Nagasaki in August 1945, the design of both its uranium- and plutonium-based fission weapons had been miniaturized so that they could be carried by a plane, albeit only by the latest and largest heavy bomber in the US inventory, the B-29 Superfortress. From the end of World War II until 1959, aircraft remained the only practical way to deliver nuclear weapons at long ranges. The speed at which bombers traveled was slow enough, and the distance between Soviet bases and US targets far enough, that US ground radars placed in strategic positions in Canada and Alaska could provide several hours of attack warning. Surprise attack was a possibility, but it was also likely that US policymakers would receive tactical warning of an incoming attack hours before it actually materialized overhead.

The introduction of intercontinental ballistic missiles (ICBMs) and submarine-launched ballistic missiles (SLBMs) changed everything. No longer could Washington and Moscow count on hours of warning before the arrival of a nuclear attack. The time between missile launch and nuclear detonation would be less than forty minutes. Missiles fired from a submarine off the coast and flown along a depressed trajectory so that they would never leave the atmosphere could strike American coastal cities in under ten minutes. Moreover, existing ground-based radars used to spot incoming bombers could not see below the horizon. As a result, Soviet ICBMs would not be detected by a ground radar until about fifteen minutes after launch, meaning US leaders would have only minutes between detection of an incoming missile strike and the start of nuclear detonations on American soil.

Nuclear war was effectively moving into the space age; in the years to come, surveillance, and eventually communication, systems would follow nuclear weapons into space. The technology required for ICBMs and space launch are practically the same. Launching any payload into low earth orbit (LEO) requires a minimum velocity of 7.8 kilometers per second (about 17,500 miles per hour). The speed required for a ballistic payload to travel halfway around the world after it is launched by the missile is only about 15 percent less than what would be required to place a payload in orbit. In this sense, the space race and nuclear arms race occurred simultaneously as the Soviet Union and the United States worked to provide tactical warning of an incoming attack in the short-fused environment created by the act of placing nuclear weapons atop ballistic missiles.

This chapter describes the US space-based nuclear command, control, and communications (NC3) infrastructure that lies at the heart of the US strategy of deterrence. It begins with an introduction to the concept of orbital mechanics, which is a fancy term that covers a discussion of how spacecraft behave in orbit and how those orbits are used for certain applications. It then describes how the characteristics of the electromagnetic spectrum serve to both constrain and enable NC3 systems. The chapter also describes the surveillance and communication satellites and ground-based radars that are critical elements of the NC3 "weapons system."

NEWTON'S CANNONBALL

When Sir Isaac Newton first imagined how an orbit would work, he used a thought experiment often referred to as "Newton's cannonball" to explain the behavior of objects circling the earth. The point of departure is Newton's law of gravitation, which accurately states that objects at sea level accelerate toward the earth at 9.8 meters per second squared (or 32.2 feet per second squared). This law predicts that objects farther from the center of the earth will be subject to less gravity, as the square of the distance between their centers of gravity. As a result, a spacecraft placed in orbit still accelerates toward the earth, but the acceleration is less than it is at sea level.

If a cannonball at sea level were placed exactly 4.9 meters (16 feet) above the ground and allowed to drop to the earth, it would take exactly one second (if we ignore the effects produced by a small amount of air friction) to reach the ground. The motion of a cannonball in other directions also is "independent" of this gravitational effect. In other words, if a cannonball were shot parallel to the ground from a height of 4.9 meters, it would still take exactly one second to reach the ground even though it is also traveling down range (horizontal) to the ground simultaneously. If the cannonball were shot horizontally at 100 meters per second, it would travel 100 meters before hitting the ground, and if it were shot at 200 meters per second horizontally, it would travel 200 meters before hitting the ground.

Over short distances, such as 100 or 200 meters, the curvature of the earth is negligible. Nevertheless, at what distance would the curvature of the earth begin to matter? How fast would the cannonball need to be shot so that the earth would curve away from the cannonball by 4.9 meters in the same amount of time as it fell 4.9 meters, causing the distance between the ball to the ground to be unchanged? The answer to that question is 7.9 kilometers each second (4.9 miles per second), or 17,671 miles per hour.

Of course, this would be impossible so close to the earth due to the dense atmosphere (not to mention obstacles such as your house). If one could travel high above the earth where the atmosphere is so thin or nonexistent that air friction becomes negligible, then it would be possible to accelerate an object to high speed. Since the force of gravity is inversely proportional to the square of the distance between the center of gravity of two objects, a spacecraft can remain in orbit high above the earth at a lower speed than at the surface of the earth. Additionally, the orbit that it maintains would be larger than if it were at the surface of the earth. The result is the spacecraft velocity will be slower and the orbital period (the time to make one full orbit) will be longer the higher a spacecraft orbit is above the earth.

Table 5.1 shows the typical velocity, orbital period, and distance from the earth's center for some circular orbit regimes. Notice that the farther a spacecraft is from the earth, the slower it travels and the longer it takes to make one full orbit. Each of these orbital regimes, however, also has characteristics that make it better for some applications than others. Each type of orbit and its importance for NC3 is then described.

TABLE 5.1. Typical Circular Orbit Velocities and Altitudes

Orbit type	Velocity	Period	Altitude above sea level
earth's surface[1]	7.9 km/sec 17,671 mph	84 min	0 km 0 mi
low earth orbit (LEO)[2]	7.8–6.9 km/sec 17,448–15,434 mph	88–127 min	160–2,000 km 100–1,243 mi
medium earth orbit (MEO)	6.9–3.07 km/sec 15,434–6,867 mph	127 min–24 hr	2,000–35,786 km 1,243 mi–22,236 mi
geostationary earth orbit (GEO) or geosynchronous orbit (GSO)	3.07 km/sec 6,867 mph	24 hr[3]	35,786 km 22,236 mi

Note: Values rounded to the nearest whole number.
1. Not possible due to thick atmosphere.
2. Typical values.
3. Technically one sidereal day, which is twenty-three hours, fifty-six minutes, and four seconds.

Low Earth Orbit

LEO ranges in altitude from just above the surface of the earth to 2,000 kilometers.[2] Of course, orbits much below 160 kilometers are impractical since the earth's atmosphere becomes too thick and causes too much drag below this altitude. For practical purposes, 160 to 2,000 kilometers is a useful range for LEO.

Placing an object into LEO orbit is relatively inexpensive, so LEO is the default orbit for most satellites unless the mission specifically requires placing the satellite into a higher orbit. As of 2021, all manned missions except the moon missions have occurred in LEO. Because LEO orbits are close to the earth, they are characterized by a short orbital period. Objects in LEO do not stay over a specific area of the earth for long, but they can revisit the same area multiple times in a single day. LEO orbits are used for most earth-sensing missions, especially when high-resolution imagery and other sensor data is needed. The possibility of obtaining high-resolution imagery or data collection using LEO, however, is offset by its rather limited field of view. LEO is a poor choice if mission requirements call for wide area coverage.

Medium Earth Orbit

Medium earth orbit (MEO) ranges in altitude from 2,000 to 35,780 kilometers. Almost all spacecraft in this orbital regime possess an orbital period close to twelve hours, which allows them to visit an area about twice a day. To achieve this orbital period, most MEO satellites are placed at an altitude between 19,100 and 23,222 kilometers.

There are three major satellite systems placed in this orbit. All of them are part of a navigation service that provides global coverage. Russia's Global Navigation Satellite System (GLONASS) is located at an altitude of 19,100 kilometers. It consists of a constellation of twenty-four operational satellites and provides positioning, navigation, and timing services free to users.[3] The United States maintains its own constellation of about thirty radio-navigation Global Positioning System (GPS) satellites at an altitude of about 20,000 kilometers. Ground-based GPS receivers can provide time and geolocation information as long as the receiver can maintain an unobstructed line of sight to four GPS satellites. Latest upgrades to the GPS constellation can give locations accurate to about one foot. Europe's Galileo satellite constellation, which is placed at an altitude of 23,222 kilometers, offers a similar capability.[4] MEO is the preferred altitude for navigation, timing, and geodetic/space environment science.

Geosynchronous Orbit and Geostationary Orbit

Set at an altitude of 35,786 kilometers, geosynchronous orbit (GEO) and geostationary orbit (GSO) spacecraft have an orbital period of exactly one sidereal day (about twenty-four hours), matching the rotational period of the earth. This allows GEO satellites to stay over the same longitude at all times and GSO satellites to remain over the equator at all times. GSO satellites thus appear stationary relative to an earth observer. This is useful because it allows unsophisticated ground terminals to send and receive communications to the GSO satellite in orbit without the aid of equipment to locate and track the position of the satellite. The classic examples of a GSO systems are DirecTV and Dish Network antennae, which can remain fixed relative to one's house, since the earth itself is rotating the dish. Another major advantage of GEO satellites is that only a few satellites are required to provide coverage of the earth. With the exception of the regions near the North and South Pole, only four satellites are typically needed to provide worldwide coverage.

Historically, GEO has been used by 90 percent of the world's communication satellites, including satellites associated with NC3 (This paradigm has changed recently as SpaceX has launched a large number of Starlink satellites to LEO rather than GEO.) Early-warning and weather satellites also are often parked in GEO, although this does create problems when coverage is needed near the poles. Nevertheless, it is possible to cover latitudes as high as 65 or even 80 degrees north or south of the equator depending on the characteristics of the signal, the performance of the ground station, and the weather.

Highly Elliptical Orbits

Highly elliptical orbits (HEO) are used to cover the polar regions. Unlike circular orbits, these orbits have high eccentricity, making them highly elliptical as the name implies. HEO also means that the spacecraft will vary in altitude from the closest point in the orbit (perigee) to the highest point in the orbit (apogee). To date, this orbit is used only to cover northern latitudes, so the perigee is always placed in the south and the apogee is always located over the northern portion of the globe. Because the apogee for these orbits is placed over the northern latitudes, the spacecraft will spend most of its time above these northern latitudes. Sensors placed in HEO can spend a good deal of time looking down on the earth and the northern latitudes.

HEO is useful in providing communication coverage for space missions. It also is useful in providing surveillance of polar regions, exactly the type of orbit needed for early warning of ICBM attack. HEO spacecraft often are used with GEO or GSO spacecraft to obtain true worldwide coverage.

THE ELECTROMAGNETIC SPECTRUM AND REMOTE SENSING

Although the relationship between surveillance and communication systems and the electromagnetic spectrum is complex, a discussion of infrared satellites, which can detect missile exhaust plumes, and phased-array ground radars, which can track objects after propulsion systems are shut down, offers a good introduction to how the properties of electromagnetic radiation shape US NC3 systems.

Detection of objects at a distance usually means detecting electromagnetic radiation. As table 5.2 illustrates, the electromagnetic spectrum includes radio waves, microwaves, infrared, visible light, ultraviolet light, X-rays, and gamma rays. All electromagnetic radiation is transmitted via photons, which are particles that lack mass and travel through free space at the speed of light at all frequencies in the electromagnetic spectrum.

The radio and microwave bands of electromagnetic radiation are used for wireless communications. Lower frequencies in the radio band are used for terrestrial communications but generally not for satellite communications. The microwave band is more useful for satellite communications. Frequencies in the infrared range are especially useful for detecting heat signatures and are used in missile early-warning satellites. The higher frequencies of the electromagnetic spectrum, such as visible light, ultraviolet light, and X-rays, find relatively few applications in the US NC3 architecture.

Each frequency within the electromagnetic spectrum reacts differently with the earth's atmosphere. Some wavelengths have a frequency that matches the resonant frequency of elements in the atmosphere such as atomic nitrogen or various forms of oxygen and water, making the atmosphere opaque at these wavelengths. Other frequencies can be reflected by the ozone in the earth's ozone layer. Attenuation, whereby energy from the radiated signal is lost by

TABLE 5.2. Electromagnetic Radiation Characteristics

Name	Wavelength	Frequency (Hz)	Photon energy (eV)
Gamma ray	<0.01 nm	>30 EHz	>124 keV
X-ray	0.01–10 nm	30 EHz–30 PHz	124 keV–124 eV
Ultraviolet	10–400 nm	30 PHz–790 THz	124 eV–3.3 eV
Visible	400–700 nm	790–430 THz	3.3–1.7 eV
Infrared	700 nm–1 mm	430 THz–300 GHz	1.7 eV–1.24 meV
Microwave	1 mm–1 m	300 GHz–300 MHz	1.24 meV–1.24 μeV
Radio	1 m–100,000 km	300 MHz–3 Hz	1.24 μeV–12.4 feV

Sources: "What Are the Spectrum Band Designators and Bandwidths?," NASA, accessed June 4, 2020, https://www.nasa.gov/directorates/heo/scan/communications/outreach/funfacts/txt_band_designators.html; "Photon Energy Calculator," Plank-Einstein Photon Energy Calculator by Omni Calculator, accessed June 4, 2020, https://www.omnicalculator.com/physics/photon-energy.

Note: eV = electron volts; EHz = exahertz; feV = femtoelectron volts; GHz = gigahertz; Hz = hertz; keV = kiloelectron volts; MHz = megahertz; meV = millielectronvolts; PHz = petahertz; THz = terragertz; μeV = microvolts.

heating molecules in the air, also is a common interaction between electromagnetic energy and the matter in the atmosphere. In these wavelengths, energy can penetrate the atmosphere but rapidly loses strength at lower altitudes or if transmission takes place over great distances. When considered as a whole, the atmosphere is opaque to many electromagnetic frequencies.

Other frequencies, by contrast, react relatively little with the earth's atmosphere and pass through more easily, meaning the atmosphere is transparent to these wavelengths. The large bands of the electromagnetic spectrum that allow most radiation to pass through the atmosphere are called "atmospheric windows." As a rule, transmitting, receiving, or sensing electromagnetic radiation over long distance through the earth's atmosphere must be done in one of these atmospheric windows. Examples of these kinds of transmission include satellite communications, terrestrial cell phone or radio transmissions, observing events on the surface of the earth from space, or using long-distance radar.

An especially important atmospheric window—infrared light—exists just below visible light in frequency with wavelengths between 700 nanometers and 1 millimeter. Although infrared light is visible to some amphibians, fish, and reptiles, it is not visible to humans. Infrared wavelengths are useful for detecting heat because the peak intensity of thermal radiation (black body radiation) emitted for hot objects up to seven thousand degrees Fahrenheit falls within the infrared range. Scientists often divide the infrared spectrum into the "near" infrared (meaning near visible light, the highest frequency), short wavelength, mid-wavelength, long wavelength, and very long wavelength (the lowest frequency).

TABLE 5.3. Common Uses of the Infrared Spectrum

Division	Wavelength	Frequency	Use case
Near infrared	0.75–1.4 μm	214–400 THz	Night-vision goggles, near-infrared spectroscopy
Short-wavelength infrared	1.4–3 μm	100–214 THz	Viewing bright rocket plumes
Mid-wavelength infrared	3–8 μm	37–100 THz	Observing flying objects below the horizon against the background of the earth; heat-seeking missiles can home in on passive infrared in this range to target jet engine exhaust plumes
Long-wavelength infrared	8–15 μm	20–37 THz	Observing objects above the horizon against the background of cold space; forward-looking infrared (FLIR) systems can obtain a completely passive picture of the outside world
Very long wavelength infrared	15–1000 μm	0.3–20 THz	Sensors and applications for this range are still experimental and challenging

Source: "Tour of the Electromagnetic Spectrum; Infrared Waves," NASA, accessed June 4, 2020, https://science.nasa.gov/ems/07_infraredwaves.
Note: THz = terragertz; μm = micrometer

Each band in the infrared spectrum has unique characteristics and uses. For viewing bright rocket exhausts from an ICBM in space, for example, short-wave infrared is used, although newer spacecraft (such as the Space-Based Infrared System) have multiple cameras that utilize multiple wavelengths to enhance the ability of operators to correctly characterize an event.

Table 5.3 summarizes the commonly used applications for each frequency of the infrared spectrum.

SPACE-BASED EARLY-WARNING SATELLITES AND GROUND SYSTEMS

From 1957 to 1959 the Soviet Union and the United States successfully tested their first ICBMs, and by January 1959 the United States had deployed the world's first operational nuclear-armed ICBM. Because ICBMs are essentially space-launch vehicles, their performance is governed by the laws of astrodynamics rather than aerodynamics. As a result, ICBM flight speeds are about 85 percent as fast as satellites in LEO, which reduces warning times to a matter of minutes rather than hours when compared with heavy bombers. Placing satellites in space is the only practical way to maximize warning of an ICBM attack. Engineers had one key advantage when it came to designing space-based missile-detection systems: ballistic missiles, space-launch vehicles, or anything that uses a rocket for propulsion has a very bright exhaust plume that is easily viewed in the infrared range of the electromagnetic spectrum.

While the US ground-based ballistic missile early-warning radars could see missiles and aircraft headed from the Soviet Union toward the American homeland, the range of these systems was severely limited by the horizon, even when situated as far north as possible. Without the ability to detect an incoming ballistic missile until several minutes into flight, the ability of the United States to respond to a Soviet ICBM attack was not particularly credible—and therefore neither was deterrence. A risk-acceptant Soviet leadership might gamble that their US counterparts might not detect an incoming ICBM attack, creating an opportunity to launch a nuclear decapitation attack and disrupt America's postattack NC3. A space-based early-warning system using infrared cameras to see the bright rocket plumes that were visible from space seconds after launch increased warning time to the maximum extent possible.

Today the US early-warning system is called the Integrated Tactical Warning and Attack Assessment System (ITW/AA). According to the 2016 edition of the *Nuclear Matters Handbook* of the Department of Defense (DOD), "ITW/AA includes rigorously tested and certified systems that provide unambiguous, reliable, accurate, timely, survivable, and enduring warning information of ballistic missile, space, and air attacks on North America."[5] ITW/AA was designed around a four-step process of surveillance, correlation, warning, and assessment. ITW/AA uses both space- and ground-based sensors for surveillance and correlation, specifically infrared heat-sensing spacecraft combined with very large phased-array ground radar.

Dual Phenomenology to Prevent False Alarms

False alarms are the bane of any ballistic missile early-warning system. If left uncorrected, a false alarm could result in an unnecessary or unauthorized nuclear attack. Additionally, if false alarms became common, national leaders might ignore valid indications of attack. From the beginning, scientists and engineers attempted to address the false alarm issue in the overall design and operations of the ITW/AA system. A requirement for verification by dual phenomenology when it came to sensor design was the result.

Dual phenomenology refers to use of two systems using different physical phenomena as the basis of sensing incoming ballistic missile threats. US space-based systems use passive infrared sensors that can "see" the infrared radiation emitted from the hot rocket exhaust as it leaves the ground. These space-based systems would probably provide US policymakers with the first tactical warning that a nuclear attack was underway. US ground-based radars would then use pulses of energy to create an echo after bouncing off a missile in flight, giving confirmation that a ballistic missile was actually inbound. Dual phenomenology can reduce the occurrence of false alarms that can occur because it is very unlikely that many naturally occurring phenomena can spook complementary systems that rely on different physical principles to monitor the environment.

Defense Support Program

The Defense Support Program (DSP) was the world's first successful satellite-based early-warning system. It replaced the Missile Defense Alarm System, which was on orbit from 1960 to 1966 but failed to provide persistent satellite early-warning coverage. The DSP system was complex and included at least four satellites in GEO that could cover the equatorial belt of the earth (to 80 degrees north and south of the equator). Added to this constellation were at least three satellites in HEO covering the area near the North Pole that could not be seen by GEO satellites. Only the Southern Hemisphere near the South Pole was left uncovered, but it was highly unlikely that ICBMs fired in the Northern Hemisphere would deviate from the shortest great-circle route that went over the North Pole.

From 1970 to 2007 twenty-three DSP satellites were launched, with newer and more capable designs replacing aging models over time. While newer satellites incorporated various advances, all DSP satellites in GEO shared a few capabilities. All had infrared cameras that from the GEO distance to the earth of 26,200 miles could see approximately one-third of the planet's surface. Since these satellites were in GEO, each would dwell over the same geographic location continually. The sensor package carried by the DSP satellites was designed to see ballistic missile launches in the infrared spectrum against the background of both the earth and space, which was visible to the satellite around the edges of its scanning area.[6] At the time the DSP constellation was designed, it was not technically possible to include a staring sensor with enough resolution to cover a third of the earth. Instead, engineers decided to include a smaller sensor that could be swept across the earth's surface as the satellite spun. All DSP satellites are spin-stabilized on their vertical axis, and the telescope carried by the satellite is offset slightly from the vertical axis so that the camera can sweep across the surface of the earth as the satellite spins, thereby covering the entire hemisphere with every revolution of the satellite.

There were five generations of DSP satellites, although the most significant changes between these models involved updates to their sensor packages. The last DSP satellite was launched in 2007.[7]

Space-Based Infrared System

The Space-Based Infrared System (SBIRS) is the replacement for DSP. The architecture of the SBIRS satellite constellation is similar to DSP with spacecraft both in GEO and in HEO, covering everywhere on the earth except the region around the South Pole. The primary mission of the SBIRS constellation, like DSP before it, is to detect and provide early warning of ICBM and SLBM launches. Unlike DSP, the SBIRS has several secondary missions, including missile defense, battlespace awareness, and technical intelligence.[8]

SBIRS spacecraft are three-axis-stabilized in order to maintain a constant orientation toward the earth. This allows the satellite to point two cameras, a scanner, and a staring sensor toward the planet. The scanning sensor alone can complete the primary mission of missile early warning, while intelligence from both the scanner and staring sensors support the secondary missions.

The first four GEO SBIRS spacecraft were launched from 2011 to 2018.[9] Two launches are planned for 2022. The United States also has placed SBIRS components as a payload on other satellites in HEO. There are enough sensors in HEO to provide continuous coverage of the great-circle routes over the North Pole.[10]

SATELLITE COMMUNICATIONS BASICS

US military satellite communications occur in the microwave band of the electromagnetic spectrum, which typically ranges from 300 megahertz (MHz) to 300 gigahertz (GHz). Using International Telecommunications Union designations, this range includes the ultra-high frequency (UHF) band (300 MHz to 3 GHz), the super high frequency (SHF) band (3 GHz to 30 GHz), and the extremely high frequency (EHF) band (30 GHz to 300 GHz).

Each of these bands experiences distinct physics phenomena that give each one distinct operational advantages and disadvantages. For this reason, the US military operates satellites in each of these bands to take advantage of their relative strengths.

Attenuation in the Microwave Band

Attenuation occurs when electromagnetic wave frequencies interact with oxygen, water, or other molecules in the atmosphere. If an electromagnetic wave has a frequency that coincides with a molecule's resonant frequency or a multiple of a resonant frequency, it will transfer energy to the molecule, causing it to become hotter. This is the phenomenon at work in household microwave ovens: electromagnetic energy in the microwave band at a resonant frequency of water is used to heat the water molecules in food. As a rule, higher frequencies are more attenuated by the atmosphere, but this is not uniform, and there are troughs and peaks in the attenuation intensity where frequencies coincide with resonant frequencies of air molecules. The effect of atmospheric attenuation varies significantly between the low UHF range and the EHF range.

Both water and diatomic oxygen are prominent absorbers of electromagnetic energy in the atmosphere. For this reason, higher frequencies such as the EHF band will have more difficulty, due to high attenuation, in an environment characterized by cloud cover or heavy fog, while the UHF band, which is less attenuated, will transmit through inclement weather more easily. No waves in the microwave band, however, can be transmitted through more than a few feet of water, so they are not useful to communicating with a submarine deep in the ocean unless the submarine is towing a communications appendage (such as a floating wire or towed communications buoy) near the surface. The only electromagnetic radiation that can transmit through bodies of water, or solid earth for that matter, are very low frequency or extremely low frequency signals. These frequencies are located below the microwave band at the bottom of the radio band.

Scintillation and Blackout

Scintillation and blackout are two effects that occur in the earth's ionosphere, which is best characterized as a plasma. Plasma is an electrically conductive medium with roughly equal numbers of negatively and positively charged particles. In the case of the earth's ionosphere, the plasma is created by ionizing X-rays and gamma rays from the sun, which eject electrons from neutral atoms in a process called "ionization." The result is a negatively charged free electron and a positively charged ion. Eventually the free electrons will recombine with the positive ions, but the steady bombardment of ionizing radiation from the sun keeps the ionosphere in a charged state. Ionization and its effects from the sun are usually not enough to greatly disturb electromagnetic waves in the UHF, SHF, or EHF bands. Nevertheless, the electromagnetic pulse produced by high-altitude detonations of large nuclear weapons may cause enough ionization to disrupt signals in these bands.[11] In other words, charged particles in the ionosphere interact with the microwave band radiation used for satellite communications.

Radio blackout occurs when a microwave passing a free electron causes the electron to oscillate. When the electron oscillates, it may bump into a neutral gas particle, generating a small amount of heat. If this happens, energy from the wave is lost. When energy loss occurs on a large scale, it can lead to radio blackout. Blackout happens predominantly in the lower ionosphere where the neutral gas density is high enough for the electrons to collide during their oscillation.

By contrast, scintillation dominates where there are significant irregularities in the structure of the plasma in the higher reaches of the ionosphere. As with radio blackout, a radio wave may cause a nearby electron to oscillate, but if the electron does not interact with a nearby gas particle, the energy from the particle is released in the same quantity as when it was absorbed. However, the direction, phase, and amplitude will change. Under normal conditions, the effects of scintillation disrupt only a small portion of the signal, and enough of the signal will pass through intact to conduct communications. Under normal conditions, the minor effects of blackout and scintillation can be overcome with adjustment (usually done automatically) by the receiver.

Significant problems can occur, however, when the ionosphere is disrupted by a large event such as a nuclear detonation in the ionosphere or a solar storm. In these events, the massive gamma ray and X-ray bursts cause irregularities in the ionosphere—dense patches of plasma that travel through less dense areas of the ionosphere. As communication signals travel through these dynamic areas, scintillation becomes highly irregular and unpredictable. The direction, phase, and amplitude of the signal also become erratic, effectively "scrambling" the transmission. Similarly, blackout conditions can occur as patches of higher-density plasma move through the lower ionosphere. As a rule, UHF will be the most affected by scintillation and blackout, SHF will be less affected, and EHF least affected.

Jamming

Jamming generally requires transmitting a noise signal at a frequency detectable by a receiver at sufficient power to drown out any meaningful signal from the transmitting station. In the US military, the term refers to intentional interruption of a signal, while "interference" refers to unintentional interruption. From a physics perspective, there is no difference between the two phenomena, and it is almost never clear at first to the satellite communications user if jamming or interference is occurring.

Jamming and interference are shaped by geographic constraints when the transmitter and receiver are using directional antennae. Directional antennae have a narrow beam and are hundreds or thousands of times more sensitive to transmissions within the beam compared to omnidirectional receivers. As a result, successful jamming usually requires that the jammer deliver a more powerful noise within this beam-width area than the legitimate signal. Movement beyond the beam width requires an increasingly powerful jamming noise to be effective until the point is reached that increasing jamming power becomes impractical.

Downlink jamming generally requires an airborne jammer that can broadcast directly within the line of sight of the ground receiving antenna. This is usually beyond the ability of all but the most advanced adversaries who can construct and operate sophisticated airborne jamming platforms. This also makes downlink jamming difficult to undertake on short notice or against unanticipated targets. To jam communications with submarines, for instance, an airborne downlink jammer would have to get between a satellite and a submarine, which would require relatively precise knowledge of the submarine's location.

A more common and likely form of jamming is uplink jamming. The antenna footprint of a satellite may be hundreds of miles wide when viewed from the surface of the earth. Therefore, an uplink jammer could be geographically quite distant from the friendly transmitting station and still successfully jam an uplink.

Additionally, the power required to jam a receiver is proportional to the bandwidth that must be jammed. For this reason, jamming EHF (which has ten times more bandwidth than SHF and one hundred times more bandwidth than UHF) is most difficult to jam. EHF signals are naturally more directional than lower frequencies, which means that a small EHF dish will produce a very narrow beam, making geographic jamming very difficult. Thus, jamming becomes increasingly difficult as frequencies increase, leaving UHF the most susceptible to jamming and EHF the least susceptible. But, given the ubiquitous impact of Murphy's law, interference still remains a common issue, especially because of the high use of UHF and SHF frequencies in commercial satellite communications.

SATELLITE COMMUNICATION SYSTEMS

The United States operates many different types of satellite communication systems. Each possesses different strengths and weaknesses. Not all these systems are dedicated on a full-time basis to the NC3 mission, but most of them play some part in providing communications to operating forces and command centers. Collectively they offer a robust communication capability that can still maintain important connectivity to deterrent forces even in the presence of jamming, blackout, or scintillation.

Thin Line versus Thick Line NC3 Communications

The US NC3 system comprises communication links that are hardened for use in a trans- and postnuclear environment (called the "thin line") as well as nonhardened communication links for use during peacetime (called the "thick line"). Inherently, the protections needed to harden a communications link and ground terminals to operate in a nuclear environment come at a high cost, both monetarily and in the usability of the system. Thin line (hardened) communications are generally more cumbersome to operate, have lower data-transmission rates than could be achieved without the protections to the signal, and the terminals are much more expensive. The thick line is comprised of communication systems that are not designed to work in a transnuclear environment (although they may recover in a postnuclear environment). However, the thick line communication systems enjoy much higher throughput, ease of use, and less expensive ground or air terminals.

During peacetime the thick line is used as the primary means of communication, while the thin line is the backup means of communication. Both thick line and thin line communication systems comprise many types of communication links, not only satellites. However, this chapter discusses only the satellite communications of these systems.

UHF Band Systems

The primary mission of UHF band satellites is to provide tactical ground, sea, and air operations worldwide with voice and data communications. There are thousands of UHF band terminals used by US and allied units and commands. The US Navy operates both the payload and bus for the US military's UHF band satellite system. The Navy Space Operations Center at Point Mugu, California, is the primary operations center for these systems. A backup operations center is the Naval Satellite Operations Center at Schriever Space Force Base in Colorado.

UHF band satellites are generally referred to as "narrowband" communication systems. Nevertheless, some systems also have "wideband" (SHF) and "protected" (EHF) communication capabilities. Lower-frequency communications have two main advantages over higher frequencies. Their signals usually suffer from less attenuation while passing through the atmosphere, especially during inclement weather. They also require relatively inexpensive receivers and transmitters. Antennae for UHF systems, for instance, include inexpensive helical antennae and parabolic dishes. UHF is also frequently used for commercial satellite communications, especially voice communications. Widespread use in the commercial sector has produced a variety of UHF band terminals that can be acquired at low cost for military applications. The low cost and relatively small size of UHF ground terminals make them ideal for tactical communications and man-portable systems.

While UHF may be best in terms of cost and its ability to function in inclement weather, it possesses several less desirable characteristics. It is relatively easy to jam UHF. Inexpensive rudimentary broadband jammers can be effective against UHF transmitters, which creates an opportunity for unsophisticated and poorly funded groups to field UHF band jammers. UHF, with its relatively long wavelength (i.e., low frequency), also has the most limited transmission rate. For this reason, it has traditionally been used for voice communications that can be encoded on the signal, while video and other more data-intensive transmissions have typically been reserved for higher frequencies that could handle more throughput. Additionally, UHF transmissions are the most susceptible to scintillation and blackouts. In a trans- or postnuclear environment, it would take longer for UHF transmission capabilities to recover than SHF or EHF satellite transmissions. Since scintillation of UHF satellite communications occurs in the ionosphere, lower-altitude line-of-sight UHF transmissions—for example, from aircraft to ground stations—should work even when the ionosphere is highly scintillated.

Fleet Satellite Communications System

The oldest UHF band system is the Fleet Satellite Communications system. Six of these satellites were placed in orbit from 1978 to 1989, and two are still in operation in 2021. The Fleet Satellite Communications system is in GEO and has a limited capacity by today's standards. Each satellite has thirty 25-kHz channels for voice communication and five 5-kHz channels for low-data-rate transmission. The last two Fleet Satellites placed in orbit were equipped with an experimental EHF payload meant to test ground EHF terminals, although this payload was turned off in 2007.[12]

Ultra High Frequency Follow-On System

The Ultra High Frequency Follow-On (UFO) system was designed to replace the Fleet Satellite Communications system. These satellites have approximately twice as many communication channels as the Fleet Satellite spacecraft. The first UFO spacecraft was launched in 1993, and the final spacecraft in the constellation was launched in 2003. There were eleven UFO satellites in total, all placed in GEO. Their capabilities included ship-to-shore communications and fleet broadcasts. The system offered many channels for 4,800-bits-per-second data transmission, 2,400-bits-per-second data/voice transmission, and 75-bits-per-second secondary communications capability. A small EHF payload with a single earth-coverage beam and a steerable spot beam were included in the system starting with the fourth satellite placed in orbit.[13]

Mobile User Objective System

Launched from 2012 to 2016, the five satellites of the Mobile User Objective System (MUOS) are the current military state-of-the-art UHF band system fielded by the United States. These GSO satellites have approximately ten times more throughput capacity than the UFO system. Notable innovations in the MUOS include a new third-generation Wideband Code Division Multiple Access (WCDMA) fifteen-foot-diameter, high-gain antenna and a secondary UHF system that is compatible with the previous generation UFO ground-user terminals (to maintain UHF communications in the event that UFO satellites are retired before all user terminals can be upgraded to the new MUOS WCDMA system). Most of the added capacity of this system is produced by its new third-generation payload and the new ground radios used to communicate with it.[14]

Wideband (SHF Band) Systems

The primary mission of wideband satellite systems is to provide high-capacity (i.e., more than UHF or EHF) communications to the US military and allied partners. SHF band terminals tend to be larger and more expensive than UHF band, so they are less common. Nevertheless, SHF ground terminals are often located at larger military command headquarters around the globe. The Space Force and Army jointly operate US military wideband systems. The communications payload on board these systems is operated by the Army Satellite Operations Brigade, located at Peterson Space Force Base, Colorado, while the satellite itself is operated by the Space Force 4th Space Operations Squadron, located at Schriever Space Force Base, also in Colorado.[15]

SHF band satellites are referred to as "wideband" because the SHF spectrum is ten times larger than the UHF (i.e., "narrowband") spectrum. SHF ranges from 3 GHz to 30 GHz. SHF, which transmits at frequencies ten times higher than UHF, is generally capable of data-rate transmissions that are about ten times faster than UHF band systems. When compared to UHF, SHF is less susceptible to jamming, scintillation, and blackouts; only sophisticated militaries are capable of jamming SHF band. SHF ground terminals are typically larger and more costly than UHF terminals. As a result, they are usually found on larger platforms, although man-portable SHF systems are now beginning to enter service. SHF is also more attenuated than UHF and less attenuated than EHF, so its performance in poor weather falls between the UHF and EHF bands. The current US SHF system is Wideband Global Satellite Communication, or Wideband Global SATCOM (WGS).[16]

Defense Satellite Communications System

The Defense Satellite Communications System, now a legacy program, was the first SHF band satellite system deployed by the US military. It is also the largest and longest-running satellite communication system fielded by the United States. From 1966 to 2003, fifty-five of these spacecraft were launched. Production occurred in three blocks. Blocks one and two included spin-stabilized spacecraft, while block three comprised three-axis-stabilized satellites. The latest version of the satellite was equipped with six independent channels that were each capable of transmission rates of 200 megabits per second. Six of these satellites remain in operation as of 2020.[17]

Wideband Global Satellite Communications

The Wideband Global SATCOM system is a state-of-the-art, high-capacity satellite that operates in the SHF band. This system is currently in block III production. WGS satellites are in GEO, and the coverage they provide has been synchronized with the remaining Defense Satellite Communications System satellites. All WGS satellites are three-axis-stabilized. Satellites in this constellation provide upward of 11 gigabits per second of transmission capacity, which is about fifty-five times the capacity of the latest version of the Defense Satellite Communications System.[18]

Protected EHF Band Systems

The mission of "protected" EHF band satellites is to provide strategic and assured communication capabilities for the National Military System, capabilities that are often described as "thin line" communications because they would need to remain operational even during and following a nuclear attack. Although these protected systems primarily rely on EHF frequencies to accomplish their mission, satellites in these constellations often incorporate systems that utilize SHF and UHF transmissions. The EHF band ranges from 30 GHz to 300 GHz, making it the most susceptible to attenuation caused by the presence of moisture in the atmosphere. This attenuation problem reduces reliability in poor weather and faces increased problems when used to communicate with users located at latitudes greater than 65 degrees. Despite these disadvantages, however, EHF transmissions are relatively unaffected by the scintillation and blackout created by nuclear detonations in the ionosphere. This ability to operate in a post- or transnuclear environment provides an enduring thin line communications capability needed to maintain NC3. Additionally, because the EHF band is 270 GHz wide, EHF systems can hop between a wider range of frequencies, "protecting" EHF bands from traditional jamming techniques.[19]

EHF band systems generally are found only in military systems. As a result, there are few commercial products to leverage for purposes of research and manufacturing, creating a situation in which all US military EHF band terminals are custom-designed and purpose-built. No commercial users appear interested in deploying frequency-hopping, ultrawideband ground terminals and satellite systems that are hardened against electromagnetic pulse. Because of the high cost of EHF terminals, they are reserved for a few select units and command centers that are most directly associated with thin line communications between legitimate command authorities and the operators of US nuclear delivery systems.

Although the newest EHF system, known as the Advanced Extremely High Frequency (AEHF) satellite system, is currently operational, several of the satellites in the US legacy protected satellite system known as the Military Strategic and Tactical Relay (MILSTAR) are still functioning. The Space Force 4th

Space Operations Squadron also operates these systems. These EHF satellites are primarily in GEO, although there are also EHF payloads on satellites in HEO to cover the northern latitudes. The HEO payloads compatible with MILSTAR are called the Interim Polar System, while the HEO payloads compatible with the AEHF satellite system are called the Enhanced Polar System.[20]

Military Strategic and Tactical Relay

From 1994 to 2003, five MILSTAR satellites were placed in orbit. MILSTAR satellites provide secure, jam-resistant, and EMP-hardened NC3 communication between commanders and US strategic forces. The first two MILSTAR satellites included a low-data-rate payload with data rates between 75 bits per second and 2,400 bits per second. The last three satellites included both a low-data-rate payload and a medium-data-rate payload, which provided rates between 4.8 kilobits per second and 1.544 megabits per second.[21]

MILSTAR and AEHF are capable of establishing satellite cross-links. By contrast, US UHF and SHF satellite constellations lack this capability. Cross-links provide increased mission robustness in the event that a ground site is disrupted or destroyed. Protected EHF band satellites can continue their mission without ground sites by using the cross-links. Additionally, the cross-link itself is extremely difficult to jam or disrupt. The frequency is not in an atmospheric window, so ground jammers would be ineffective, and it would be impractical to build satellite jammers to dwell within the cross-link.

AEHF Satellite System

In 2021 the AEHF system works in conjunction with MILSTAR, which will eventually be phased out—leaving the AEHF satellite system as the sole US nuclear-hardened, protected satellite capability. Six AEHF satellites were launched into GSO from 2010 to 2020, providing worldwide coverage. AEHF satellites incorporate a new "extreme data rate" transmission system that can transmit at rates of up to 8.192 megabits per second.[22] This new transmission system requires a host of updated user-terminal systems. For aircraft, a Family of Advanced Beyond Line-of-Sight-Terminals (FAB-T) are being deployed across the force, which include the Command Post Terminal for command aircraft and the Force Element Terminal for the B-52. For nonairborne platforms, several terminals are being developed and deployed: the Single-Channel Anti-Jam Man-Portable Terminal, the vehicle-mobile Secure Mobile Anti-Jam Reliable Tactical Terminal,[23] and the Submarine High Data Rate system.

Interim Polar System and Enhanced Polar System

The Interim Polar System is the counterpart to MILSTAR in highly elliptical orbit, providing coverage at latitudes farther north than 65 degrees. The

Interim Polar System is not found on a dedicated satellite; instead, the system is hosted as a secondary payload on other US national satellites in HEO. The Interim Polar System became operational in February 2007. In 2020 three satellites were in orbit. Two satellites usually are in view of the mission area at any given time, thereby providing continuous coverage.[24]

The Enhanced Polar System is the replacement for the Interim Polar System —it is the counterpart to the AEHF satellite system in HEO, covering latitudes farther north than 65 degrees. Like the Interim Polar System, the Enhanced Polar System also is hosted as a secondary payload on other US national satellites rather than using dedicated satellites. The Enhanced Polar System also incorporates the Enhanced Polar System transmission system for substantially increased throughput.[25]

GROUND RADARS

Ground radars include radar in the radio spectrum and light detection and ranging (LIDAR) in the optical and infrared spectrum. Radars and LIDARs transmit energy and then observe a small fraction of the returned energy that is reflected by an object, which is called its radar cross section. This signal can reveal many characteristics of the target, such as its size or orientation. Radars usually transmit in pulses. The time lapse between transmission and receipt of the radar return can reveal the distance from the radar to the object. Reflected radar transmissions experience Doppler shift depending on the speed of the target, thereby also allowing the velocity and movement of the object relative to the radar to be determined. The bearing and azimuth from the object to the radar also is measurable. Thus, a single radar observation can reveal radial velocity, bearing, and azimuth to a target. A series of rapid observations can reveal the three-dimensional location and trajectory of an object. If the object is in a ballistic trajectory, then its approximate point of impact can be determined. Multiple sensors can increase the accuracy of these measurements.

Distant Early Warning Line

The first early-warning radar built by the United States was the Distant Early Warning (DEW) Line, a series of ground radars built across northern Alaska, northern Canada, and Greenland. There were also two other radar lines in Canada, the first called the Mid-Canada Line, which was approximately halfway between the DEW Line and the United States, and the Pinetree Line, which ran along the US-Canada border. Construction of all these radar systems began in 1954, and they became operational in 1957. The Mid-Canada Line and the Pinetree Line were operational for only a few years, but the DEW Line remained in use until the system was modernized and became the North Warning System in 1993. All three of these radar systems were optimized to detect aircraft approaching the United States from the north. None could detect ICBMs.[26]

Ballistic Missile Early Warning System

The first radar system capable of detecting ballistic missiles was the Ballistic Missile Early Warning System. This system included three radar sites and was fully operational by 1961. This system's primary mission was to detect ballistic missile launches from the Soviet Union that were headed toward the United States on a polar trajectory. Until the launch of DSP satellites in 1970, this was the only system that could provide tactical warning of ballistic missiles launched by the Soviet Union. The Ballistic Missile Early Warning System could provide only between ten and twenty-five minutes of warning time before the impact of incoming warheads, and without the dual phenomenology provided by DSP satellites. As a result, false alarms were common.

Precision Acquisition Vehicle Entry Phased Array Warning System

The Precision Acquisition Vehicle Entry Phased Array Warning System (PAVE PAWS) was a long-range early-warning radar designed to warn of ballistic missiles launched by ballistic missile submarines. The first two radars of this type were built at Beale Air Force Base in California to monitor launches from the Pacific and on Cape Cod, Massachusetts, to monitor launches from the Atlantic.

PAVE PAWS was a giant leap forward in ballistic missile warning radar. A single phased-array radar face can monitor 120 degrees of coverage. Each of the sites had two radar faces allowing for a total of 240 degrees of coverage. The range of these radars is impressive at three thousand miles, but they are still limited by the horizon. The radars also were highly automated, requiring only three personnel to operate.[27]

After the success of the original two sites, more were identified to host new phased-array warning radars under the PAVE PAWS expansion program. From 1986 to 1987, such radars were added at Robbins Air Force Base, Georgia, and Eldorado Air Force Base, Texas, to warn of SLBM launches against the United States from the southeast and the Gulf of Mexico. These radars were subsequently decommissioned in 1995 as part of the Cold War drawdown. The radar at Eldorado was eventually moved to Clear Air Force Base in Alaska to replace the old Ballistic Missile Early Warning System that had been deployed there since the 1960s.[28] PAVE PAWS radars were replaced by the AN/FPS-123 Solid State Phased Array Radar System.

Solid State Phased Array Radar System

The Solid State Phased Array Radar System is the latest addition to the US ground-based early-warning system. The system was deployed to locations including Beale Air Force Base, California; Cape Cod Air Force Base, Massachusetts; Thule, Greenland; Clear, Alaska (both Thule and Clear with AN/FPS-120 radars); and Fylingdales in the United Kingdom. The entire system became fully operational in 2001 when the radar at Clear was added and the last Ballistic Missile Early Warning System station, which was less than a mile away, was decommissioned.[29]

The primary mission of the Solid State Phased Array Radar System is to provide ballistic missile early-warning data for the Integrated Tactical Warning and Attack Assessment system. As a secondary mission, it is a collateral sensor for the US Space Surveillance Network, which is led by the Combined Space Operations Center at Vandenberg Space Force Base, California. Each of the five sites in the Solid State Phased Array Radar System has been upgraded to the Upgraded Early Warning Radar (AN/FPS-132), which adds fidelity to missile detection for missile defense. With this upgrade, the system gained a second primary mission of missile defense in addition to its traditional mission of missile warning. Data from each site is now also sent to the Ballistic Missile Defense System. The system still maintains its secondary mission of space surveillance. For missile warning, data is sent to the Missile Warning Center at Cheyenne Mountain, Colorado, where data from both ground radar and space early-warning satellites enters a fusion process for verification using dual phenomenology. The Missile Warning Center turns this data into tactical warning of missile attack and forwards this information into the decision-making venues used by US national leaders.[30]

Precision Acquisition Radar Attack Characterization System

The Precision Acquisition Radar Attack Characterization System is a single-face, 120-degree-coverage AN/FPS-116 radar that was originally built at Cavalier Air Force Base, North Dakota, as part of the Safeguard missile-defense system defending US missile fields. The Safeguard system was decommissioned in 1976 shortly after this radar was built. Since that time, it has provided data to the Missile Warning Center and has served as a collateral sensor for the Space Surveillance Network.[31]

CONCLUSION

As nuclear weapons moved into space with the advent of the ICBM, sensors and communication systems followed. Today the US NC3 system is dependent on space-based sensors for the detection and initial assessment of missile launches and satellite relays that provide thin line communication capabilities encountered in a trans- or postnuclear environment. The general capabilities and limitations of these systems are well known because they are governed by the physics underlying orbital mechanics and the propagation of electromagnetic energy.

This brief introduction to these communication, surveillance, and early-warning systems highlights how succeeding generations of systems often leveraged the systems they were replacing to build redundant capabilities or to expand coverage. The ideas governing operation of a system and its overall design thus hark back to the analog era and are focused on maintaining operations following the ultimate insult, a full-scale nuclear attack. By contrast, today these systems face a different array of threats stemming from direct cyberattacks, insider threats, and creeping obsolescence. The sunk costs represented by these existing systems, however, make it difficult to simply start from scratch when it comes to future NC3 systems. The fact that these systems were never intended to operate in a cyber context, let alone face a concerted cyberattack, might actually constitute a strength because their analog elements tend to be prima facie resistant to cyber assaults. Still, at a time when human mediation is largely absent from sensor and communication systems, it is interesting that the United States relies on so many "humans in the loop" when it comes to operating these systems and monitoring and fusing the data that they produce. One is left to wonder if the cyber age will transform NC3 much like the missile age before it, placing an increasing premium on speed when it comes to sensing, fusing, assessing, and communicating—the primary NC3 mission that provides the backbone of nuclear command, control, and communications.

NOTES

1. Albert Einstein to F. D. Roosevelt, August 2, 1939, "Einstein Letter," Franklin D. Roosevelt Presidential Library and Museum Archives, http://www.fdrlibrary.marist.edu/archives/pdfs/docsworldwar.pdf.
2. United Nations Office for Outer Space Affairs, Steering Group and Working Group 4, *IADC Space Debris Mitigation Guidelines*, IADC-02-01, September 2007, http://www.unoosa.org/documents/pdf/spacelaw/sd/IADC-2002-01-IADC-Space_Debris-Guidelines-Revision1.pdf.
3. G. M. Polischuk, V. I. Kozlov, "The Global Navigation Satellite System GLONASS: Development and Usage in the 21st Century," Defense Technical Information Center, December 2002, https://apps.dtic.mil/dtic/tr/fulltext/u2/a484380.pdf.
4. "Catalog of Earth Satellite Orbits," NASA Earth Observatory, September 4, 2009, https://earthobservatory.nasa.gov/features/OrbitsCatalog.
5. *Nuclear Matters Handbook: 2016* (Washington, DC: Office of the Deputy Secretary of Defense for Nuclear Matters, 2016), 76, https://www.lasg.org/Nuclear-Matters-2016.pdf.
6. "Defense Support Program Satellites," US Air Force, November 23, 2015, https://www.af.mil/About-Us/Fact-Sheets/Display/Article/104611/defense-support-program-satellites/.

7. "Defense Support Program Satellites."
8. "Space Based Infrared System," US Air Force Space Command, March 22, 2017, https://www.afspc.af.mil/About-Us/Fact-Sheets/Display/Article/1012596/space-based-infrared-system/.
9. "U.S. Military Satellite Launched to Fortify against Missile Attacks," *Spaceflight Now*, January 20, 2018, https://spaceflightnow.com/2018/01/20/u-s-military-satellite-launched-to-fortify-against-missile-attacks/.
10. "Space Based Infrared Surveillance SBIRS," Lockheed Martin, accessed June 4, 2020, https://www.lockheedmartin.com/en-us/products/sbirs.html.
11. Samuel Glasstone, *The Effects of Nuclear Weapons* (Washington, DC: Government Printing Office, 1977), 487.
12. "Legacy Satellite Communications (Legacy SATCOM)," Naval Warfare Systems Command.
13. "Ultra High Frequency Follow-On," US Navy Program Executive Officer for Space, Communications and Sensors, March 1, 1999, https://www.globalsecurity.org/space/library/report/1999/uhf_follow-on_fact_sheet.pdf.
14. "Mobile User Objective System," Office of the Secretary of Defense, January 30, 2020, https://www.dote.osd.mil/Portals/97/pub/reports/FY2019/navy/2019muos.pdf?ver=2020-01-30-115519-503.
15. Air Command and Staff College, *AU-18 Space Primer* (Maxwell AFB, AL: Air University Press, 2009), 189, https://www.airuniversity.af.edu/Portals/10/AUPress/Books/AU-18.PDF.
16. Air Command and Staff College, 186–87.
17. "Defense Satellite Communications System," Air Force Space Command, March 27, 2017, https://www.afspc.af.mil/About-Us/Fact-Sheets/Display/Article/1012656/defense-satellite-communications-system/.
18. "WGS: Wideband Global SATCOM," Space Flight 101, August 30, 2021, https://spaceflight101.com/spacecraft/wgs-wideband-global-satcom/.
19. "EHF: Extremely High Frequency," GlobalSecurity.org, accessed June 4, 2020, https://www.globalsecurity.org/space/systems/ehf.htm. Air Command and Staff College, *AU-18 Space Primer*, 190–92.
20. "4th Space Operations Squadron," Schriever Air Force Base, July 2020, https://www.schriever.spaceforce.mil/About-Us/Fact-Sheets/Display/Article/275820/4th-space-operations-squadron/. See also "Enhanced Polar System," Northrup Grumman, accessed June 4, 2020, https://www.northropgrumman.com/space/enhanced-polar-system/.
21. "Milstar Satellite Communications System," US Air Force, November 23, 2015, https://www.af.mil/About-Us/Fact-Sheets/Display/Article/104563/milstar-satellite-communications-system/.
22. "Advanced Extremely High Frequency System," US Air Force Space Command, March 22, 2017, https://www.afspc.af.mil/About-Us/Fact-Sheets/Display/Article/249024/advanced-extremely-high-frequency-system/.
23. "Secure Mobile Anti-Jam Reliable Tactical Terminal (SMART-T)," Raytheon Technologies, accessed May 31, 2020, https://www.raytheon.com/capabilities/products/smart-t.
24. "Interim Polar System Reaches Full Operational Capability," US Air Force, February 6, 2007, https://www.af.mil/News/Article-Display/Article/128112/interim-polar-system-reaches-full-operational-capability/.

25. "4th Space Operations Squadron Gains Enhanced Polar System," US Air Force, September 27, 2019, https://www.af.mil/News/Article-Display/Article/1973294/4th-space-operations-squadron-gains-enhanced-polar-system/.
26. Samuel Edward Twitchell, *The Incomplete Shield: The Distant Early Warning Line and the Struggle for Effective Continental Air Defense, 1950–1960* (Ames: Iowa State University, 2011), 33.
27. "PAVE PAWS Radar System," US Air Force, November 23, 2015, https://www.af.mil/About-Us/Fact-Sheets/Display/Article/104593/pave-paws-radar-system/.
28. David Winkler, *Searching the Skies: The Legacy of the United States Cold War Radar Program* (Langley AFB, VA: US Air Force Air Combat Command, June 1997), https://apps.dtic.mil/dtic/tr/fulltext/u2/a331231.pdf.
29. "Clear AFS, Alaska," GlobalSecurity.org, accessed May 31, 2020, https://www.globalsecurity.org/space/facility/clear.htm.
30. "12th Space Warning Squadron, Peterson Space Force Base," accessed May 31, 2020, https://www.peterson.spaceforce.mil/About/Fact-Sheets/Display/Article/326224/12th-space-warning-squadron/.
31. "Perimeter Acquisition Radar Attack Characterization System," Air Force Space Command (Archived), March 22, 2017, https://www.afspc.af.mil/About-Us/Fact-Sheets/Display/Article/1126406/perimeter-acquisition-radar-attack-characterization-system/.

PART III

SIX

CYBER OPERATIONS AND NUCLEAR ESCALATION

A DANGEROUS GAMBLE

Jon R. Lindsay

Credible nuclear deterrence requires reliable nuclear command, control, and communications (NC3). For the same reason, strategic adversaries have incentives to hack into NC3 to gain technical intelligence in peacetime or combat advantages in wartime. All human and technological components of NC3 are potential targets, although not all are equally accessible or vulnerable. The implications for strategic stability are ambiguous. An adversary that gains intelligence about the reliability of NC3 might be able to distinguish credible threats from nuclear bluffs, which could be stabilizing. Yet the same intrusions that inform might also disrupt. Deliberate interference with NC3 can be destabilizing if it raises the chances of miscalculation or malfunction in a nuclear crisis.

As digital modernization increases the complexity of NC3, classic strategic trade-offs become more wicked. Digital systems have the potential to enhance the efficiency and reliability of communication and computation. However, more efficient networks also enable more efficient exploitation for intelligence. Improvements in NC3 capabilities that enhance the reliability of nuclear options might improve the credibility of threats, assuming that information about improvements can be shared with the targets of threats. Yet the increased complexity of digital systems can also undermine mutual information and create new error potentials, which heightens risks of escalation and accident. Actors who want to assess the reliability of complex NC3 will need ever more intelligence, which encourages intrusions into NC3 systems. At the same time, the active penetration of digital systems for intelligence also opens the possibility of manipulating the data in and functionality of the same systems, while complicating offensive planning. Indeed, the introduction of new vulnerabilities and interaction effects tends to complicate all types of cyber operations: exploitation for intelligence, disruptive attacks, and network defense. The increasing complexity of cyber-nuclear interactions thus heightens the risks of opportunistic exploitation, intentional sabotage, and accidental miscalculation for everyone. For these reasons, cybersecurity has emerged as a critical factor in modern NC3.

While digital technology does raise pressing security concerns about NC3, it is important to appreciate that NC3 security is not simply a technical matter. There are serious organizational and political problems emerging in the intersection of the cyber and nuclear domains. Separately, each of them have profoundly different operational, strategic, and proliferation characteristics. Combined, they create numerous pathways to nuclear escalation, some deliberate and some inadvertent, some familiar and some new. In general, there are two distinct categories of risk that emerge from the combination of cyber operations and nuclear weapons. One category, which is very familiar in critiques of nuclear deterrence theory, emphasizes failures of human beings to live up to the ideals of rational decision-making models. The other, which is somewhat less familiar, highlights perverse incentives that emerge from strategic rationality itself.

In the first case, the increasing sociotechnical complexity of NC3 can create confusion and uncertainty during a nuclear crisis. Military operators and political decision-makers may respond to this situation in less than rational ways. All people make mistakes and misperceive under conditions of stress and ambiguity. Information overload, misinformation, and disinformation could lead to premature or ill-considered decisions to release nuclear weapons. Moreover, because hackers are people too, even the best hackers will make mistakes sometimes. Malware that malfunctions when the attacker is counting on it to do something else might create problems for either the target or the attacker. Failures to understand the consequences of complexity in tightly coupled digital NC3 systems, and the software that exploits them, could then result in dangerous unintended consequences.[1]

In the second case, by contrast, cyber-nuclear interactions can generate rational incentives to escalate a militarized crisis to nuclear war. Whereas the previous category of risk involves sins of omission (because actors stumble into dangerous situations they cannot comprehend), here actors are guilty of sins of commission (because they rationally expect to be better off through threats or escalation). Offensive hacking depends on secrecy. Intrusions to disrupt NC3, which must be planned in advance, cannot be revealed to the target if they are to remain viable when needed in the future. Unfortunately, secrecy and deception tend to undermine the clear communication on which credible deterrence depends. As Dr. Strangelove notes in the eponymous classic, "The whole point of the doomsday machine is lost if you keep it a secret!" Preparation or use of cyber operations to limit damage in a nuclear war can, ironically, increase the risks of starting a nuclear war in the first place. The interdependence of conventional and nuclear command and control might also create rational incentives to escalate once a conventional war begins.[2]

This chapter provides a high-level overview of the interaction of cyber operations and nuclear weapons. It first outlines potential vulnerabilities of NC3 to cyber interference. Next it contrasts the operational, strategic, and proliferation characteristics of the nuclear and cyber domains. Then it summarizes the cyber and nuclear capabilities of the acknowledged nuclear weapons states plus Iran, which are the actors most likely to be implicated in cyber-NC3 operations as either attackers or targets. Finally, it describes twenty-one pathways to escalation in the complex gamble of cyber-nuclear operations.

CYBER VULNERABILITIES OF NUCLEAR WEAPONS

NC3 is the nervous system of nuclear deterrence. It connects some of the most complex sociotechnical information systems in existence to the most devastating weapons ever created. Many treatments of NC3 focus only on the challenges of early warning and command and control in a crisis, but it is important to appreciate that there are vital information-processing functions and technologies that enable and influence performance not only in crises but also in preparation and not only in the narrow technical channels of military command and control but also in the broader political information-processing environment. Thus, it is useful to take a wide view and envision NC3 as an interaction of several different functions and vulnerabilities. I list these in roughly temporal order, from preparation for a nuclear crisis to fighting a nuclear war:

- *Capabilities acquisition*: Sensors, data-processing systems, communication links, and digital components in weapons platforms are all products of upstream research, development, test, evaluation, and procurement processes. The supply chains and manufacturing facilities that produce capabilities, the supercomputers that model and evaluate their performance, and the technical personnel and managers of these systems are all potential intelligence targets. A hostile adversary might exploit these vectors well in advance of a crisis to preposition capabilities for sabotage that can be activated later on. Upstream friction could also undermine readiness (or proliferation) and increase financial costs of fielding a fully functional deterrent. Finally, hostile intelligence gathering targeting capabilities enables the enemy to devise countermeasures, which may or may not be revealed prior to a crisis.

- *Strategic assessment*: National intelligence collection, analysis, and reporting, together with political assessment and decision functions, enable those who direct (and take direction from) the National Military Command System to determine the context, nature, extent, and stakes of a nuclear crisis. Upstream of a crisis, many of the same organizations also contribute to the formulation of nuclear war plans. Increasingly planning has a cyber dimension as planners consider the defense of computer networks and offensive cyber operations before and during a crisis. Vulnerabilities include the loyalty of trusted personnel, the reliability and complexity of the information environment, perceptions of attribution and intention informing military contingency plans, and the security of war plans themselves.
- *Early warning*: Space satellites and air- or ground-based sensors monitor enemy nuclear forces and potential nuclear combat areas in peacetime and wartime. It is imperative to detect and interpret events such as enemy missile launches to understand whether deterrence has failed and determine how much time is available for response prior to impact. Early warning can be strategically stabilizing if it discourages the enemy from mobilizing for a surprise attack. Direct (kinetic) or information (nonkinetic) attacks on early-warning infrastructure—satellites in orbit, ground-control stations, connective communication links—can potentially create early-warning false positives (spoofing an attack) or false negatives (blinding detection of an attack).
- *Operational control*: Systems aggregate intelligence data for political leaders and military commanders and enable them to send instructions to operational units in the field. Secure, authenticated, redundant communication networks tie everything in the operational NC3 system together. Hostile intelligence operations could compromise legitimate access to NC3 data and functionality, the integrity of authorized and authenticated data and commands, or the confidentiality in operational communications. Under the right conditions, the compromise of confidentiality, integrity, or access could result in undesirable outcomes including unauthorized launch, accidental launch, launch failure, or targeting error.
- *Tactical systems*: Nuclear forces deployed on land, in the air, or under the waves must be able to receive and authenticate instructions and send back status reports. Platform diversity and dispersal ensures that at least some nuclear forces can survive an enemy attack and be available for retaliation. Thus, the nuclear triad is supposed to provide the secure second-strike capability that is the sine qua non of stable deterrence. In addition to the supply-chain vulnerabilities discussed above

(e.g., inserting digital components more likely to malfunction on command), attack vectors include tactical command and control networks and weapons system telemetry. Adverse consequences include launch failure, premature launch, guidance failure and targeting, and self-destruction on the ground or in flight.

All of these physical and organizational (sociotechnical) components together form a complex distributed information system that controls the use and nonuse of nuclear weapons. This system must meet stringent criteria. To provide a credible deterrent, a nuclear arsenal must *always* be ready when orders are given by legitimate authority, but it must *never* be usable by unauthorized persons or by accident. The "always-never" criteria pose a dilemma because weapons must be promptly available to authorized users who make threats to use them, yet the same users must be able to reassure targets that they will not be used if the target complies with the threat. Weapons that are ready to launch at a moment's notice or triggered automatically are more likely to be used inadvertently, which would violate the "never" criterion. Weapons that are decoupled from NC3 and covered with safeguards against unauthorized launch might not be available in time during a nuclear crisis, and they risk destruction by enemy preemption. This violates the "always" criterion.

Modern NC3 systems use technical means and organizational procedures to mitigate the always-never dilemma through redundant communications, concealed and dispersed forces, multiple contingency plans and detailed standard operating procedures drilled into military organizations, and rigorously tested and exercised technical architectures.[3] Indeed, advanced information technologies can potentially improve NC3. An expanded range and number of sensors can improve early warning, while the ability to aggregate and analyze data from sensors and other information sources can improve the ability to distinguish true warnings from false indications. Robust networks can connect multiple command centers and dispersed weapons systems to improve survivability and enhance collective situational awareness. Better cryptographic authentication protocols can improve trust among people in the system. High-fidelity targeting data and precision-guided weapons can increase confidence in destroying enemy targets or intercepting enemy missiles. Monitoring, reporting, auditing, and authentication schemes enable network operators to detect and correct data-processing problems.

Unfortunately, the price of more sophisticated NC3 is more complex failure modes, which are harder to understand, and a larger attack surface, which is harder to defend. Remote intrusions and the target's reaction to them have the potential to undermine either the "always" criterion by disabling weapons launch or the "never" criterion by initiating unauthorized launch. These possibilities are not just science fiction, even if the reality is far more complicated than the plots of movies such as the 1983 classic *WarGames*. Indeed, concerns about offensive cyber operations targeting NC3 are all too plausible. Vulnerabilities have been discovered in historical NC3 systems that could potentially be exploited by a sophisticated adversary. Nuclear safety experts have compiled a disconcerting list of computer glitches, loose components, early-warning radar faults, and human mistakes that have not only resulted in close calls but also revealed the potential for malicious interference.[4] In 2013 the commander of US Strategic Command stated he was "very concerned with the potential of a cyber-related attack on our nuclear command and control and on the weapons systems themselves."[5]

Historical experience further suggests that some political actors have the willingness and ability to hack nuclear systems. A Cold War program known as Canopy Wing combined electronic warfare and information operations to degrade Soviet nuclear and conventional control. According to Warsaw Pact officials who became aware of the program through espionage, it "sent ice-cold shivers down our spines."[6] The revelation of the Stuxnet malware in 2010 demonstrated American and Israeli willingness to conduct intrusions into nuclear infrastructure and disrupt it while also highlighting the operational challenges of crafting and conducting remote covert sabotage.[7] The Israeli military reportedly used cyber operations to disable Syrian air defenses during its 2007 raid on a Syrian nuclear facility.[8] The United States, furthermore, may have conducted cyber and electronic warfare operations to "remotely manipulate data inside North Korea's missile systems."[9] While this was reportedly part of a US counterproliferation initiative, as distinguished from a counterforce measure, this episode highlights the potential utility of employing cyber and electronic warfare measures "left of launch" (i.e., disrupting or disabling enemy weapons prior to use) in an actual warfighting scenario.

Fortunately, this historical experience has also encouraged increased attention to engineering reliable systems through the years. Redundancy and resilience emerge as recurrent defensive principles across multiple categories of NC3 failure, whether the result of accident or attack. NC3 systems may thus employ parallel or backup sensors, communication links, authentication protocols, and weapons to identify and overcome errors caused by malicious hacking. Insofar as cyberattacks target single points of failure or corrupt key data, reducing the number and exposure of critical nodes and increasing error detection and correction are usually priorities. System heterogeneity is another principle that can be used to avoid technical monocultures that are easier to target, although the system-engineering integration challenges mount considerably with heterogeneity.

Just as attack vectors implicate technical systems, psychological perceptions, or some combination, defenses usually incorporate some combination of technical and policy measures. Defensive measures range from preventive action before a crisis to active mitigation during a crisis. Mitigations respond to perceived vulnerabilities in each NC3 segment. Confidence in capabilities acquisition might be improved by onshoring logistics and vertically integrating supply chains to reduce exposure to hostile intelligence. Redundant supplies and verification protocols reduce the impact of and complicate the achievement of enemy compromise. The integrity of strategic assessment in policy and intelligence organizations is improved through various measures, including counterintelligence monitoring and investigation, use of multiple political and intelligence advisers and all-source analytical fusion to control bias or compromise, proactive public affairs and active defense strategies to counter disinformation, and crisis hotline arrangements. Early-warning systems might be enhanced by fielding multiple redundant overlapping sensors employing multiple detection phenomenology feeding into all-source intelligence fusion. Operational control can be improved by fielding redundant communication and authentication channels in case one network goes down. Yet it is also important to limit connections and exposure to potentially hostile access. Throughout the NC3 system, cybersecurity best practices should be employed, such as active network monitoring and human-reliability screening and training. Finally, the reliability of tactical systems is typically achieved by expanding and diversifying the arsenal (i.e., relying on redundancy or overkill) as well as rigorous and continuous testing and evaluation practices.

Achieving security, reliability, and resilience is expensive. These defensive measures usually impose serious financial and information-processing burdens on human organizations, potentially undermining the efficiency of operations. Redundancy and heterogeneity can also increase the risk of "normal accidents" if tightly coupled systems with nonlinear interactions end up operating outside of designed scenarios.[10] In NC3 as everywhere with complex systems, reliability is an ongoing balancing act full of painful trade-offs. NC3 is inherently complex, and the complexity only increases as we factor in strategic interaction between the nuclear and cyber domains.

COMPARING THE NUCLEAR AND CYBER DOMAINS

While cyber warfare is sometimes likened to a new weapon of mass destruction capable of great societal disruption, this comparison is misleading.[11] The operational characteristics of the cyber and nuclear domains are strikingly different in terms of the nature of capabilities involved and the material and organizational requirements for weaponization (see table 6.1). These are general

TABLE 6.1. Comparison of Operational Factors in the Nuclear and Cyber Domains

Operational factor	Nuclear weapons	Offensive cyber operations
Damage mechanism	Direct blast, fire, radiation	Indirect influence and espionage
Damage severity	Extreme—cities, populations, planet	Generally low; higher levels possible
Reversibility	Low—devastation, lingering effects	High—repair, redirect, reinstall
Delivery	Stand-off weapons, missiles	Remote access, social engineering
Payload	Thermonuclear detonation	Control, persistence, exfiltrate, disrupt
Feasibility of defense	Limited due to low probability of interception and high cost of misses	Difficult but possible using counterintelligence methods
Timeline	Rapid delivery with instant devastation	Tactically fast but operationally slow with indefinite persistence
Command and control	Centralized	Decentralized
System complexity	Complicated but well characterized	Extreme diversity and connectivity
System jurisdiction	National command authority	Globalized civil society
Targeting	Deliberate planning process	Detailed intelligence and extensive planning
Reliability	Production, testing, models, exercise	Custom engineering each use

tendencies, and there are plenty of nuances and exceptions in practice. Yet ideal types can be useful for conceptualizing the essence of the danger. This section summarizes the differences for tactical operations, strategic interactions, and capability proliferation in these two domains. These differences highlight the potential for tensions and complexity when cyber operations are combined or interacting with nuclear weapons. Given these extreme differences, it would be rash to simply assume that strategic dynamics of either domain will remain unchanged through interaction with the other.

At the tactical level, nuclear weapons create severe and irreversible damage (with exceptions such as an airburst for demonstration), and they do it very quickly. These extreme tactical effects give nuclear weapons their outsize strategic importance. By contrast, cyber operations generally create little to no damage (with exceptions such as massive critical infrastructure attack), and once discovered their effects can often be remediated. Moreover, most cyber operations are conducted over a long period of time, maintaining persistence where they can collect information or exert influence indefinitely (quite in contrast to the popular trope about cyber warfare being at the speed of electrons). Defense against nuclear warheads speeding in from outer space is extremely difficult, and the costs of missing even one are extremely high: a city annihilated and millions of lives lost. Missile defenses are improving but still unreliable, and left-of-launch cyber and electronic warfare methods are fraught with difficulty. Cyber defense is also widely thought to be difficult (and relatively harder than offense) since attackers craft their intrusions to evade defenses and complicate attribution; however, network monitoring and counterintelligence techniques can shift the balance. Indeed, the offense-defense balance starts to look more favorable for defense against complex, high-value targets.[12]

One striking difference in the management of the two domains is the centralization of most states' nuclear enterprises, including an elaborate regime of tests and exercises, to realize always-never criteria. Cyber command and control tends to be more distributed, leveraging networks of compromised computers in the target network and possibly on the Internet. Cyber operations rely on the commercial technologies and shared connections of a global domain rather than the specialized and highly controlled technologies of the nuclear realm. Nuclear weapons can be tested on an instrumented range or computationally simulated with precise scientific models to create confidence in each standardized weapon design. But almost every cyber operation relies on custom engineering for each new target and considerable intelligence preparation (potentially including human intelligence) to tailor the intrusion and payload for novel circumstances.

Operational aspects inform but do not necessarily determine the strategic utility of particular types of weapons. The political utility of a technical capability ultimately depends on incentives for action or restraint based on expectations of how other actors will behave. Strategic concepts for nuclear weapons are perhaps more mature than for cyber operations, which is not surprising since the strategic studies community in many ways was a product of the nuclear revolution. Furthermore, the problems of intelligence and subterfuge have received comparatively little attention in the field of international relations.[13]

Modern social scientific understandings of the causes of war and the credibility of deterrence emphasize the importance of information.[14] The main reason that nuclear and cyber strategic dynamics differ so much is because the nuclear and cyber domains have markedly different informational characteristics. The basic strategic facts about nuclear weapons are easily appreciated. The high costs of nuclear use and potential retaliation make nuclear threats most credible when used to defend vital interests such as regime survival but less credible for compellent threats that seek to revise the status quo.[15] Nuclear weapons can and must be revealed to establish a credible deterrent threat. By contrast, the implications and even capabilities of cyber operations are murky to most people, even commanders with all the right clearances and accesses. Cyber intrusions, which rely on secrecy and careful preparation, cannot be revealed if the attacker wants them to remain viable for a future contingency. The "cyber commitment problem" refers to the unsuitability of cyber means for coercion due to the fact that revelation of the threat, which is needed to separate credible threats from bluffs, would enable the target to patch or reconfigure its networks to mitigate the threat.[16] The imperative to maintain access to target systems and preserve the viability of shared networks is a reinforcing source of restraint in the cyber domain distinct from the fear of retaliation (usually in different domains—e.g., economic sanctions or a conventional military response).[17]

These extreme informational differences tend to push nuclear and cyber operations to the opposite ends of the conflict spectrum. A threat to use nuclear weapons is tantamount to threatening total war, owing to the severe costs of a "limited" nuclear war and the escalatory risks involved. Such a threat is most credible in defense of vital interests yet less credible for peripheral interests (or, as some would argue, for compellence). Cyber operations, by contrast, can be used to pursue marginal revision in the distribution of power and benefits by conducting intelligence and covert action in peacetime as well as war, where they can be a force multiplier for action in the other domains (land, sea, air, space). The interaction of the cyber and nuclear domains has different consequences depending on which is the main domain of action. Nuclear threats can serve implicitly or explicitly to bound the severity of cyberattacks (as suggested by the 2018 Nuclear Posture Review from the Donald Trump administration). Yet NC3 targeting cyber operations, which rely fundamentally on deception, tend to undermine the stability of nuclear deterrence, which relies on transparency.[18]

These operational and strategic characteristics result in very different proliferation dynamics for nuclear and cyber capabilities, as summarized in table 6.3. The operational factors discussed above (see table 6.1) imply quite different financial, technical, organizational, and market barriers to entry. Cyber operations do require a little more than just technical expertise and an Internet connection—namely, the organizational capacity to collect intelligence and conduct covert activity—but this is slight compared to the scientific and military infrastructure required for nuclear weapons. The strategic factors (see table 6.2) result in additional disincentives to acquire nuclear

TABLE 6.2. Comparison of Strategic Factors in the Nuclear and Cyber Domains

Strategic factors	Nuclear weapons	Offensive cyber operations
Intellectual concepts	Mature	Immature
Informational quality	Can be revealed without reducing utility (and must be revealed for deterrence)	Deceptive sources and methods require secrecy to remain viable
Commitment problem	High costs of retaliation	Revelation undermines capability
Political usefulness	Enhance status quo stability	Marginal revision of power balance
Warfighting utility	Limited (counterforce school)	Force multiplier (C4ISR)
Deterrence utility	Credible protection of vital interests	Limited (reputation for cyber ability)
Compellence utility	Less credible for revising status quo	Limited (ransomware)
Interdependence	Mutual exposure	Shared protocols, networks, trade
Political logic	Mutual assured destruction	Intelligence and covert action
Conflict spectrum	High end	Low end
Incentives for restraint	Nuclear retaliation and escalation	Loss of access and cross-domain action
Cross-domain effects	Offensive cyber operations undermine strategic stability	Nuclear deterrence bounds the severity of cyberattacks

Note: C4ISR = command, control, communications, intelligence, surveillance, and reconnaissance.

weapons—namely, the risk of preventative war and sanctions from powers who would prefer not to be coerced by them.[19] Deterrence and counterproliferation might be backed up by a normative system of arms control treaties and inspection regimes. By contrast, there are few strategic disincentives to the acquisition of cyber capabilities and many incentives for states looking for a way to work around the strengths of their adversaries. Given the reliance on deception for cyber operations, cyber arms control proposals are inherently incredible (i.e., they require participants to promise not to lie, which is a good way to cover lying behavior).

Supply- and demand-side barriers have limited nuclear proliferation to (currently) only a handful of states, and there are strong disincentives for any

TABLE 6.3. Comparison of Proliferation Factors in the Nuclear and Cyber Domains

Proliferation factor	Nuclear weapons	Offensive cyber operations
Financial barriers	Higher	Lower
Technical barriers	Expertise, fuel cycle, labs, testing	Computer science expertise
Operational barriers	Delivery systems, NC3	Intelligence and operations
Market barriers	Tightly controlled	Thriving commercial market
Strategic barriers	Risk of preventative war and sanctions	None
Dual-use	Nuclear energy	Ubiquitous digital networks
Norms	"Nuclear taboo" and historic nonuse	Weak norms and endemic usage
Arms control treaties	NPT, PTBT, OST, START, etc.	Cybercrime, economic espionage
Enforcement	Intelligence, inspections, sanctions	Infeasible: secrecy and deception
Capable actors	Nine nuclear weapon states	Many states and nonstate actors
Terrorist threat	High barriers but "loose nuke" risk	Attractive and available at low end

Note: NC3 = nuclear command, control, and communications; NPT = Non-Proliferation Treaty; PTBT = Partial Test Ban Treaty; OST = Outer Space Treaty; START = Strategic Arms Reduction Treaty

of them to proliferate to terrorists.[20] Cyber proliferation is comparatively unrestrained, however, especially at the low end of the conflict spectrum where cyber criminals and spies alike can and do flourish. Low-end activity, moreover, including planting propaganda and agitating on social media, could potentially be destabilizing in a nuclear crisis if it muddied political and intelligence assessments of the situation and enemy intentions. The attribution problem, and thus the risk of misattribution, is also greater at the lower end, but then the consequences are lower too (unless admixed with crises and operations in other domains).[21]

For good reasons, there are high barriers to acquiring and using nuclear weapons. Once acquired, they are most useful for deterrence because they improve mutual information about the high costs of war. The barriers to acquiring and using cyber capabilities, by contrast, are much lower. Because cyber operations depend fundamentally on secrecy and deception, they are better used in support of military or intelligence operations rather than coercive signaling (deterrence or compellence). In almost every respect, the cyber and nuclear domains are complementary—that is, they have nearly opposite characteristics. This means that combinations can interfere in interesting, or alarming, ways. A full analysis of these complementarities is beyond the scope of this chapter, but they are summarized here simply to demonstrate how stark the differences are, which is suggestive of ways in which the integration of more cyber systems into NC3 might complicate what we think we know about good old nuclear deterrence.

CYBER CAPABILITIES OF NUCLEAR WEAPONS STATES

Offensive cyber operations targeting NC3 are far more technically demanding than other types of cyber operations. They require lengthy reconnaissance to gather detailed intelligence, specific technical expertise on the NC3 and weapons systems of the enemy state, testing and rehearsal to assure commanders that the operation will work as intended, and some assessment of the enemy organization's routines and human behavior to understand how the target will behave with or compensate for degraded NC3. The Stuxnet operation targeting Iranian nuclear enrichment, for example, took many years of careful preparation and many intelligence resources, and that was simply targeting the fuel cycle.[22] Targeting the NC3 systems of an operational deterrent should be expected to be even more difficult and sensitive.

Many cyber operations that might target NC3 in principle never materialize due to technical hurdles and operational requirements. Any sensitive targeted operation must be carefully planned and monitored via supporting command and control networks to receive feedback on the progress of the intrusion and to push updates and instructions to the attack code, and external sources of intelligence are needed to search for indications of compromise. These are difficult tasks for even mature signals and human intelligence agencies such as the National Security Agency and the Central Intelligence Agency. Not coincidentally, states with the requisite organizational capacity for sophisticated cyber operations also happen to be nuclear weapons states.

Moreover, there are also strategic reasons why nuclear weapons states are more likely to be interested in a cyber-NC3 capability. The risks involved in cyber-NC3 operations are significant—operational failure, counterintelligence compromise, inadvertent escalation—and must be offset by some potential benefit in a nuclear warfighting scenario or for gathering intelligence to support that eventuality. Those actors who do decide to take the risks of penetrating enemy NC3 will almost certainly want some sort of insurance policy (i.e., other counterforce capabilities or a robust nuclear deterrence posture) to offset potential compromise of offensive cyber operations. Furthermore, states that believe that they enjoy coercive benefits from having a mature nuclear deterrent will tend to resist the entry of new entrants to the nuclear club since nuclear proliferation to rivals would constrain their freedom of action. The creation of cyber effects against NC3 becomes attractive as a means for limiting proliferation or degrading immature deterrents. For operational and strategic reasons, therefore, NC3 intrusions are most likely to be conducted by nuclear powers with the ability and willingness to backstop cyber operations with other forms of power.

Table 6.4 lists the acknowledged nuclear weapons states plus Iran, which is the state most likely to make a dash for the bomb given the unraveling of the Joint Comprehensive Plan of Action during the Trump presidency. The size and posture of the nuclear arsenals of these states vary considerably. The former Cold War superpowers are in a class unto themselves with large and varied arsenals. Both of them have somewhat ambiguous postures but for different reasons. The United States provides extended deterrence to its allies and thus cannot make a no-first-use pledge, relies on a wide range of nuclear options for countervalue and counterforce strikes, and reserves the right to threaten nuclear retaliation against catastrophic nonnuclear attacks. Russia has no meaningful extended-deterrence commitments but has a large arsenal of nonstrategic nuclear weapons that it might brandish in a compellent role or to "escalate to deescalate." States such as China and India have minimal deterrence postures with declaratory pledges for no first use, which is generally believed to be good for strategic stability. Others, as discussed with the United States and Russia, also hope to use their arsenals for something more than simply deterring nuclear attacks on the homeland, including deterring nonnuclear attacks, extending deterrence to allies, and coercive diplomacy. More ambiguous and aggressive postures, which are designed to make nuclear weapons more usable in this expanded range of situations, carry increased risks of strategic instability.[23]

These states also vary in their proficiency at cyber offense and cyber defense. The United States stands head and shoulders above the rest in terms of intelligence capacity and political-economic advantages in cyberspace. Russia and China have even larger programs, although their comparative advantages in information warfare or "active measures" (Russia) and political surveillance and industrial espionage (China) are not necessarily fungible to offensive cyber operations targeting NC3. States coded as "maturing" probably lack the ability to achieve a deep and dangerous penetration into a target's NC3 (especially targets with "leading" or better cyber defense); they also may have difficulty detecting and mitigating a penetration (especially by "leading" or better attackers).

The rightmost columns in table 6.4 offer a rough assessment of the risks of nuclear escalation due to relative cyber offensive and defensive capabilities in the context of rival nuclear balances. Nuclear rivalries can be assessed for

TABLE 6.4. Acknowledged Nuclear Weapons, State Nuclear, and Cyber Capabilities

State	Warheads (deployed)[1]	Nuclear posture	Cyber offense[2]	Cyber defense[3]	Nuclear rivals	Cyber-nuclear risk in rivalries
USA	6,450 (1,750)	Ambiguous: extended deterrence and counterforce	Top	Top 0.91 (2nd)	Russia, China, DPRK, (Iran)	Moderate
Russia	6,850 (1,600)	Ambiguous: strategic triad and nonstrategic arsenal	Leading	Leading 0.79 (10th)	USA, China, UK, France	Moderate
China	280	Minimal, NFU	Leading	Maturing 0.62 (32nd)	USA, India, Russia	Moderate
UK	215 (120)	General	Leading	Leading 0.78 (12th)	Russia	Low
France	300 (280)	General	Maturing	Leading 0.81 (8th)	Russia	Low
India	130–140	Minimal, NFU	Maturing	Maturing 0.68 (23rd)	Pakistan, China	Low
Pakistan	140–150	Asymmetrical	Maturing	Maturing 0.45 (66th)	India	Moderate
North Korea	10–20	Ambiguous, asymmetrical	Maturing	Maturing 0.53 (52nd)	USA	High
Iran	0	Latency	Maturing	Maturing 0.49 (59th)	USA	High

Note: DPRK = Democratic Peoples' Republic of Korea; NFU = no first use; UK = United Kingdom; USA = United States.
1. "World Nuclear Forces," in Stockholm International Peace Research Institute, *SIPRI Yearbook 2018: Armaments, Disarmament and International Security* (Oxford: Oxford University Press, 2018), https://www.sipri.org/yearbook/2018/06.
2. Author assessment.
3. International Telecommunication Union, *Global Cybersecurity Index 2017*, https://www.itu.int/dms_pub/itu-d/opb/str/D-STR-GCI.01-2017-R1-PDF-E.pdf. The Global Cybersecurity Index (GCI) is a composite measure (with rank across countries included) of legal, technical, organizational, capacity building, and cooperation to enhance national cybersecurity for both the government and private sector. Singapore is the only state to receive a higher GCI than the United States.

the potential for strategic instability resulting from cyber-nuclear interactions. Cyber-NC3 interactions are most relevant strategically when the attacker has nuclear weapons, and cyber-NC3 destabilization is most likely to be felt in a brinksmanship crisis between nuclear rivals. The most dangerous situation is an asymmetrical dyad where a small nuclear arsenal with weaker cyber defenses faces a stronger nuclear power with potent cyber offense capability, such as North Korea versus the United States. Defenders with larger arsenals or more competent cyber defense would tend to reduce the incentives for rivals to engage in NC3 cyberattacks. States such as the United States, Russia, and China all face moderate risk because while they have retaliatory forces or competent cyber defenses, they also face an adversary with the capability and possibly the motivation to intrude into NC3 systems.

While space precludes detailed discussion, this variation in nuclear and cyber capabilities and postures is suggestive of considerable complexity in any given dyad for any given crisis scenario. To increase the complexity further, we now turn to the various mechanisms by which these actors might find themselves drawn into an escalatory scenario exacerbated by offensive cyber operations.

TWENTY-ONE WAYS TO DIE

The combination of offensive cyber operations and nuclear weapons creates many different pathways for escalation, which imperils strategic stability. Strategic stability in this context refers to the marginal risk of the outbreak of nuclear war or escalation of a war to a higher level of intensity as a result of cyber-nuclear interactions.[24]

Table 6.5 lists twenty-one different ways in which cyber operations can exacerbate the risks of nuclear escalation. The columns distinguish these mechanisms by the time period when they are most salient (peace, crisis, or war). The rows distinguish them by the actor responsible for the decision to escalate the use of nuclear weapons, which may or may not be the same actor that makes the decision to conduct cyber operations. Those that involve rational incentives to escalate, as contrasted with subrational psychology, are indicated with an asterisk. Space constraints preclude a detailed analysis of the risks and likelihood of each pathway, but this conjectural summary is at least suggestive of the multiple and potentially interacting routes to escalation inherent in cyber-nuclear operations. The pathways to Armageddon could be multiplied indefinitely by combining these mechanisms with each other and focusing on effects in specific segments of the nuclear enterprise. No claim is implied here that these mechanisms constitute a mutually exclusive or collectively exhaustive typology. I highlight twenty-one of them simply to underscore the uncertainty and luck involved in any cyber-nuclear gamble.

TABLE 6.5. Cyber-Nuclear Escalation Mechanisms by Actor and Timing

Actor	Peace	Crisis	War
The cyberattacker escalates with nuclear weapons	1. Surprise nuclear first strike uses cyber operations to paralyze NC3: "cyber bolt from the blue"	2. Reliance on secrecy that cannot be revealed for coercion: "the cyber commitment problem"* 3. Overconfidence in cyber counterforce capability	4. Closing window of cyber effectiveness due to the invalidation of planning assumptions caused by damage or wartime reserve modes*
Either the cyberattacker or target escalates	5. Accidental launch due to mishap or malfunction in NC3 computers	6. Information overload, panic, and confused decision-making resulting from system failure: "fog of cyberwar" 7. Closing window for damage limitation: "first-move advantage"*	8. Nuclear retaliation in response to a massive cyberattack 9. Deliberate launch of nuclear weapons, hitting the wrong targets
The target of cyberattack escalates	10. Inability to distinguish cyberattacks from intelligence probes ("the cybersecurity dilemma")		
	11. Compromised preventative attack heightens resolve of nuclear proliferator 12. Capitulation in a prior cyber-nuclear crisis results in improved capability or resolve next time	13. Cyber activity creates false early-warning indications that pressure target to launch 14. Target misattributes source of cyberattack and mistakenly retaliates 15. Compromised cyber preemption heightens target hostility or resolve	16. Closing window for retaliation due to attacks on nuclear forces / NC3: "use it or lose it" 17. Closing window for nuclear use due to attacks on dual-use C3I during a conventional war: "entanglement" 18. Escalating during a losing war in hopes of favorable terms: "gambling for resurrection"
Nuclear escalation encouraged by a third party	19. Deliberate but unauthorized launch by an insider threat or external hacker 20. Cyberattack masquerading as third party to prompt retaliation: "false flag"		
	21. Chronic disinformation and influence operations distort planning and assessment, creating a crisis-prone environment		

Note: C3I = command, control, communications, and intelligence; NC3 = nuclear command, control, and communications.
* Rational incentives to escalate.

The risks of breakdown in complex systems and human confusion in the fog of war have received the lion's share of attention in the literature on organizational reliability.[25] NC3 architects are generally familiar with these sorts of risks even if they have not, or ultimately cannot, eliminate them completely. Because NC3 systems interface directly with human decision-makers, degradation of NC3 under cyberattack carries the potential to degrade the quality of decision-making. This might be described as "the fog of cyber war" (scenario 6). Cyberattacks might degrade the quality of incoming warning data and reports from operational units and outgoing requests for information and instructions to units. Time pressure, fear, panic, exhaustion, and organizational politics—fog and friction—can all degrade the quality of decision-making in crisis or war. Most analysis of cyber-nuclear risk falls into this general category.[26] A variant of this problem might emerge not from cyberattacks on NC3 per se but on the intelligence and assessment functions, perhaps even including social media manipulation that contributes to a climate of hostility and mistrust (scenario 21), which might complicate assessment of the nature and stakes of the crisis.[27] The fog of war in cyberspace can surely be an exacerbating factor in many of the other scenarios.

It is important to appreciate that some version of subrational or bounded rational thinking is usually invoked in typical crisis-escalation scenarios that stress the potential for misperception, miscalculation, and error. Indeed, many of the scenarios listed in table 6.5 involve some deviation from strictly rational utility maximization. Actors may be risk averse for gains and risk accepting for losses. They may think "hot" or emotionally under pressure. They may use heuristics and "thin slice" rather than gather or use all the information available. Bounded rational thinking has been demonstrated in experiments and found to be relevant in historical case studies.[28] How decision-makers react to the information revealed depends on assumptions about rationality.

Indeed, only three scenarios in table 6.5 feature fully rational incentives, marked with an asterisk. It is possible that cooler heads and more rational thinkers might avoid disaster in the other eighteen scenarios. For instance, as systems begin malfunctioning, and as it becomes obvious that the enemy has launched a cyberattack degrading NC3 reliability, a rational victim might realize that the balance of power is no longer favorable. A rational victim experiencing a degrading cyberattack might thus be willing to compromise short of war. The three rationalist mechanisms are thus in some ways more concerning. Less appreciated than the fog of cyberwar but in some ways more worrisome is the potential for rational miscalculation that results from strategic information asymmetries created by cyber operations. Reliance on pervasive digital computer networks can increase the complexity of the system, which increases intrinsic operational uncertainty. More problematically, hackers must rely on stealth and deception to exploit NC3, which increases strategic information asymmetry. Anything that contributes to information asymmetry regarding the balance of power and resolve is a potential source for bargaining failure or war.[29]

In the "cyber commitment problem" (scenario 2), for example, the enemy attack on NC3 can never be revealed to the target in advance because its effectiveness depends on secrecy.[30] Effective deterrence requires an actor to reveal its willingness and capacity to punish the target under some particular circumstances. Deterrence, as well as negotiated settlements to crises that restore deterrence, depend on common knowledge about the balance of power, mutual interests, and the expected costs and outcomes of war. Unfortunately, a cyberattack that disables NC3 cannot be revealed to the target for coercion before or during a crisis since the target could take steps to disarm the intrusion. Thus, the target stands fast, believing it can win a contest of brinksmanship, and the attacker also stands fast, believing it can win a counterforce exchange. Eventually the attacker decides that war is inevitable and moves to preempt or limit damage with a combination of cyber and nuclear means.

The other two plausibly rationalist mechanisms in table 6.5 involve closing windows of opportunity. Since cyber operations targeting NC3 depend on careful planning and detailed intelligence, circumstances that threaten to undermine the conditions for their effectiveness are particularly worrisome. Even if the cyber information asymmetry is not implicated in the initiation of a nuclear war, the closing window of cyber viability (scenario 4) creates rational pressures to use capabilities while they are still available for counterforce or damage limitation. On the other side, an actor may calculate that a rival known to have advanced cyber capabilities will begin to initiate counterforce attacks and rush to launch damage-limitation strikes while NC3 is still viable (scenario 7), even if the forces themselves are not at risk. This is akin to the classic scenario described by Thomas Schelling where both sides rush to execute a disarming first strike.

Additional window mechanisms can be activated by more bounded rational thinking. For instance, cyberattacks on networks that are used for both conventional C3 and NC3 might be attacked in a conventional war for conventional benefits. However, the (nuclear-conventional) "entangled" target becomes worried that these attacks are actually preparatory to nuclear war (misinterpreted warning, scenario 13) or are degrading the usability of nuclear forces ("use it or lose it," scenario 16) or are degrading the opportunity to attack enemy nuclear forces if needed (damage limitation window, scenario 7).[31]

The plausibility of these scenarios varies depending on the complexity of the operations involved and the behavioral assumptions needed to get to nuclear escalation. The most plausible appear to be the fog of cyber warfare (scenario 6), damage-limitation window (scenario 7), cyber commitment problem (scenario 2), and foiled prevention (scenario 11). The last of these is, interestingly, a peacetime risk factor created using cyber operations to prevent nuclear proliferation. The inadvertent compromise of this operation, as in the Stuxnet attack against Iran, increases the resolve of the proliferator to acquire a weapon. Most of the other scenarios can be considered merely possible risks because they require numerous supporting assumptions to significantly raise the chances of cyber-enabled nuclear escalation. Some, such as the false flag (scenario 20) and the bolt from the blue (scenario 1), require quite heroic political and operational assumptions. These are left as an exercise for the reader.

Plausibility aside, the magnitude of the risk also varies. Consider once again the example of foiled prevention (scenario 11)—the discovery of an adversary's attempt to use cyber operations to degrade a latent nuclear capability. This event heightens mistrust and tension in future nuclear crises, should they transpire, but by itself is a very indirect risk factor for escalation. By contrast, the most dangerous scenario is perhaps the cyber commitment problem (scenario 2). The confluence of hidden operations (which produce information asymmetry) and strategic rationality (which makes the expected value of war greater than the expected value of settlement) makes it a dangerous eventuality indeed, since even perfectly rational actors will have incentives to initiate a nuclear war for the sake of damage limitation as the crisis bargaining range closes. In most other scenarios, a sober appraisal of costs and benefits would be more likely to reveal incentives to avoid or mitigate escalation. The risk analysis then turns on the sobriety of the very human individuals and institutions that implement competing NC3 systems.

CONCLUSION

The interaction between cyber operations and nuclear weapons is incredibly complex. The complexity and danger of this interaction is only partly a function of technology. There are also significant political, economic, and strategic factors associated with the cyber and nuclear domains. The expanding attack surface of modern NC3 systems creates new opportunities for exploitation but also for miscalculation and mistake. At the same time, the operational challenges associated with exploiting those vulnerabilities under actual operational and political conditions cannot be underemphasized.

The cyber and nuclear domains have radically different operational, strategic, and proliferation characteristics. One implication is that not every state will have the same capability to conduct cyber operations against enemy NC3. Nonstate actors are unlikely to have much capability at all for technical operations against the most sensitive systems, although they can certainly contribute to a degraded strategic information environment. Civilian information technologies and organizations, moreover, can also become inadvertent accomplices for sophisticated state cyber operations targeting NC3 systems. Another implication of cyber-nuclear complementarity is that age-old verities of nuclear deterrence cannot be taken for granted in the digital age.

In every case, analysis of the specific political and technological context of interaction is vital for understanding specific risks of cyber-nuclear interaction. Not all nuclear rivalries will be destabilized to the same degree by cyber operations, given asymmetrical NC3 vulnerabilities, cyber capabilities, and expected consequences. In rivalries where cyber-NC3 interactions do manifest, furthermore, not all pathways to escalation are equally plausible or dangerous. The sheer variety of pathways in combination with the complexity of the systems involved and the political complexity of any crisis, however, should give one pause.

A third nuclear weapon dropped in anger would be a major historical catastrophe. Nuclear deterrence may have helped humanity avoid this event so far. Improving the reliability of NC3 does have the potential to improve nuclear deterrence. Advocates of deterrence should thus support the digital modernization of NC3. Unfortunately, digital systems in modern NC3, and in the broader information environment of international politics, create many new risk factors. The same systems adopted to improve security and control could end up undermining both. The combination of cyber and nuclear capabilities has the potential to create a proverbial doomsday device that could be triggered despite the wishes of everyone to avoid it.

NOTES

This chapter builds on and refines a paper presented on January 22–23, 2019, at a workshop at Stanford University titled "NC3 Systems and Strategic Stability: A Global Overview," sponsored by the Nautilus Institute, Technology for Global Security, and Stanford's Preventive Defense Project. The original paper was posted as "Cyber Operations and Nuclear Weapons," NAPSNet Special Report, June 20, 2019, at https://nautilus.org/napsnet/napsnet-special-reports/cyber-operations-and-nuclear-weapons/. This chapter significantly revises the original.

1. Analyses of NC3 risks emphasizing complexity and confusion include Stephen J. Cimbala, *Nuclear Weapons in the Information Age* (New York: Continuum International Publishing, 2012); and Andrew Futter, *Hacking the Bomb: Cyber Threats and Nuclear Weapons* (Washington, DC: Georgetown University Press, 2018).
2. Analyses of NC3 risks emphasizing rational incentives to escalate include Avery Goldstein, "First Things First: The Pressing Danger of Crisis Instability in U.S.-China Relations," *International Security* 37, no. 4 (2013): 49–89; James M. Acton, "Escalation through Entanglement: How the Vulnerability of Command-and-Control Systems Raises the Risks of an Inadvertent Nuclear War," *International Security* 43,

no. 1 (August 1, 2018): 56–99; and Erik Gartzke and Jon R. Lindsay, "Thermonuclear Cyberwar," *Journal of Cybersecurity* 3, no. 1 (February 2017): 37–48.
3. Paul J. Bracken, *The Command and Control of Nuclear Forces* (New Haven, CT: Yale University Press, 1983); Christopher A. Ford, "Playing for Time on the Edge of the Apocalypse: Maximizing Decision Time for Nuclear Leaders," in *Deterrence: Its Past and Future; Papers Presented at Hoover Institution, November 2010*, ed. George Shultz, Sidney D. Drell, and James E. Goodby (Stanford, CA: Hoover Institution, 2011).
4. Shaun Gregory, *The Hidden Cost of Deterrence: Nuclear Weapons Accidents* (London: Brassey's, 1990); Scott D. Sagan, *The Limits of Safety: Organizations, Accidents, and Nuclear Weapons* (Princeton, NJ: Princeton University Press, 1995); Eric Schlosser, *Command and Control: Nuclear Weapons, the Damascus Accident, and the Illusion of Safety* (New York: Penguin, 2014).
5. Testimony of Gen. C. Robert Kehler, USAF, "Department of Defense Authorization for Appropriations Request for Fiscal Year 2014 and the Future Years Defense Program," hearing, US Senate Committee on Armed Services, March 12, 2013, 202, https://www.armed-services.senate.gov/imo/media/doc/stratcom_cybercom_fullcomm_hearing_031213.pdf.
6. Benjamin B. Fischer, "CANOPY WING: The U.S. War Plan That Gave the East Germans Goose Bumps," *International Journal of Intelligence and CounterIntelligence* 27, no. 3 (2014): 439.
7. Jon R. Lindsay, "Stuxnet and the Limits of Cyber Warfare," *Security Studies* 22, no. 3 (2013): 365–404.
8. David A. Fulghum, "Why Syria's Air Defenses Failed to Detect Israelis," *Aviation Week*, Ares (blog), October 3, 2007.
9. David E. Sanger and William J. Broad, "Trump Inherits a Secret Cyberwar against North Korean Missiles," *New York Times*, March 4, 2017.
10. Charles Perrow, *Normal Accidents: Living with High Risk Technologies*, 2nd ed. (Princeton, NJ: Princeton University Press, 1999).
11. Joseph S. Nye Jr., "Nuclear Lessons for Cyber Security?," *Strategic Studies Quarterly* 5, no. 4 (2011): 18–38.
12. Rebecca Slayton, "What Is the Cyber Offense-Defense Balance? Conceptions, Causes, and Assessment," *International Security* 41, no. 3 (January 1, 2017): 72–109; Jon R. Lindsay, "Tipping the Scales: The Attribution Problem and the Feasibility of Deterrence against Cyber Attack," *Journal of Cybersecurity* 1, no. 1 (2015): 53–67.
13. Fortunately this is changing with a new generation of scholarship on secret statecraft. See, for example, Austin Carson, *Secret Wars: Covert Conflict in International Politics* (Princeton, NJ: Princeton University Press, 2018); Lindsey A. O'Rourke, *Covert Regime Change: America's Secret Cold War* (Ithaca, NY: Cornell University Press, 2018); Michael Poznansky, *In the Shadow of International Law: Covert Intervention in the Postwar World* (New York: Oxford University Press, 2020).
14. Robert Powell, *Nuclear Deterrence Theory: The Search for Credibility* (Cambridge: Cambridge University Press, 1990); James D. Fearon, "Rationalist Explanations for War," *International Organization* 49, no. 3 (1995): 379–414; Erik Gartzke, "War Is in the Error Term," *International Organization* 53, no. 3 (1999): 567–87; Robert

Powell, "Nuclear Brinkmanship, Limited War, and Military Power," *International Organization* 69, no. 3 (2015): 589–626.
15. Todd S. Sechser and Matthew Fuhrmann, *Nuclear Weapons and Coercive Diplomacy* (New York: Cambridge University Press, 2017). See also Matthew Kroenig, *The Logic of American Nuclear Strategy: Why Strategic Superiority Matters* (New York: Oxford University Press, 2018).
16. Erik Gartzke and Jon R. Lindsay, "The Cyber Commitment Problem and the Destabilization of Nuclear Deterrence," in *Bytes, Bombs, and Spies: The Strategic Dimensions of Offensive Cyber Operations*, ed. Herbert S. Lin and Amy B. Zegart (Washington, DC: Brookings Institution Press, 2018), 195–234.
17. Jon R. Lindsay, "Restrained by Design: The Political Economy of Cybersecurity," *Digital Policy, Regulation and Governance* 19, no. 6 (2017): 493–514.
18. Gartzke and Lindsay, "Cyber Commitment Problem."
19. Nuno Monteiro and Alexandre Debs, "The Strategic Logic of Nuclear Proliferation," *International Security* 39, no. 2 (October 1, 2014): 7–51.
20. Scott D. Sagan, "The Causes of Nuclear Weapons Proliferation," *Annual Review of Political Science* 14, no. 1 (2011): 225–44, https://doi.org/10.1146/annurev-polisci-052209-131042; Keir A. Lieber and Daryl G. Press, "Why States Won't Give Nuclear Weapons to Terrorists," *International Security* 38, no. 1 (July 1, 2013): 80–104.
21. Lindsay, "Tipping the Scales."
22. Slayton, "What Is the Cyber Offense-Defense Balance?"
23. Vipin Narang, *Nuclear Strategy in the Modern Era: Regional Powers and International Conflict* (Princeton, NJ: Princeton University Press, 2014).
24. The term is contested. Generally, see Elbridge A. Colby and Michael S. Gerson, eds., *Strategic Stability: Contending Interpretations* (Carlisle Barracks, PA: Strategic Studies Institute, US Army War College, 2013).
25. Sagan, *Limits of Safety*; Diane Vaughan, *The Challenger Launch Decision: Risky Technology, Culture, and Deviance at NASA* (Chicago: University of Chicago Press, 1996); Perrow, *Normal Accidents*; Scott A. Snook, *Friendly Fire: The Accidental Shootdown of U.S. Black Hawks over Northern Iraq* (Princeton, NJ: Princeton University Press, 2000); Karl E. Weick and Kathleen M. Sutcliffe, *Managing the Unexpected: Sustained Performance in a Complex World*, 3rd ed. (Hoboken, NJ: John Wiley & Sons, 2015).
26. Cimbala, *Nuclear Weapons*; Andrew Futter, "Hacking the Bomb: Nuclear Weapons in the Cyber Age," International Studies Association Annual Conference, New Orleans, 2015.
27. "Three Tweets to Midnight: Nuclear Crisis Stability and the Information Ecosystem," Stanley Center for Peace and Security, October 2017, https://www.stanleyfoundation.org//resources.cfm?id=1646&title=Three-Tweets-to-Midnight:-Nuclear-Crisis-Stability-and-the-Information-Ecosystem.
28. J. M. Goldgeier and E. Tetlock, "Psychology and International Relations Theory," *Annual Review of Political Science* 4, no. 1 (2001): 67–92. See also Janice Gross Stein, "The Micro-Foundations of International Relations Theory: Psychology and Behavioral Economics," *International Organization* 71, no. S1 (April 2017): 249–63.
29. Fearon, "Rationalist Explanations for War." See also Gartzke, "War Is in the Error Term."

30. Gartzke and Lindsay, "Cyber Commitment Problem."
31. Goldstein, "First Things First." See also Caitlin Talmadge, "Would China Go Nuclear? Assessing the Risk of Chinese Nuclear Escalation in a Conventional War with the United States," *International Security* 41, no. 4 (April 1, 2017): 50–92; and Acton, "Escalation through Entanglement."

SEVEN

TECHNOLOGY THREATS TO NC3
PAST LESSONS AND CURRENT CHALLENGES

Wade L. Huntley

History demonstrates that technical shortcomings in the US nuclear command, control, and communications (NC3) system can be minimized but not eliminated with certainty.[1] New, emerging information technologies provide significant new efficiencies and functionalities, but they also are creating novel potential vulnerabilities and threat vectors for US adversaries to exploit using the contemporary technologies of the cyber domain. Adversaries that may have an interest in compromising US NC3 can seek to utilize a variety of means to identify vulnerabilities and devise exploitations. Subtle exploitations potentially may be combined to impinge upon the reliability and assurance of the National Military Command System at critical points. Nongovernmental analysts have sought to delineate the technical challenges cyber technologies may pose for US NC3 systems.[2] US policymakers increasingly appreciate that security requires thorough and ongoing exploration of new as well as traditional threats to US NC3 to establish the reliability of these systems in actuality and in the eyes of any potential adversary.[3]

To explore these issues, this chapter first reviews selected past incidents of NC3 shortfalls that are particularly indicative of the importance of reliable computer and communication capabilities. The chapter then spotlights selected contemporary concerns about cyber vulnerabilities to the National Military Command System.

TESTS OF NUCLEAR SAFETY

The fundamental purpose of the National Military Command System is to meet the twin criteria of the "always/never" requirement: US nuclear forces must always be available for use when needed but must never be utilized accidentally, mistakenly, or by unauthorized individuals.[4] Over the history of US nuclear weapons possession, a number of shortfalls of this surety and safety requirement have been publicly documented.[5] The most notorious of the incidents are those that generated false alarms of nuclear attack, moving decision-makers toward possible use of nuclear capabilities. An array of factors account for these incidents. Two such incidents have been traced specifically to unpredictable behavior in computer and communication equipment.

Early on the morning of June 3, 1980, computers at the North American Air Defense Command (NORAD) headquarters in Colorado Springs, Colorado, signaled to Strategic Air Command (SAC) in Omaha and the National Military Command Center in the Pentagon that a Soviet missile attack was underway. Initial response procedures were implemented: fighters were launched, strategic bomber and tanker crews were ordered to their stations and started their engines, and the National Emergency Airborne Command Post at Andrews Air Force Base taxied into position for takeoff.[6]

National Security Adviser Zbigniew Brzezinski was alerted. Some years later, Brzezinski recalled being awoken around three o'clock in the morning by his military assistant, Brig. Gen. William Odom, to be told the United States was under attack by two hundred Soviet nuclear missiles. In a droll later account, Brzezinski explained that his responsibilities for coordinating nuclear response options provided him three minutes to confirm the attack and notify the president, who would then have four minutes to decide on a response. Brzezinski further observed that the size of the reported attack, two hundred missiles, "was an interesting number because that means it's a selective counterforce strike, which means that the presidential decision would be a little more difficult." Nevertheless, while Brzezinski mulled which response options he might recommend to President Jimmy Carter, confirmations of the attack were not forthcoming. By his third minute, "it was clear that this was a false alarm. So I did nothing. I went back to sleep."[7]

Evidence disconfirming the reported attack was apparent because "key missile warning sensor systems" had not detected the incoming missiles, pointing to a false alarm generated in the NORAD computer system.[8] On June 6, 1980, a second, similar false alarm took place but was disconfirmed sooner due to precautionary measures following the first incident.[9] After the second incident, technicians identified the problem as a defective computer chip in a communication system. At that time, NORAD routinely sent messages into the network to test the communication lines; the messages were missile-attack warnings but with the number of missiles launched set to "0000." The faulty chip (which a Pentagon official said cost forty-six cents[10]), was randomly placing a number "2" in the variable, signifying a positive number of missiles launched (200, 2200, etc.) and hence indicating a real attack.[11] Thus, the number of 200 missiles conveyed in the first false alarm, which Brzezinski had interpreted as indicating a counterforce attack that would complicate presidential decision-making, was in fact only a random artifact of the particular fault in the computer chip.

These episodes followed a related incident that had occurred seven months earlier. On November 9, 1979, computers at NORAD headquarters reported indications of a large-scale missile attack on the United States by the Soviet Union, first from submarines and then from Soviet land sites. NORAD promptly relayed the attack warning to SAC, other high-level command posts, and officials in Washington. A threat assessment conference, including the SAC commander at Offutt Air Force Base, Nebraska, and the chairman of the Joint Chiefs of Staff, recognized that the attack pattern fit Pentagon assumptions of Soviet war plans. Per prepared guidelines, US intercontinental ballistic missile crews were put on highest alert, nuclear bombers were activated, and the National Emergency Airborne Command Post took off from Andrews Air Force Base, Maryland, though without President Carter on board.[12]

Many accounts have conveyed the basic finding that the cause of the false alarm was mistaken insertion into an operational computer of a training tape containing a scenario for a large-scale nuclear attack.[13] Department of Defense (DOD) officials stated the following day that the alert was not taken seriously enough to warrant notifying top civilian or military officials and was handled by "middle-level" officers.[14] But the full story is more complicated. In his cover letter to NORAD's report on the incident to the Air Force chief of staff, NORAD commander Lt. Gen. James Hartinger relayed that "the precise mode of failure of the Message Generator/Recorder on 9 November could not be replicated," and so it was unclear whether the incident was caused by a "human error, computer error, or combination of both."[15] Bureaucracy may also have had a role: a NORAD summary of a briefing and discussion session with Sen. Gary Hart conveyed that the new 427M computer in operation was still undergoing developmental testing, which was taking place on the operational system rather than in a separate, isolated system because of "lack of funds" to procure an additional computer facility for that purpose.[16] In sum, the 1979 and 1980 episodes both occurred during a years-long period of problematic implementation of a computer system upgrade. The 1979 incident, in particular, reflected a "normal accident" insofar as complex and tightly coupled systems allowed an unexpected human-machine interface to produce an unanticipated and in this case inexplicable outcome.[17]

These incidents are well known because shortfalls of the safety requirement that US nuclear weapons never be utilized accidentally or mistakenly could be catastrophic. But the complementary surety requirement that US nuclear weapons always be available for use when needed has also experienced episodes of failure. Such failures are inherently less newsworthy because they do not raise the specter of imminent, accidental, or unauthorized nuclear use, but they are no less salient to the security of the National Military Command System.

The computer-related incidents discussed in this section carry new implications in the cyber age. Traditionally, securing the National Military Command System on both sides of the always/never requirement has focused on technical reliability and physical protection, particularly in the event of actual nuclear combat. Accordingly, the causes in each of the incidents reviewed above turned out to be internal. Nevertheless, each case expressed effects that can now be generated by external actors using cyber means, at least in theory. That prospect opens a new dimension of challenges to sustaining the always/never requirement of the National Military Command System now and into the future. Moreover, the kinds of effects that cyber penetration of NC3 might generate create novel strategic implications that have yet to be fully fathomed.[18]

VULNERABILITIES OF THE DIGITAL AGE

Recent assessments have cataloged the need for renovating the obsolescent information technologies of the National Military Command System.[19] In this context, the potential vulnerabilities to deliberate malicious intrusion of both existing systems and more sophisticated updated systems have also gained increasing attention within the DOD and among outside observers. A seminal 2013 Defense Science Board examination of cyberthreats across the US military noted that most nuclear weapons systems had not been evaluated against "top tier" cyberthreats and urged prioritization of the "cyber resiliency of the nuclear deterrent" against a "full spectrum" of threats, including supply chains, insiders, communications, and other elements.[20]

Estimates of the prospects for successful malicious penetration of the National Military Command System are necessarily speculative and deductive. One early demonstration of this potential, however, was the Eligible Receiver exercise in 1997. Eligible Receiver 97 was one of a series of no-notice interoperability exercises, conducted under the authority of the Joint Chiefs of Staff, planned and executed with little or no notice to the participants to evaluate command, control, communications, computers, and intelligence (C4I) and interoperability issues. Eligible Receiver 97 was the first of this type of exercise to focus on information systems and operation. For this exercise, National Security Agency director Lt. Gen. Kenneth Minihan received authorization from Gen. John Shalikashvili, the chairman of the Joint Chiefs of Staff, for the National Security Agency "Red Team" to test the cyber vulnerability of US military networks by launching actual attacks against those networks without the knowledge of the targets.[21]

The Red Team was prohibited from using National Security Agency capabilities; it was restricted to using only publicly available techniques and tools. Nevertheless, the Red Team was able to penetrate the National Military Command Center in the Pentagon on the first day of the exercise and the rest of the targeted military networks in less than one week. The team was able to gain root access to over thirty government networks and key data-storage drives. The team blocked services, manipulated emails, disrupted phones, and altered data. Yet most officers in charge of the systems did not know they had been hacked. Most alarmingly, the exercise uncovered evidence that foreign agents had already penetrated the networks for real.[22]

The postmortem of the exercise concluded that the DOD was almost completely unprepared and defenseless against cyberattacks. To be sure, many of the easiest vulnerabilities, such as poor password generation and protection, are now subject to more stringent operational standards. Nevertheless, more sophisticated offensive capabilities were available in 1997, and these capabilities have advanced considerably since the turn of the century. As one knowledgeable analyst recently observed,

> Eligible Receiver 97 . . . showed that the [Defense] Department was able to see into the future, articulate the principal vectors of challenge, and begin to form the priority organizational, doctrinal and capability responses necessary to ensure US mission effectiveness. The velocity of change, however, has attacked the very methods that were selected to close a clearly anticipated vulnerability. . . . Protection measures failed to improve at the same rate as offensive cyber potential. As a result, much of the promise of Eligible Receiver 97 remains unachieved.[23]

An additional enduring lesson of Eligible Receiver 97 is the challenge of maintaining defensive vigilance when the most dangerous threats are also the most invisible.

CYBER CONCERNS TODAY: HARDENING THE HARDWARE

In the context of growing concerns for cyberthreats to US critical infrastructure generally, specific attention has been drawn to the potential vulnerabilities to cyber intrusions of the National Military Command System. In particular, international analysts typically skeptical of cybersecurity alarmism observe the potent if unlikely security consequences of cyber-enabled intrusion into countries' exercise of nuclear command and control (NC2).[24]

Cyberthreats to NC3 can be interpreted in terms of broader conceptualization of threats in the cyber domain. A key feature of the domain is the "operational reach and the opportunity to compromise the integrity of critical infrastructures in direct and indirect ways *without a physical presence*."[25] Although cyberspace is intricately connected to the physical environments (land, sea, air and space), it is this capacity to take militarily relevant actions without a physical presence at the site of the target (often termed "non-kinetic" action) that constitutes cyberspace as a warfighting domain and distinguishes it from other domains.[26] Thus, cyberthreat vectors for NC3 systems may include their physical elements (computers, communication hardware, etc.) but also the nonphysical elements, including logical components (software, databases, etc.) and personnel management (access authority, identity verification, etc.). Potent threats may incorporate all these elements—for example, a corrupted individual gaining unauthorized access to implant exploitative software that impacts physical system operation.

The physical network elements of the National Military Command System are extensive, sophisticated, and critical. Command centers include the primary National Military Command Center located within the Pentagon; the Global Operations Center located at US Strategic Command headquarters at Offutt Air Force Base, Nebraska; the E-4B National Airborne Operations Center kept continuously ready to launch within minutes from random basing locations; and the E-6B Take Charge and Move Out Airborne Command Post that can serve as a backup command post for all three legs of the US nuclear triad. These command centers receive sensor information from the Integrated Tactical Warning and Attack Assessment System, which is required to provide "unambiguous, reliable, accurate, timely, survivable, and enduring warning information" on strategic attack.[27] Relaying command decisions relies on the Strategic Automated Command Control System, operated and maintained by the 595th Strategic Communications Squadron at Offutt Air Force Base, which provides force distribution and emergency action messaging capabilities as well as rapid retargeting of intercontinental ballistic missiles.[28]

All these facilities utilize a redundant network of communications capabilities that include "a myriad of terrestrial, airborne, and satellite-based systems ranging in sophistication from the simple telephone, to radio frequency systems, to government and non-government satellites."[29] This NC3 system must function optimally to achieve the fundamental always/never requirement for the National Military Command System. Toward this end, the DOD's unofficial *Nuclear Matters Handbook* describes the NC3 architecture as comprising a "thick-line" layer of day-to-day capabilities providing "robust command and control over nuclear and supporting government operations," and a "thin-line" layer that is required to provide "assured, unbroken, redundant, survivable, secure, and enduring connectivity" among principal decision-makers under all threat environments and wartime conditions. In particular, "the thin-line NC3 architecture must be sustained and supported during any modernization effort to ensure presidential requirements can be met."[30]

The need for modernization of the NC3 hardware has been a palpable concern over the past decade. This need was particularly symbolized by the continued reliance of the Strategic Automated Command Control System equipment, as recently as 2016, on eight-inch floppy-disk drives dating to the 1960s.[31] As such, US NC3 systems have been undergoing considerable upgrading. In its 2017 review of these efforts, the Government Accountability Office (GAO) concluded that the DOD was making positive progress but encouraged "identifying and communicating performance measures, milestones, and risks" associated with these efforts, in order to ensure that "underlying problems are addressed, and risks are mitigated or accepted."[32]

Although it may seem incongruous to accept any risks in the maintenance and modernization of a system expected to maintain an absolute minimum of performance even under conditions of nuclear war, in fact no complex system can be guaranteed to be 100 percent unbreakable.[33] All efforts to improve reliability and security in complex systems face marginally increasing resource demands and diminishing marginal returns. Calibrating uncertainties with respect to anticipating future risks in unpredictable circumstances is therefore a critical challenge.

In this context, one of the most critical potential physical cyber vulnerabilities for the National Military Command System and NC3 systems may be the supply chain of hardware procurement in this period of modernization. Once in place, NC3 equipment is subject to extensive physical and operational security. Nevertheless, many key systems depend upon commercial off-the-shelf procurement for budgetary reasons, necessitating reliance on essential communications hardware originally manufactured to standards dictated by commercial viability. Hence, "this antecedent cyber vulnerability is imported into the defense sphere, thereby weakening resilience and reducing the credibility of our deterrent. [Commercial off-the-shelf] technologies convey vulnerability and risk to customers (government, businesses or consumers), with few standards-based responses in place to accelerate resilience and resistance to commonly used techniques."[34] Moreover, many US-owned and trusted companies in the traditional defense industrial base rely on supply chains including numerous vendors and subcontractors, some that are not US-owned or US-domiciled.[35] While the utilization of commercial off-the-shelf technologies creates a unique avenue for surreptitious corruption of this hardware in manufacturing and shipment, the prevalent use of subcontractors and extended supply lines poses security challenges for more customized components as well. Supply-chain security across an array of critical infrastructure components is now a ubiquitous challenge receiving increasing US government attention.[36]

CYBER CONCERNS TODAY: SEQUESTERING THE SOFTWARE

The physical elements of NC3 systems operate by virtue of the logic programming (software), electronic data, and networked interactions that the physical elements support. The capability to transmit information electronically does not by itself constitute a distinct cyberthreat; electronic information transmission has had military applications since the invention of the telegraph.[37] Rather, it is the advent of software programming enabling transmitted information to undertake instructed action remotely—the combination of computers and networking—that creates a warfighting capacity within the virtual information environment.[38] As noted above, the distinguishing feature of cyberspace is the potential for malign actors to utilize computational networking to take destructive or coercive actions *without a physical presence*. These virtual elements constitute a distinct threat vector for NC3 systems.

Contemporary computational networks provide a number of techniques for meaningful remote action. A distributed denial-of-service (DDoS) attack is a relatively simple technique utilizing a collection of often thousands of controlled networked computers to simultaneously contact a targeted node, disabling it through sheer volume of information flow. DDoS attacks have been put to militarily useful effect in recent incidents.[39]

Among the most sophisticated techniques are those that utilize vulnerabilities in a target's computational systems of which no actors except the adversary are aware. Knowledge of such "zero-day" vulnerabilities is particularly powerful because the target is, by definition, ignorant of the vulnerability and because its exploitation can often be hidden from the target as well. When targeted computational nodes themselves operate physical systems, adversaries can exploit such capabilities to create physical destruction without the target even knowing that they have been attacked.[40]

The National Military Command System computational network is in principle subject to these types of vulnerabilities, but its design also presents certain idiosyncratic features that make it relatively less susceptible to attack at the virtual level. For example, communications within the network rely on robust encryption to deny adversaries even observation, let alone manipulation, of the content of those communications. Ironically, the antiquated nature of some of the technology—such as Strategic Automated Command Control System legacy utilization of floppy-disk drives dating to the 1960s—can provide a degree of defensive sturdiness, insofar as simple systems contain fewer subtle vulnerabilities and may be less familiar to adversaries seeking to discover and exploit such vulnerabilities. Known weaknesses in legacy NC3 systems are less risky because they are isolated.[41]

Idiosyncrasy may provide some defense, but it falls short of surety. The security provided by robust encryption depends on the encryption keys and the communicating devices remaining uncompromised, pointing again to potential vulnerabilities from reliance on commercial off-the-shelf equipment and from use of nonmilitary systems, such as commercial satellites, within the NC3 systems. And clearly the considerable costs of time, resources, and unrealized capabilities imposed by antiquated hardware and software preclude relying on whatever incidental defensive benefits such capabilities provide. As the preceding discussion of Eligible Receiver 97 showed, older systems were already vulnerable enough, and the capabilities of adversaries intent on exploiting any available vulnerabilities in these systems have continued to progress.

Modernization of the US NC3 enterprise creates the possibility not only of introducing new, modern vulnerabilities in software systems but also of increasing the exposure of vulnerabilities in network-centric environments.[42] Reliance on commercial off-the-shelf hardware and software increases the prospects of introducing zero-day vulnerabilities because adversarial researchers have already had opportunities to search for and stockpile such vulnerabilities.[43] Hence, tangible trade-offs of costs and performance in the process of modernization may also carry hidden costs of increasing inherently unpredictable risk quotients for introducing future vulnerabilities. Moreover, even custom-tailored software systems may be exposed to extended supply-chain vulnerabilities. The potential widespread impact of supply-chain corruption was powerfully demonstrated by the revelation in December 2020 that Russian hackers had accessed tens of thousands of US government and private-sector networks by compromising updates to network-monitoring software provided by a single common vendor.[44]

PROSPECTS FOR EXPLOITATION

It is not likely that an adversary, once discovering such zero-day vulnerabilities in the National Military Command System, would quickly exploit them. Exploitation of such vulnerabilities is likely to reveal the vulnerability to the target, enabling the targeted party to remediate the vulnerability.[45] As a result, such exploitations are unlikely to be utilized by the adversary, or experienced by the target, in the course of day-to-day circumstances. Any adversary that achieved such penetration would be motivated to preserve the capability for an opportune moment when its effects could be leveraged to support broader critical objectives.[46] Thus, vulnerabilities in NC3 systems are more likely to be exploited as "logic bombs"—malware lying in wait to be deployed at the most opportune moment.

Adversaries could place such logic bombs in US NC3 systems to disable US nuclear forces at the threshold of nuclear conflict. But adversaries might utilize such logic bombs to create effects that reinforce more conventional efforts in the context of a wider conflict, when neutralizing US nuclear attack or deterrence capabilities creates a critical disability impinging on broader US strategic objectives. Of course, any opportunity for an adversary to exploit a generated disability of US nuclear forces would last only as long as it took for the United States to overcome the disability, after which the exploitation would not only be neutered in the present but also blocked for the future.[47] Adversaries would therefore be motivated to spring the exploitation with precise timing in circumstances that would be worthy of the effort to develop the exploitation in the first place.[48] Nevertheless, even a temporary nuclear disabling could facilitate an adversary's conventional action at a key moment or enable coercing concessions that would be difficult to later reverse.[49]

Exploiting both physical and virtual cyber vulnerabilities often involves digital identity misrepresentations within the affected networks. Such fraudulent cyber-personas, whether produced automatically or human-engineered, share the feature of presenting a trustable identity to access network elements. Fraudulent cyber-personas may cloak either outside adversaries or corrupted insiders, or both.

The DOD's depiction of the National Military Command System highlights that it "relies on a collection of activities, processes, and procedures performed by appropriate military commanders and support personnel who, through the chain of command, allow for senior-level decisions on nuclear weapons employment."[50] The performance of personnel in defined roles—roles that in some cases may be filled by different individuals and that are independent of those individuals—reflects the criticality of authentication of legitimate identities within the National Military Command System.

Fraudulent cyber-personas could enable adversaries to interfere with operations within the NC3 systems. Simply discovering a target's user-account password can enable an adversary to access or manipulate data, disrupt activities, and perhaps create destructive physical effects. More ambitiously and dangerously, adversaries could attempt to intrude and substitute ("spoof") a false persona for a real one. The most critical spoof would, of course, be the identity of the president of United States, who has the ultimate authority for US nuclear weapons utilization. Fortunately, protections to ensure the identities of agents and the authenticity of directives within the communication networks are already robust for purposes of nuclear surety.[51] Thus, in contrast to most other organizations, the design of the National Military Command System is relatively more robust against cyber-persona attacks.

For this reason, a more fundamental concern is the insider threat. Insider threats are individuals who, either willfully or inadvertently, act in ways that create vulnerabilities to the organization. Willful corrupted insiders, depending on where they are placed, can overcome otherwise reliable defenses. Inadvertent insider threats expose vulnerabilities of inadequate operational security and sometimes the inherent limits imposed by the fallibility of human nature.

Across many governmental and commercial organizations, insider threats can imperil the cybersecurity of both physical and virtual network elements. Willfully or inadvertently, insiders can facilitate the corruption of supply chains and help adversaries reach networks that are isolated ("air-gapped") from the global Internet. Willfully or inadvertently, insiders can convey critical details of the design and operation of software systems and networks and provide adversaries with access to those logical systems.

Within the National Military Command System, programs to ensure personnel reliability are highly developed.[52] Nevertheless, misses could prove critical, particularly when instrumental to leveraging other cyber vulnerabilities. Because of the importance of maintaining the secrecy of the specifications and operational details of NC3 systems, insider-facilitated espionage could be all the more damaging. The absolute importance of keeping communications secure from software attack and identity misrepresentation highlights the potential vulnerability of insider access to encryption information, particularly insofar as communications may pass through nonmilitary devices, such as commercial satellites.

Above all, the greatest vulnerability of the National Military Command System to insider disruption involves the critical value of time. As illustrated by Zbigniew Brzezinski's experience discussed above, procedures for US response to a detected nuclear attack are finely honed and provide only a few minutes for agents at each stage of the process to exercise their responsibilities. At many stages of this process, an insider-instigated interruption could delay or distort legitimate US nuclear use or could block the prevention of unintended and unauthorized US nuclear use. In these contexts, it would not matter if the insider action were quickly discovered; a delay of the process by only a few minutes could make all the difference.

CONCLUSION

Cyberthreats to contemporary NC3 systems are a challenge that Cold War designers of the systems could not anticipate. But these threats should not be exaggerated. The scope of potential vulnerabilities and the consequences of their exploitation should be neither glorified nor gainsaid. Careful assessment of the details of potential vulnerabilities and mitigation efforts is not within the purview of the present analysis.[53] The preceding discussion has provided a survey of central issues, the challenges they raise, and the strategic implications they entail as a foundation for such assessment. As important, the discussion has sought to highlight how some cyber-exploitation risks to NC3 systems have implications that reach well beyond the traditional concern that these systems continue to perform reliably in the event of actual nuclear conflict.

NOTES

1. Nuclear command and control (NC2) refers to the exercise of authority and direction over all facets of military nuclear weapon operations. NC3 refers to the integrated system of facilities, equipment, procedures, and personnel enabling the execution of these functions. See Secretary of the Air Force, "Air Force Nuclear Command, Control, and Communications (NC3)," Air Force Instruction 13-550, April 16, 2019, 4–5, https://static.e-publishing.af.mil/production/1/af_a10/publication/afi13-550/afi13-550.pdf.
2. For examples, see Page O. Stoutland and Samantha Pitts-Kiefer, *Nuclear Weapons in the New Cyber Age: Report of the Cyber-Nuclear Weapons Study Group*, Nuclear Threat Initiative, September 2018, https://media.nti.org/documents/Cyber_report_finalsmall.pdf; and Beyza Unal and Patricia Lewis, *Cybersecurity of Nuclear Weapons Systems: Threats, Vulnerabilities and Consequences*, Royal Institute of International Affairs, January 11, 2018, https://www.chathamhouse.org/2018/01/cybersecurity-nuclear-weapons-systems.
3. See, e.g., Secretary of the Air Force, "Air Force Nuclear Command, Control, and Communications," 19–21. For a recent appraisal of US congressional attention to DOD assessments of the cyber resilience of US NC3 systems, see Theresa Hitchens, "Congress Fears DoD Not Prepared for NC3 Cyber Attacks," *Breaking Defense*, December 11, 2020, https://breakingdefense.com/2020/12/congress-fears-dod-not-prepared-for-nc3-cyber-attacks/.
4. For a recent articulation, see David A. Deptula and William A. LaPlante, *Modernizing U.S. Nuclear Command, Control, and Communications*, report by the Mitchell Institute for Aerospace Studies and the MITRE Corp. (Arlington, VA: Air Force Association, February 2019), 4.
5. Matt Stevens and Christopher Mele, "Causes of False Missile Alerts: The Sun, the Moon and a 46-Cent Chip," *New York Times*, January 13, 2018, https://www.nytimes.com/2018/01/13/us/false-alarm-missile-alerts.html; "Close Calls with Nuclear Weapons," Union of Concerned Scientists fact sheet, April 2015, https://www.ucsusa.org/nuclear-weapons/hair-trigger-alert/close-calls; Patricia Lewis, Benoît Pelopidas, and Heather Williams, *Too Close for Comfort: Cases of Near Nuclear Use and Options for Policy*, Royal Institute for International Affairs, 2014, https://www.chathamhouse.org/publications/papers/view/199200; Eric Schlosser, *Command and Control: Nuclear Weapons, the Damascus Incident, and the Illusion of Safety* (New York: Penguin, 2013); Scott D. Sagan, *The Limits of Safety: Organizations, Accidents, and Nuclear Weapons* (Princeton, NJ: Princeton University

Press, 1993). For a recent review critical of the salience of these incidents, see Bruno Tertrais, "'On The Brink'—Really? Revisiting Nuclear Close Calls since 1945," *Washington Quarterly* 40, no. 2 (Summer 2017): 51–66. This chapter is not concerned with how "close" any of these "close calls" actually were; its focus is the subset that exhibited information system fallibility.

6. Eric Schlosser, "World War Three, by Mistake," *New Yorker*, December 23, 2016, https://www.newyorker.com/news/news-desk/world-war-three-by-mistake; "Close Calls," 4; Schlosser, *Command and Control*, 367–68; William Burr, "The 3 A.M. Phone Call," National Security Archive, George Washington University, March 1, 2012, https://nsarchive2.gwu.edu/nukevault/ebb371/; "Fact Sheet," DOD, n.d. [circa June 7/8, 1980], declassified from secret, https://nsarchive2.gwu.edu/nukevault/ebb371/docs/doc%2013%20circa%206-7-80.pdf.; "Missile Alerts Traced to 46¢ Item," *New York Times*, June 18, 1980, https://timesmachine.nytimes.com/timesmachine/1980/06/18/111247462.html; Sagan, *Limits of Safety*, 228–38.

7. "A Conversation with Zbigniew Brzezinski," video, Council on Foreign Relations, March 30, 2012, https://www.youtube.com/watch?v=oTKOqH0mF9c&feature=youtu.be&t=8m43s, 8:43–13:44); cf. Schlosser, "World War Three, by Mistake." See Schlosser, *Command and Control*, 367–68, for a more detailed account, including an apparent update from Odom to Brzezinski, prior to confirming the false alarm, that the attack was actually 2,200 missiles. A two-hundred-missile selective counterforce strike would have meant the Soviet Union was retaining the bulk of its nuclear forces for a potential subsequent attack on US cities, depending on the US reaction to the initial strike. In this situation, calibrating the response for escalation concerns would have been central to presidential decision-making, whereas managing prospects for further escalation would not be an issue if the Soviet Union had launched an all-out first strike. Brzezinski added that President Carter, when informed the next morning, was angered by not being notified in real time, despite having approved the procedures that were followed.

8. "Fact Sheet," DOD, n.d. [circa June 7/8, 1980], declassified from secret, https://nsarchive2.gwu.edu/nukevault/ebb371/docs/doc%2013%20circa%206-7-80.pdf, 1; cf. Burr, "3 A.M. Phone Call."

9. Following the second incident, "NORAD was instructed to use an alternate computer, the Mission Essential Backup Computer, as the prime computer." "Fact Sheet," 1980, 2.

10. "Missile Alerts Traced to 46¢ Item."

11. Comptroller General of the United States, *NORAD's Missile Warning System: What Went Wrong?*, report to the chairman, Committee on Government Operations, House of Representatives, MASAD-81-30 (Washington, DC: GAO, May 15, 1981), http://www.gao.gov/assets/140/133240.pdf, 13; Schlosser, *Command and Control*, 367–68; cf. Sagan, *Limits of Safety*, 231–32. Among other remedies, NORAD stopped using blank warning messages to test communication lines. Comptroller General of the United States, *NORAD's Missile Warning System*, 14.

12. "Close Calls," 4; Schlosser, *Command and Control*, 365–66; Burr, "3 A.M. Phone Call."

13. Comptroller General of the United States, *NORAD's Missile Warning System*, 3; Schlosser, *Command and Control*, 366; cf. "Close Calls," 4.

14. A. O. Sulzberger, "Error Alerts U.S. Forces to a False Missile Attack," *New York Times*, November 11, 1979.

15. Lt. Gen. James V. Hartinger, commander in chief, Aerospace Defense Command, letter to Gen. Lew Allen, chief of staff, US Air Force, March 14, 1980, declassified from secret, National Security Archive, https://nsarchive2.gwu.edu/nukevault/ebb371/docs/doc%2011.pdf; cf. Burr, "3 A.M. Phone Call."
16. NORAD, message to assistant secretary of defense C3 and Joint Chiefs of Staff, December 20, 1979, declassified from secret, National Security Archive, https://nsarchive2.gwu.edu/nukevault/ebb371/docs/doc%2010%2012-20-79.pdf; cf. Hartinger, letter to Allen; Burr, "3 A.M. Phone Call." A subsequent GAO report found no link between acquisition procedures and the computer problems. Nevertheless, the report also conveyed that NORAD had by 1981 constructed a software development and testing facility isolated from the operational missile warning system, to prevent a repeat of the November 1979 incident. See Comptroller General of the United States, *NORAD's Missile Warning System*, 6, 13–14.
17. Scott D. Sagan, "Learning from Normal Accidents," *Organization and Environment* 17, no. 1 (March 2004).
18. For a seminal effort to flesh out strategic implications at the nuclear-cyber nexus, see Erik Gartzke and Jon R. Lindsay, "Thermonuclear Cyberwar," *Journal of Cybersecurity* 3, no. 1 (2017): 37–48. See also the following chapter in this volume.
19. GAO, *Processes to Monitor Progress on Implementing Recommendations and Managing Risks Could Be Improved*, Report to Congressional Requesters, GAO-18-144, October 2017, https://www.gao.gov/assets/690/687596.pdf; cf. GAO, *Federal Agencies Need to Address Aging Legacy Systems*, Report to Congressional Requesters, GAO-16-486, May 2016, https://www.gao.gov/assets/680/677436.pdf, 15.
20. Defense Science Board, *Resilient Military Systems and the Advanced Cyber Threat* (Washington, DC: DOD Task Force, January 2013), 7–8; cf. Gartzke and Lindsay, "Thermonuclear Cyberwar"; Jared Dunnmon, "Nuclear Command and Control in the Twenty-First Century: Maintaining Surety in Outer Space and Cyberspace," in *Project on Nuclear Issues: A Collection of Papers from the 2016 Nuclear Scholars Initiative and PONI Conference Series*, ed. Mark Cancian, Center for Strategic and International Studies (Lanham, MD: Rowman & Littlefield, 2017); Alexandra Van Dine, "After Stuxnet: Acknowledging the Cyber Threat to Nuclear Facilities," in Cancian, *Project on Nuclear Issues*.
21. Fred Kaplan, "Inside 'Eligible Receiver,'" *Slate*, March 7, 2016, https://slate.com/technology/2016/03/inside-the-nsas-shockingly-successful-simulated-hack-of-the-u-s-military.html; "Eligible Receiver," GlobalSecurity.org, accessed September 1, 2021, https://www.globalsecurity.org/military/ops/eligible-receiver.htm. Exercises attacking operational US military targets were authorized by President George H. W. Bush's 1990 National Security Directive 42. Kaplan, "Inside 'Eligible Receiver.'"
22. David Mussington, "Eligible Receiver at 20: Enduring Meaning of a Foundational Exercise," LinkedIn, November 13, 2017, https://www.linkedin.com/pulse/eligible-receiver-20-enduring-meaning-foundational-b-david/; Kaplan, "Inside 'Eligible Receiver'"; "Eligible Receiver," GlobalSecurity.org.
23. Mussington, "Eligible Receiver at 20." David Mussington was a participant in the original project and has continued working in this area. Mussington, personal correspondence to author.
24. Gartzke and Lindsay, "Thermonuclear Cyberwar."
25. US Joint Chiefs of Staff, "Cyberspace Operations," Joint Publication 3-12, June 8, 2018, I-1 (emphasis added).

26. The discussion here is cognizant of the debate over whether describing cyberspace as a "warfighting domain" is sensible in the first place.
27. Office of the Deputy Assistant Secretary of Defense for Nuclear Matters (ODASD[NM]), *Nuclear Matters Handbook 2020 [Revised]*, https://www.acq.osd.mil/ncbdp/nm//NMHB2020rev/, 16–17. Note that the foreword states that the handbook is "unofficial" and "neither authoritative nor directive, although every effort has been made to ensure that it is accurate and comprehensive."
28. "595th Command and Control Group," fact sheet, US Air Force Global Strike Command, January 26, 2018, https://www.afgsc.af.mil/About/Fact-Sheets/Article/1424762/595th-command-and-control-group/.
29. ODASD(NM), *Nuclear Matters Handbook*, 17.
30. ODASD(NM), 19.
31. GAO, *Federal Agencies Need to Address*; Andrew Futter, "The Double-Edged Sword: US Nuclear Command and Control Modernization," *Bulletin of the Atomic Scientists*, June 29, 2016, https://thebulletin.org/2016/06/the-double-edged-sword-us-nuclear-command-and-control-modernization/.
32. GAO, *Processes to Monitor Progress*.
33. Sagan, *Limits of Safety*.
34. Mussington, "Eligible Receiver at 20."
35. Secretary of the Navy, *Cybersecurity Readiness Review*, March 2019, https://www.navy.mil/strategic/CyberSecurityReview.pdf, 8.
36. David J. Lynch, "Biden Orders Sweeping Review of U.S. Supply Chain Weak Spots," *Washington Post*, February 24, 2021, https://www.washingtonpost.com/business/2021/02/24/biden-supply-chain; White House, "Remarks by President Biden at Signing of an Executive Order on Supply Chains," February 24, 2021, https://www.whitehouse.gov/briefing-room/speeches-remarks/2021/02/24/remarks-by-president-biden-at-signing-of-an-executive-order-on-supply-chains/.
37. Tom Standage, *The Victorian Internet: The Remarkable Story of the Telegraph and the Nineteenth Century's On-Line Pioneers* (London: Bloomsbury, 1998).
38. For an early anticipation of such "cyberwar," see John Arquilla and David Ronfeldt, "Cyberwar Is Coming!," *Comparative Strategy* 12, no. 2 (Spring 1993): 141–65.
39. David Hollis, "Cyberwar Case Study: Georgia 2008," *Small Wars Journal*, January 6, 2011.
40. Ralph Langner, *To Kill a Centrifuge: A Technical Analysis of What Stuxnet's Creators Tried to Achieve* (Arlington, VA: Langner Group, 2013).
41. Deptula and LaPlante, *Modernizing U.S. Nuclear*, 26.
42. Deptula and LaPlante, 27, 31.
43. Lillian Ablon and Andy Bogart, *Zero Days, Thousands of Nights: The Life and Times of Zero-Day Vulnerabilities and Their Exploits* (Santa Monica, CA: RAND Corp., 2017), https://www.rand.org/pubs/research_reports/RR1751.html.
44. David E. Sanger, Nicole Perlroth, and Julian E. Barnes, "As Understanding of Russian Hacking Grows, So Does Alarm," *New York Times*, January 5, 2021, https://www.nytimes.com/2021/01/02/us/politics/russian-hacking-government.html; cf. Jake Williams, "What You Need to Know about the SolarWinds Supply-Chain Attack," SANS Institute, December 15, 2020, https://www.sans.org/blog/what-you-need-to-know-about-the-solarwinds-supply-chain-attack/; Steven J. Vaughan-Nichols, "SolarWinds: The More We Learn, the Worse It Looks," ZDNet, January 4, 2021, https://www.zdnet.com/article/solarwinds-the-more-we-learn-the-worse

-it-looks/; Kevin Mandia, "Global Intrusion Campaign Leverages Software Supply Chain Compromise," FireEye Stories Blog, December 13, 2020, https://www.fireeye.com/blog/products-and-services/2020/12/global-intrusion-campaign-leverages-software-supply-chain-compromise.html.
45. For exploration of this important aspect of zero-day vulnerabilities, see Ablon and Bogart, *Zero Days*.
46. Gartzke and Lindsay, "Thermonuclear Cyberwar," 38, 42, 45.
47. See Gartzke and Lindsay, 44.
48. Adversaries' patience would be further tested by the uncertainty that the vulnerability could be discovered and neutralized before it could be used at all.
49. A temporary nuclear disabling might also have the less tangible but longer-term effect of instilling a loss of US confidence in the integrity of its systems. Subsequent to such an attack, every malfunction or instance of odd behavior could be perceived as a possible attack. Additional capabilities and procedures to insulate and diagnose misbehaving systems could create new resource and operational burdens. However, means for adversaries to take advantage of such increased systemic drag are not apparent.
50. ODASD(NM), *Nuclear Matters Handbook*, 248.
51. ODASD(NM), ch. 8.
52. ODASD(NM), 97–98.
53. Deptula and LaPlante, *Modernizing U.S. Nuclear*, 12.

EIGHT

TECHNOLOGY THREATS TO NC3
A FUTURE SCENARIO

Wade L. Huntley

This chapter presents a fictional scenario that threads together some of the emerging risks discussed in this volume into a narrative aiming to illustrate the novel threat possibilities that those risks pose. In particular, the scenario spotlights the limitations of two aspects of conventional wisdom. First, maintaining the safety and surety of nuclear command, control, and communications (NC3) systems in the event of major strategic war is rightly a primary concern. However, this scenario shows how compromise of (NC3) systems—in particular, the surety requirement—can be critical even in more readily imaginable conflicts far from the cusp of nuclear conflict. Second, the necessarily secretive and transitory nature of cyber exploitations does make it difficult to use cyber effects to coerce future behavior.[1] However, this scenario shows how an adversary, with foresight and timing, might exploit cyber vulnerabilities to generate unique coercive power at an opportune moment. The preceding chapter in this volume noted that even a temporary disabling of command and control of nuclear forces could create coercive leverage at a key inflection point of a conventional security crisis, exerting a decisive influence on its outcome. The scenario in this chapter illustrates that prospect.

The scenario is not intended to be predictive and deliberately includes features that are factually strained. Rather, the scenario is intended to be plausible and provocative. While unlikely to occur as depicted, the scenario spotlights the dangers posed in failing to meet the broader range of contemporary challenges to the future security of NC3 systems. The chapter presents the scenario as a fictional, real-time story to better depict how timing can be the critical factor in adversarial exploitation of any cyber compromise of the National Military Command System.

A SCENARIO OF THE NEAR FUTURE

The winter of 2027 was a bitter one in the Old World. The early winter had brought layers of heavy snow across Europe, followed by weeks of record low temperatures, seemingly locking the continent under a deep sheet of ice.

The international climate of the continent was no warmer. The continuing decline in US-Russian relations was casting an ever-lengthening shadow over the region. For several years, US policies had followed through on commitments to resist Russian encroachments, with actions including intensified support for Ukraine's democratic government; bolstered North Atlantic Treaty Organization (NATO) nuclear and conventional military postures; and adopted a "zero tolerance" policy on Russian cyber intrusions. The stance had been met by the Kremlin with increasing acrimony and belligerence, including vociferous hostility toward NATO activities; deepened diplomatic overtures to China and Iran; a naval buildup in the Arctic Ocean, newly navigable as a result of global warming; and increasingly aggressive air and naval activities in the Baltic Sea.[2] In 2026 Russia had refused negotiations to replace the expiring New Strategic Arms Reduction Treaty and had implemented a full blockade of the Ukrainian Sea of Azov ports of Berdyansk and Mariupol.[3]

By fall of 2026, European states lay severely fractured in the aftermath of the United Kingdom's calamitous "no deal" Brexit, the nationalistic responses across Europe to the 2020–23 global pandemic, and tenacious economic doldrums across the European Union. Turkey, Poland, and Hungary, with authoritarian-leaning governments strengthening their grips on power, increasingly found warmth in the receptive bear-hug of the Kremlin. In Poland the ruling party, Law and Justice, frustrated in earlier efforts to reduce dependence on Russian gas imports and still struggling to reestablish authority following the 2025 Easter Uprising, was deepening its ties to the Kremlin behind a facade of concern for the "Russia threat."[4] Turkey's full activation of its S-400 air defense system, purchased from Russia, and increased obstruction of NATO's defense planning in the Baltics had led to a spiraling decline in its relations with other NATO allies.[5]

Germany and France, economically roughed up and observing smaller NATO allies to the east pull away, leaned increasingly on one another and into the resurgent US commitment to NATO. In Germany the conservative government, still struggling to find an able successor to Angela Merkel and stem the rising popularity of the far-right Alternative for Germany party, had turned to a policy of strengthening its NATO leadership role as a tamer outlet for growing domestic nationalism.[6] But as the record-cold winter set in, countries dependent on imports of Russian natural gas saw prices rise steeply, and in many cases they experienced intermittent supply stoppages, including interruptions in the five-year-old Nord Stream 2 pipeline, that seemed a bit too correlated to international developments for coincidence.[7]

The Lithuanian, Latvian, and Estonian governments were particularly sensitive to Russian encroachments. The continued unexplained technical failures of Lithuania's liquefied natural gas terminal in Klaipėda, its third-largest city, had left all three countries even more highly dependent on Russian natural gas imports.[8] Russian gas interruptions to these countries increased in frequency, though always just briefly enough and with just enough excuses to avoid triggering a broader political crisis. This "campaign" of gas price increases and cutoffs dragged down the Baltic economies and chilled homes, leaving the populations frigid, frightened, and resentful of both Russia's bullying and their own governments' impotence.

The White House was in the midst of formulating an energy support plan for the Baltic states when the Baltic Crisis began.

At approximately one o'clock on the morning of January 1, 2027, in Daugavpils, Latvia's second-largest city, a sizable group of young Latvians with nationalist sentiments left a large public New Year's Eve celebration, collected tools and paint, and headed to the Russian cemetery and monument on the eastern side of town.[9] While one contingent felled the roadside monument with chains pulled by two trucks, groups of others set off into the cemetery, vandalizing and defacing tombstones as they roamed.

A passing Latvian of Russian descent, angered by the melee, contacted a group of friends and returned with them to the scene, aiming to stem the destruction. But they had underestimated the size and ferocity of the alcohol-fueled crowd. The resulting violence left three of the Russian Latvians dead, and four others were taken to hospital by their retreating comrades.

By dawn, news of the bloody skirmish was spreading virally on social media within Daugavpils's Russian community, roughly half its population.[10] Police arriving on the scene arrested nine of the hooligans, but most had already fled, and those arrested claimed no knowledge of any of the violence. Hundreds of Russian Latvians gathered, setting up a vigil for the three killed, trying (but failing) to replace the monument, and demanding justice.

The city government, led by a rising star in the pro-Russian Harmony party, reacted quickly.[11] Police investigators began aggressively canvassing the city's non-Russian communities to find any individuals who had been present at the scene. Soon dozens of youths were in police custody undergoing intensive questioning in an effort to identify the assailants, while police continued to search for more witnesses. The chaotic and aggressive police reaction sparked anger and resentment in the native Latvian population. By day's end, some headed to the scene of the vigil in counterprotest, and more fighting broke out. As darkness fell, police reinforcements struggled on the choked, narrow highway to reach the scene. Violence flared throughout the night, and morning found another eleven dead and thirty-seven injured.

By the morning of Saturday, January 2, the rioting was international news. The Kremlin issued a series of increasingly vituperative statements accusing the Latvian government of insensitivity to the interests and safety of ethnic Russians and calling on neighboring countries to pressure the government to extend greater protections to them. Social media exploded in activity, quickly coalescing around pop-up personas calling for radical action to achieve political autonomy for the beleaguered Russian minorities in all the Baltic states.

In Riga, Latvia's capital, the pro-Western government was caught flatfooted. The significant Russian population in the capital region was restive, and Moscow cleverly had not immediately curtailed natural gas supplies there, leaving the leadership wary of triggering that reaction. Privately the government began desperately pleading for support from NATO allies. But other European capitals also were taken by surprise by the sudden crisis. Only the strongly anti-Russian government in Berlin offered speedy reassurances.

In Washington the senior White House staff coalesced quickly and met throughout the day. The White House issued several statements supporting Latvian government efforts to maintain peace and warning Russia against disruptive interference. But action was hampered by analytical gaps as key Baltic specialists in the intelligence community had to be recalled in the middle of the long New Year holiday weekend. The political situation in Latvia was suddenly murky and volatile, and early analysis of the exploding social media frenzy showed signs of deliberate provocation by coordinated agents. Although the intelligence services had noticed the telltale signs of Russian cyber and social media activities in Georgia and Ukraine, they also suspected that Russia had improved its deception capabilities.[12] In the early hours and days of the crisis, it was not possible to identify and attribute the sources of the most insidious disinformation and pro-Russian radicalism in the social media circulation.

By Saturday evening, violent disturbances had spread farther in eastern Latvia and to the more heavily Russian regions around Riga. Latvia's national civil authorities could not keep up and appeared to be losing control over law and order in several areas. Then, overnight, came the first reports, from US signals, imagery, and ground intelligence sources, of Russian troop movements toward Latvia's eastern border and what might be paramilitary activities in the rural eastern Latvian district of Zilupe. The fast action dismayed policymakers who had hoped recent efforts to improve Baltic defenses would better deter "overt, opportunistic aggression."[13] But it also seemed to validate an analytical consensus that domestic political forces in Moscow could drive, or even require, an aggressive response to any opportunity to assert Russian nationalist interests, regardless of NATO's deterrence posture.[14]

At three o'clock on the morning of Sunday, January 3, the US president convened the senior national security staff in the Situation Room.[15] The German government, privy to some of the same intelligence, had just conveyed its intent to declare Russian activities a threat to the security of the Baltic allies and was seeking US partnership to jointly call for an emergency meeting of NATO's North Atlantic Council to invoke the collective-defense provisions of the North Atlantic Treaty's Article 5.[16] The president was instinctively supportive, and the discussion raised little dissent: although the situation remained opaque, there was broad consensus that a quick and strong posture signaling preparation to respond would dampen any hopes the Kremlin might have of catching the alliance off guard. The president approved a joint communiqué with Germany to be sent immediately to all other NATO governments, with specific reassurances to the Latvian government.

The US national security leadership then turned its attention to more active response options. It was morning in Europe and becoming clear that the Latvian government response was hamstrung by widespread breakdowns in civil authorities' communication systems. Indications of sabotage to these systems, by cyber or other means, were growing. Marauding groups of ethnic Russian protesters were shutting down normal life in the streets of Riga, and information from the greater Daugavpils region was becoming disjointed and conflicting. The most worrisome development was confirmation of paramilitary activities emanating from the Zilupe district, with some reports referring to "men in white," based on descriptions of teams in unmarked snow-camouflage uniforms. Civil unrest was one thing; an organized insurgency, possibly Russian-supported, was something else. The pattern resembled the experience in eastern Ukraine in 2013 and 2014, in which unconventional warfare tactics aimed to mask Russian responsibility.[17] Ukraine was not a NATO member, but Latvia was, so the same activity posed a more fundamental challenge to the alliance. But the tactic could still impede application of the NATO charter promising common defense against clear "armed attack."[18] The president decided to order the US Special Operations Command to prepare to implement a range of response options with or without a NATO sanction, commenting, "We will fight fire with fire."[19]

At 5:31 a.m., the chair of the Joint Chiefs of Staff (JCS) returned to the Situation Room after a brief absence. The ashen look on his normally determined face drew everyone's attention.

"Madam President, we have another problem. We have just lost communication with a portion of our intercontinental ballistic missile force."

The senior national security officials in the room peered back in stunned silence. The president leaned forward slowly in her chair. "General, what exactly do you mean?"

The JCS chair, who had come to appreciate the president's get-to-the-point style, conveyed the essentials: the 91st Missile Wing at Minot Air Force Base in North Dakota had gone into Launch Facility Down (LF Down) status; launch crews could not communicate with the wing of 150 Minuteman III missiles controlled at the base. He knew that the president already understood that this was one of three wings constituting the full US intercontinental ballistic missile (ICBM) force.[20]

The president replied, "I know this has happened before.[21] What's the prognosis this time?"

"We are right now implementing the safety guidelines to secure the weapons.[22] We've begun the diagnostics."

The president knew the JCS chair had risen to flag rank through leadership on information security and understood the technology.

"This time it's the full wing, not just a squadron," the JCS chair continued. "First indications are the bug is trickier than the last time. Last time we knew the machine to isolate from the start. Right now we're still looking for the root of the problem."

A fervent discussion ensued. Any loss of control over nuclear weapons, even if there was no risk of accidental use, was always a serious matter. Coming on the cusp of a potential showdown with Russia in the Baltics was terrible timing. But most US nuclear forces remained fully operational, and the LF Down condition at Minot could be kept secret for now. The president looked up at the line of world times displayed on the wall. The North Atlantic Council would convene at 1:00 p.m. in Brussels, in about one hour. She then leaned back in her chair. "OK," she said, "nothing changes in Europe." She turned to the JCS chief. "General, get this fixed."

With that, most senior national security officials returned their attention to the Baltic developments. At this point, Russian troop movements toward its border with eastern Latvia were unmistakable. Officials debated whether the Kremlin was simply posturing or if it would really dare to move regular troops into a NATO country on so little pretext. At the president's order, the secretary of defense was activating planned options to activate the rapid conventional deployment to the Baltic borders that had been heavily bolstered in recent years.[23] But the president did not want to depend on the threat of escalation to deter outright Russian action, as increased tactical nuclear weapons posturing by both Russia and NATO after the demise of the Intermediate-Range Nuclear Forces Treaty had increased the stakes of any direct military conflict. US special operations teams prepositioned in Europe were now ready to deploy, and hundreds of specialists across the capital were now poring over real-time intelligence to develop effective but nonescalatory options in the fluid environment.

At 6:42 a.m., the secretary of state, who had been tasked with coordinating the North Atlantic Council meeting due to begin in minutes, suddenly burst into the Situation Room. The eyes of the normally inexpressive career diplomat sparked with concern.

"Madam President, you have to hear this. We have just received this private cable directly from the Kremlin. You all have to hear this. Now." He began to read:

> To the US President:
> The Russian Federation and the United States share an interest in stability and peace in Europe. Conflict can be avoided if each side can accurately gauge their interests and strengths.[24] For this reason we now inform you that we are aware of the current disability of your nuclear ICBM forces in your state of North Dakota. This disability was deliberately caused by an intrusion into your nuclear command and control systems . . .

"Oh, my God," someone gasped.

The secretary of state paused for a moment, then continued:

> This disability was deliberately caused by an intrusion into your nuclear command and control systems by an independent entity. This entity has conveyed this and other information to us through our intelligence services.

"Independent, my ass!" It was the national security adviser, known for his quick mind and quick temper. "We know the APTs [advanced persistent threats] that could try something like this. Every one with Russian leanings is directly tied to the Russian government!"[25]

The secretary of state went on reading:

> This independent entity has informed us that it has the capability to initiate further disabilities in your systems at any time, as it chooses. We are convinced this claim is valid.[26]

Several gasps were audible. The president turned directly to the JCS chair, who began answering before the president asked. "Madam President, we have no evidence of further intrusions, but we don't even know the LF Down's cause yet—we've only been on this about ninety minutes. We can't say for sure this outage is malicious, but that would explain a couple of the forensic oddities we've found so far." The JCS chair paused. "Until we get to the bottom of it, I can't rule out further compromise."[27]

The president turned back to the secretary of state. "OK, what else?"

The secretary of state continued:

We wish to dissuade this entity from such a reckless action, which would increase uncertainties and raise risks of nuclear conflict.[28] But our ability to make this effort will depend upon the US acting with care and consideration regarding current circumstances in European states of mutual interest. If, on the other hand, the US government behaves aggressively, we cannot control whether this entity may take further action—including perhaps passing information of the current US nuclear disability to other interested governments and to the world public.

The secretary of defense and national security adviser exchanged fretful looks. The two had weeks earlier returned from a tour of key Asian allies. Focused diplomacy and reconciled trade issues had bolstered US relations throughout the Western Pacific but had also deepened the fissures with China's increasingly aggressive government. The introduction of People's Liberation Army ground forces into Hong Kong in 2025 in response to mass demonstrations on the thirtieth anniversary of the Sino-British Joint Declaration had cemented negative perceptions of expanded Chinese military activities in the South China Sea and Indian Ocean and increased concerns over the disintegrating relationship between Beijing and Taipei. Meanwhile, North Korea's public test of a submarine-launched ballistic missile demonstrated a clear capability to reach any US target as well as advances in warhead reentry guidance.[29] The recent tour to gird US assurances to Japan and South Korea had been successful, but both countries had placed particular emphasis on the reliability of US nuclear extended deterrence as the cornerstone of the alliance relationship in the face of a menacing China.[30] The two officials' minds raced at the potential repercussions for both deterrence and reassurance if countries in this region learned that US nuclear launch capabilities had been compromised.

The secretary of state finished reading the Russian missive:

We are fully hopeful that the enlightened US government will choose a wise and prudent course of action to maintain stability and peace in Europe and throughout the world. We will observe carefully the outcomes of the deliberations currently taking place between the US government and its NATO allies.

Signed: President of the Russian Federation.

"It's an ultimatum," the secretary of defense stated grimly. "They want to stop an Article 5 declaration. They want us to stand down in the Baltics."[31]

"Indeed," the secretary of state replied. "Having this card up their sleeve might explain why they've been so quickly aggressive in the first place."[32]

"Disingenuous crap," the national security adviser snarled. "It's just a deniability pretense. Just like the little white men. They know we know it's them. Slippery bastards!"

The president leaned forward and looked around the room. "Options?"

The national security adviser was quickest. "We should just ignore it. Most of our nuclear forces are unaffected. Nothing's changed on the ground. The rest of it . . ." His voice trailed off for a moment. "The rest of it is just words."

The secretary of defense took a deep breath. "That's taking a big risk. They knew about the LF Down almost as soon as we did; that's a strong indication the intrusion is real. The threats to take down more of the forces or pass the knowledge to Beijing or Pyongyang—those are plausible threats until we can get back on top of our systems. And we don't have time for that." He pointed to the clocks on the wall. "The North Atlantic Council meeting just got underway. We need to direct our ambassador now. If we go forward in Latvia with Article 5 and the special ops teams and then we lose more ICBMs, what then? How do we keep escalating if we've lost the top rung of the ladder? The cost of backing off then will be even higher. And if the Russians tell the Chinese or North Koreans and they see our deterrent in Asia in a noose just as we are getting hip deep into the Baltics, we're just inviting a whole second crisis there. The worst is that if they believe our nuclear posture is compromised—and especially if they think it is more compromised than it really is—they might even consider a first-strike nuclear attack."

He paused for a moment, his eyes surveying the room, to let that sink in. "And even if we avoid all that, public knowledge of the malicious compromise of our NC3 systems will kneecap our deterrence posture and allies' confidence for years, maybe decades. Some have been restless to get their own nuclear weapons for a long time; compromise of our extended-deterrence posture could be the tipping point."[33] He then fixed his gaze on the national security adviser. "That's a lot to risk on hoping it's just words."

The national security adviser hesitated before replying. "But if we back off in the Baltics now, we're undermining our deterrence promises to NATO just at the moment they are most needed. We would also be kneecapping our deterrence assurances to our East Asian allies. Don't think they wouldn't take that lesson! That's today. That's for real, not hypothetical. And besides, what's to stop them from blabbing to the world anyway?"

The JCS chair weighed in. "We will figure out the LF Down. This leverage over us won't last long. Once we're back online, the Russians would have a lot less to gain by blabbing. And they don't have a big interest in sparking conflict in Asia, apart from the leverage now." He knew most in the room had seen the recent intelligence reports of deep Russian concern over rising Chinese influence over Central Asia, where China's Belt and Road Initiative had undermined

Russia's ties, swamping Russia's gamble that it could partner with China's outreach to the region.[34] The recent intelligence reports conveyed clearly the Russian leadership's private perception that US resistance to China's expansion in Asia had some utility to Russia's interests. "So, it's plausible they mean it when they say they'd keep it to themselves if we do what they want."[35] Then his tone turned more fatalistic. "But for the moment, I guess we're damned if we do, damned if we don't." The room went quiet.

The secretary of state began tapping a pen. Then the seasoned diplomat began to speak, slowly, choosing his words carefully. "We're not quite damned if we do, damned if we don't. The reputational outcomes are not quite equal. If our adversaries or the world see our nuclear posture compromised, that's hardware, that's at the core, that's a blow to our deterrence reputation that could take decades to repair. Deterrence is, after all, in the eye of the beholder. Even when we get full confidence in our NC3 again, it will still be hard to convince everyone else, especially our allies. On the other hand, if we stand down now in the Baltics, the reputational cost is not so much to the military infrastructure or the country as a whole but rather only to the . . . the political leadership."

Everyone in the room grasped the meaning. If the US government backed away from the Baltics now without offering a good reason, the avalanche of backlash would land fully on the White House. Everyone in the room would be bruised. To preserve the public reliability of the US nuclear deterrent, none of them would be able to explain the true rationale, perhaps ever. But the president, whose foreign policy was built on bolstering US resistance to Russian encroachments, would suffer the most. She would appear to have completely buckled at the most crucial moment. US long-term nuclear credibility would be shielded, but her personal credibility on the world stage, and likely in the eyes of the American public, would be destroyed.

The president, once again, leaned back in her chair. This time, she paused a moment, eyes closed. All eyes were on her, and the moment seemed an eternity. Then she looked back at her secretary of state. "Thank you, Sam. That's helpful. Please inform our North Atlantic Council ambassador that our stance is shifting. And get our friend the German chancellor on the phone. He should hear this directly from me."[36]

The president and national security staff hoped that the incapacitation of the ICBM wing could be solved quickly enough to shed the shackle on a more forceful US response in the Baltics, but this was not to be. The Air Force had restored control over the ICBM wing within hours but had not isolated the source of the compromise and could not guarantee nonrecurrence. The national security adviser considered this good enough and over the next two days increasingly agitated to reconsider the decision and take the chance of a forceful NATO response. But it was already too late. US opposition to an

Article 5 declaration in the Baltics that Sunday stymied even a coordinated diplomatic response by the NATO allies. Meanwhile, public reaction in both Europe and the United States was immediate and withering. Only leftist antiwar advocates and rightist nationalists favored the US stance. As the secretary of state predicted, many analysts could find no explanation for US reticence other than presidential spinelessness. By Tuesday the opportunity for decisive US leadership to coalesce a united NATO response was already gone.

Within a week the Baltic situation had stabilized but not favorably. In Latvia paramilitary units, now operating more openly, effectively controlled the eastern third of the country as well as certain areas in and around Riga. Without effective NATO backing, the government lost public support and fractured. Harmony party representatives navigated for control, led by the charismatic longtime mayor of Riga, an ethnic Russian.[37] Disturbances also broke out in Klaipėda, home to Lithuania's second-largest population of ethnic Russians, effectively shutting down the country's main Baltic Sea port.[38] In Estonia paramilitary forces emerged from the heavily ethnic-Russian northeastern county of Ida-Viru, which effectively became autonomous and a source of further instability along the Gulf of Finland to the outskirts of the capital of Tallinn. The Kremlin had succeeded in placing a client government in one Baltic state and paralyzing the governments of the other two.

By the spring, as the winter ice began cracking, so did NATO. Although the president was the target of much enmity, some European leaders began to see a trend of US ambivalence toward the alliance across administrations, realizing long-held expectations among some analysts.[39] In May Turkey formally withdrew from NATO and began collaborating openly with Russia to suppress Kurdish forces across Syria and Iraq.[40] In the summer US intelligence discovered a concerted German crash program, with some support from France, to develop its own nuclear weapons.[41] Later, intelligence sources in Moscow conveyed that the Russian government had learned of, and was dismayed by, this news. Privately the secretary of state was crestfallen by this development but took solace in the absence of any indications of invigorated nuclear weapons interest in either Japan or South Korea following the president's political harakari. US intelligence found no evidence of awareness in Asian capitals of the compromise of US nuclear forces.

US nuclear and cyber technicians worked desperately to get to the bottom of the LF Down condition and within weeks succeeded. Combing the systems at Minot proved frustrating until analysts realized the problem was external to the base. Through a series of complex simulations, the analysts found the source of the missile error responses in signals initiated within the Strategic Automated Command Control System (SACCS), the primary network for transmission of emergency action messages and communications between

Strategic Command and the nuclear missile forces. Analysts then traced the source of the signaling to a small computer chip that had been surreptitiously altered in manufacturing and installed as part of a major upgrade to the SACCS system begun in 2014.[42] This became the most important instance of adversarial supply-chain corruption of a US military system ever discovered.

It took a little more time for analysts to determine how the LF Down had actually been triggered. The SACCS network was "air-gapped" (creating a separate finite network) with an independent power supply in anticipation of nuclear attack. But concurrent to the upgrade, one SACCS facility at Offutt Air Force Base had also installed a new Wi-Fi–capable soda machine.[43] The Wi-Fi broadcasting had been disabled, but hidden circuitry allowed the machine to receive and relay incoming Wi-Fi signals into the building's power system (as can many simple home routers); the corrupt SACCS chip was designed to monitor the SACCS power supply to receive these signals. The Wi-Fi signal to the soda machine likely came from beyond the base perimeter and was probably less than one second in duration—an unnoticed anomaly in the base signals-monitoring system. Investigators discovered that the soda machine had been "thrown in free" as part of the SACCS upgrade and happily accepted by cost-conscious program managers.

Once the intrusion was fully understood, it was simple (if somewhat costly) to cleanse the systems. Changes were made to hardware design and operational procedures to prevent any repeat of this kind of attack, as is typical in such cases.[44] Forensic analysts also realized that because the soda machine was only a receiver, the communications linkage could only operate one-way; unlike many forms of cyber intrusion, the malware could not "phone home." Lacking any evidence of any other intelligence leakage from the National Military Command System equipment or personnel, investigators concluded that the perpetrators probably relied on external indicators, such as altered activity patterns at the base garnered by satellite imagery or human observation, to detect whether the instruction to trigger the LF Down was successful. The perpetrators likely were not sure the sabotage worked. Hence, the Russian communiqué on the morning of January 3, and in particular the threat to broaden the launch-capability outage, was that much bluff.[45]

Federal investigators eventually learned that Russian agents had utilized public governmental contracting information to identify DOD suppliers for the SACCS modernization, then used cyber espionage of these firms' financial data to position shell companies posing as US-source firms to win key subcontracts. Most of the involved executives and technicians were unwitting, but a few key perpetrators had left the country shortly after the Baltic Crisis erupted.

The entire episode remained top secret and tightly compartmentalized. Despite the necessary number of individuals involved in the analysis and investigation of the penetration, the full consequences were much more narrowly known, and the information did not leak. The public image of the safety and surety of the US nuclear posture had been preserved.

The president never recovered politically. Strong stances toward Russia that had been heralded before the Baltic Crisis were now widely perceived as false bravado. Diminished influence on the world stage also undercut the administration's domestic effectiveness, stripping the White House of most political power beyond its formal tools. By autumn 2027, facing the increasing likelihood of primary challenges within her party, the president announced she would not run for reelection in 2028.

Two weeks before the 2029 inauguration, the incoming president and select senior national security nominees met with their departing counterparts, including some officials who had already left the administration. That day, the new president, of the opposite party, learned the full story of the cyber intrusion of the US NC3 system that had enabled Russia to coerce the United States not to resist its Baltic incursion. The confab, scheduled for midafternoon, lasted through a rush-organized dinner and deep into the evening. Media speculated dreamily about the nature of the discussions during what came to be known as the "Long Meeting." The only public hint was that, from that day forward, the new president never again spoke critically of his predecessor.

CONCLUSION

The preceding scenario will not happen. There is little chance of the exact confluence of these events. Moreover, certain technical details are intentionally inaccurate. But this story is not meant to be predictive. Scenarios provide value by creating plausible, anticipatory, and thought-provoking depictions of possible futures that highlight critical and underrecognized features of a problem. In that vein, the scenario here offers a number of potential implications. The following discussion summarizes several of the most prominent.

One implication is that the primary importance of the safety and surety of nuclear weapons command and control extends well beyond contexts involving potential nuclear weapons use. Typically the "always/never" requirement applies either to preventing unauthorized theft or use of nuclear weapons or to protecting NC3 systems in the event of nuclear conflict.[46] The scenario here involves neither of these contexts. Rather, in the scenario, compromise of the safety and surety of the US NC3 systems fundamentally impacts the outcome of a major international crisis that involves neither an immediate concern over unauthorized use nor an imminent nuclear weapons use.

The lesson is that, in the cyber age, exploitation of NC3 vulnerabilities can sway the outcomes of a much broader range of more easily imaginable international conflicts. Although some of the most powerful cyber exploitations depend on subterfuge and deception, an adversary's careful wielding of its successful disabling of US capabilities opens possibilities to coerce US behavior in conventional crises (including crises involving other nuclear-armed states in which nuclear use is not yet imminent). These possibilities may further incentivize adversaries to pursue disabling US NC3 for nonnuclear purposes, which can fuel destabilizing behavior even if such attempts ultimately are thwarted.

This prospect points to a second implication, the flip side of the first. The potential for a cyber compromise of NC3 systems to impact broader crises underscores the prospective contributions of cyber capabilities to overall power in international conflicts. These contributions are not self-evident.[47] The transitory and self-revealing nature of cyber exploitations limits their use for coercion, as compared to espionage, disruption, and other direct effects.[48] To use cyber compromise of NC3 systems for coercion should be even harder: once the target knows of the penetration, it will be highly motivated to act as quickly as possible to limit and remediate the effects.

The scenario here shows that achieving cyber coercion by NC3 infiltration may be hard, but when possible its effects can be decisive. Here the scenario builds on a prospect anticipated by Erik Gartzke and Jon Lindsay:

> If the successful compromise [of NC3] is detected but not mitigated, then the target learns that the balance of power is not as favorable as thought. This possibility suggests fleeting opportunities for "coercion" by revealing the cyber coup to the target in the midst of a crisis while the cyber attacker maintains or develops a favorable military advantage before the target has the opportunity to reverse or compensate the NC3 disruption.[49]

Note that in the scenario Russia is also utilizing its cyber disruption of US NC3 to wield two additional elements of coercive power. First, it is brandishing its limited "cyber coup" to credibly threaten wider US nuclear disability. Second, it is dangling the prospect of revealing these disabilities to other US adversaries and allies, to the significant detriment of US security interests beyond the immediate crisis. Both of these capacities to inflict further damage provide immediacy to the coercive leverage, an essential quality given the transitory nature of the NC3 incapacitation.

A third implication flows from this second one. Due to the nature of cyber exploitation, many of the most powerful cyber tools available to state actors must be kept secret to remain effective, bringing secrecy and deception to the forefront of cyber strategy.[50] Often the secrecy of what capabilities are and how they are utilized is treated one-dimensionally: exposure is exposure. In this scenario, however, revelation of the compromise of US NC3 systems to

US decision-makers *without* revealing that compromise publicly established a level of shared secrecy. That level of shared secrecy was central to the coercive power of the exploitation. Indeed, the threat of revelation to US adversaries and allies was itself an instrument of coercion. US sensitivity to the public exposure of its compromised NC3 system created a vulnerability that Russia could exploit only by revealing it *privately* to US decision-makers while colluding in public secrecy.[51] The lesson here is that secrecy in cyberspace is multilayered. The level of shared bilateral secrecy offers its own range of threats, opportunities, and crisis dynamics, adding a further dimension to the potential role of deception in cyber strategy and cyber operations.

A fourth implication involves the effects of these first three conditions on adversarial incentives. An NC3 compromise timed to provide an opportunity to influence US behavior in a conventional crisis would still be a fleeting resource. The combination of the advantage provided and the perishability of the opportunity could incentivize an adversary to act more aggressively or more precipitously in the crisis than that adversary otherwise would have. Indeed, the potential obsolescence of the latent NC3 exploitation, and the "use-it-or-lose-it" logic that it induces, could help tempt an adversary to initiate the crisis in the first place.[52] These characteristics of surreptitious penetration can further incentivize crisis initiation due to the one-sided nature of the knowledge of the strategic advantage; "by providing the option of a sneak attack, the intelligence about the opponent's [vulnerability] has *guaranteed* a violent resolution to the dispute."[53]

A final implication concerns the dynamics of US leadership decision-making in major international crises. In the legal organization of command and control of US military forces, no power is both as critical and as centralized as the presidential authority over the use of nuclear weapons. By intention, vesting this authority in that single individual is an element of surety: while other components of the NC3 enterprise aim to provide accurate information and to carry out actions as quickly and efficiently as possible, the locus of ultimate decision is vested in the one person charged with apprehending and effecting the interests of the nation as a whole.

This organization of decision-making, while perhaps minimizing possible intrusions by the vagaries of human frailty, nevertheless ultimately depends on the prudence, acumen, and integrity of the holder of the office of president of the United States. Electoral selection cannot prevent all venality, amorality, and stupidity, but historically these are aberrant traits.[54] All presidents, though, have exhibited to some degree a natural human concern for present reputation and future historical remembrance.[55]

The scenario, at its climax, hinges on a contest of such human qualities. It places the weight of ultimate decision on the tension between the personal interest in permanent reputation and the national interest in permanent preservation. Disclosure of the compromise of US NC3 in the midst of the Baltic Crisis would risk opportunistic provocations by adversaries, lost faith by allies, and long-term reputational costs to the country. The president can hope to forestall this outcome only at the cost of the public appearance of individual trepidation. Pursuit of the national interest requires a personal act of bravery entailing the lifelong burden of a reputation for cowardice. In making this person the first woman to hold the US presidency, the scenario implies that this president bears the additional burden of attaching that stigma to any woman who might seek that office in the future.[56]

The depth of this dilemma is made possible by the opportunities for the coercive manipulation of secrecy provided in the space where prospects for cyber exploitation meet the safety and surety requirements of the US NC3 enterprise. The importance of securing these systems against the dynamic threats of evolving information technologies still focuses on the longstanding priority of maintaining exquisite control over the nuclear weapons themselves. But today this importance also includes ensuring that US national security never ultimately depends, as in this scenario, on a president's self-sacrificing integrity.

NOTES

1. See Erik Gartzke and Jon R. Lindsay, "Thermonuclear Cyberwar," *Journal of Cybersecurity* 3, no. 1 (2017): 37–48.
2. A preponderance of military incidents involving Russia already take place in the Baltic Sea. See "Russian Military Incident Tracker," American Security Project, accessed September 1, 2021, https://www.americansecurityproject.org/us-russia-relationship/russian-military-incident-tracker/.
3. Anders Åslund, "In Ukraine, It's No Longer about Little Green Men," *Politico*, November 28, 2018, https://www.politico.eu/article/in-ukraine-its-no-longer-about-little-green-men-russia-agression-azov-sea-kerch-strait/.
4. Vladimir Afanasiev, "Poland Reverts to Russian Gas Pipeline Imports in Q3," *Upstream*, November 22, 2020, https://www.upstreamonline.com/production/poland-reverts-to-russian-gas-pipeline-imports-in-q3/2-1-916732; Vitaly Yermakov, "Poland Counts the Cost of Turning Down Russian Gas Taps," *Financial Times*, June 16, 2020, https://www.ft.com/content/78d764c1-b60d-478d-9c7e-a4a9d860edcb; Joanna Hosa, "'Polarus' in the Making: How the Polish Government Is Learning from Russia," European Council on Foreign Relations, November 18, 2020, https://ecfr.eu/article/polarus-in-the-making-how-the-polish-government-is-learning-from-russia/; Mateusz Mazzini, "Poland's Historical Revisionism Is Pushing It into Moscow's Arms," *Foreign Policy*, February 12, 2019, https://foreignpolicy.com/2019/02/12/polands-historical-revisionism-is-pushing-it-into-moscows-arms-smolensk-kaczynski-pis-law-justice-holocaust-law/; Alexandra Yatsyk, "Russia as a Bogeyman in Poland's 2019 Domestic Political Wars," Program

on New Approaches to Research and Security in Eurasia (PONARS Eurasia), October 4, 2019, https://ponarseurasia.org/russia-as-a-bogeyman-in-poland-s-2019-domestic-political-wars/.

5. See Max Hoffman, "Flashpoints in U.S.-Turkey Relations in 2021," Center for American Progress, January 19, 2021, https://www.americanprogress.org/issues/security/reports/2021/01/19/494738/flashpoints-u-s-turkey-relations-2021/.

6. Kate Connolly, "Merkel's Successor Faces Uphill Struggle to Unite His Party," *The Guardian*, January 17, 2021, https://www.theguardian.com/world/2021/jan/17/angela-merkel-successor-armin-laschet-faces-an-uphill-struggle-to-unite-his-party; "Germany: Poll Shows Low Support for New CDU Head as Merkel Successor," *Deutsche Welle*, January 18, 2021, https://www.dw.com/en/germany-poll-shows-low-support-for-new-cdu-head-as-merkel-successor/a-56256832; Matthew Karnitschnig, "Everybody Loves Merkel. Her Likely Successors? Not So Much," *Politico*, July 19, 2020, https://www.politico.com/news/2020/07/19/germany-angela-merkel-successor-372333.

7. Russia was the largest supplier of natural gas to the EU, both in 2019 and 2020. See "EU Imports of Energy Products: Recent Developments," Eurostat, January 22, 2021, 4, https://ec.europa.eu/eurostat/statistics-explained/SEPDF/cache/46126.pdf; and Eurostat Statistics Explained, https://ec.europa.eu/eurostat/statistics-explained/index.php/EU_imports_of_energy_products_-_recent_developments. Completion of the Nord Stream 2 pipeline, expected by 2022, is likely to deepen Germany's reliance on Russian gas imports and divide its interests from other European states, particularly Ukraine. In July 2021 the US dropped its objections to completing the pipeline, despite President Joe Biden's expressed conviction that "Russia should not be able to use energy as a weapon." See Lara Jakes and Steven Erlanger, "In Deal with Germany, U.S. Drops Threat to Block Russian Gas Pipelines," *New York Times*, July 21, 2021, https://www.nytimes.com/2021/07/21/us/politics/nord-stream-2.html.

8. The liquefied natural gas terminal development is real. See "Lithuania Boosting Ties with U.S. LNG Suppliers," LNG World News, December 14, 2018, https://www.lngworldnews.com/lithuania-boosting-ties-with-us-lng-suppliers/; "Russia's Gazprom Holds 54 Percent of Lithuania's Gas Market in 2017," *Baltic Times*, January 24, 2018, https://www.baltictimes.com/russia_s_gazprom_holds_54_pct_of_lithuania_s_gas_market_in_2017/.

9. The Daugavpils memorial site exists. For information, an image, and a map location, see "Liberation Memorial Daugavpils," Traces of War, accessed September 1, 2021, https://www.tracesofwar.com/sights/12426/Liberation-Memorial-Daugavpils.htm. Cf. "Russians in Latvia," Wikipedia, accessed September 1, 2021, https://en.wikipedia.org/wiki/Russians_in_Latvia.

10. "Daugavpils," Wikipedia, accessed September 1, 2021, https://en.wikipedia.org/wiki/Daugavpils#Demographics.

11. The Harmony party is real, and the Daugavpils government since 2019 has been led periodically by the party's local leader, Andrejs Elksniņš. In June 2021 the Harmony party won municipal elections with a wide plurality and formed a government through a coalition with Latvia's Russian Union (LKS), dedicated to "defending the interests of the Russian cultural and linguistic community of Latvia." However, the attitudes attributed to such figures in this scenario are purely fictional. See Gaļina Kudrjavceva, "Elksnins to Form Coalition with Latvia's Russian Union in

Daugavpils," LETA Latvia Information Agency, June 8, 2021, https://www.leta.lv/eng/regions/news/item/218B9BF5-136E-44E5-B2DF-6DD76F8581DD/; "Aleksey Vasilyev Has Become the First Vice Mayor of Daugavpils!," Latvian Russian Union, August 2, 2021, https://rusojuz.lv/en/aleksey-vasilyev-has-become-the-first-vice-mayor-of-daugavpils/; "Andrejs Elksniņš," Wikipedia, accessed September 1, 2021, https://en.wikipedia.org/wiki/Andrejs_Elksni%C5%86%C5%A1; and "Social Democratic Party 'Harmony,'" Wikipedia, accessed September 1, 2021, https://en.wikipedia.org/wiki/Social_Democratic_Party_%22Harmony%22.
12. Emilio J. Iasiello, "Russia's Improved Information Operations: From Georgia to Crimea," *Parameters* 47, no. 2 (2017), https://ssi.armywarcollege.edu/pubs/parameters/issues/Summer_2017/8_Iasiello_RussiasImprovedInformationOperations.pdf.
13. David A. Shlapak and Michael W. Johnson, *Reinforcing Deterrence on NATO's Eastern Flank: Wargaming the Defense of the Baltics*," RAND Research Reports (Santa Monica, CA: RAND Corp., 2016), 8, https://doi.org/10.7249/RR1253.
14. On the inability of a Russian leadership based on strong defense of Russian interests to back off from a crisis without potentially fatal consequences for the image that sustains it in power, see Aleksandar Matovski, "The Logic of Vladimir Putin's Popular Appeal," in *Citizens and the State in Authoritarian Regimes*, ed. Karrie Koesel, Valerie Bunce, and Jessica Weiss (Oxford: Oxford University Press, 2020).
15. Michael Donley, Cornelius O'Leary, and John Montgomery, "Inside the White House Situation Room," Center for the Study of Intelligence, June 27, 2008, https://www.cia.gov/library/center-for-the-study-of-intelligence/csi-publications/csi-studies/studies/97unclass/whithous.html.
16. "The North Atlantic Treaty," North Atlantic Treaty Organization, April 4, 1949, https://www.nato.int/cps/ie/natohq/official_texts_17120.htm; "Collective Defence: Article 5," North Atlantic Treaty Organization, June 12, 2018, https://www.nato.int/cps/en/natohq/topics_110496.htm.
17. US Army Special Operations Command, *"Little Green Men": A Primer on Modern Russian Unconventional Warfare, Ukraine 2013–2014* (Fort Bragg, NC: US Army Special Operations Command, 2016), https://www.jhuapl.edu/Content/documents/ARIS_LittleGreenMen.pdf; Åslund, "In Ukraine, It's No Longer."
18. "The North Atlantic Treaty"; cf. US Army Special Operations Command, *"Little Green Men,"* 3.
19. See Jen Judson, "Countering 'Little Green Men': Pentagon Special Ops Studies Russia 'Gray Zone' Conflict," *Defense News*, May 15, 2017, https://www.defensenews.com/digital-show-dailies/sofic/2017/05/15/countering-little-green-men-pentagon-special-ops-studies-russia-gray-zone-conflict/.
20. Hans M. Kristensen and Robert S. Norris, "United States Nuclear Forces, 2018," *Bulletin of the Atomic Scientists*, March 5, 2018, https://www.tandfonline.com/doi/full/10.1080/00963402.2018.1438219.
21. See "Air Force Loses Contact with 50 ICBMs at Wyoming Base," Nuclear Threat Initiative, October 27, 2021, https://www.nti.org/gsn/article/air-force-loses-contact-with-50-icbms-at-wyoming-base/; Eric Schlosser, "World War Three, by Mistake," *New Yorker*, December 23, 2016, https://www.newyorker.com/news/news-desk/world-war-three-by-mistake.
22. US Air Force, "Air Force Instruction 91-114: Safety Rules for the Intercontinental Ballistic Missile System," November 1, 2018, https://fas.org/irp/doddir/usaf/afi91

-114.pdf, 4. This document states that there are no releasability restrictions on its publication.
23. See Shlapak and Johnson, "Reinforcing Deterrence," 7–10.
24. James Fearon, "Rationalist Explanations for War," *International Organization* 49, no. 3 (Summer 1995): 379–414; cf. Gartzke and Lindsay, "Thermonuclear Cyberwar," 41.
25. An APT designates a particular cyber actor, usually associated to some degree with a government, on the basis of forensic detection of indicative traits in multiple significant activities. On Russian APTs, see "Advanced Persistent Threat Groups," FireEye, accessed September 1, 2021, https://www.fireeye.com/current-threats/apt-groups.html#russia; Catalin Cimpanu, "You Have around 20 Minutes to Contain a Russian APT Attack," ZDNet, February 19, 2019, https://www.zdnet.com/article/you-have-around-20-minutes-to-contain-a-russian-apt-attack/; Catalin Cimpanu, "Russian APT Comes Back to Life with New US Spear-Phishing Campaign," ZDNet, November 16, 2018, https://www.zdnet.com/article/russian-apt-comes-back-to-life-with-new-us-spear-phishing-campaign/.
26. Retention of a capacity to inflict further harm after an initial use of force is a long-recognized vital ingredient to successful coercion. See Thomas Schelling, *Arms and Influence* (New Haven, CT: Yale University Press, 1966), ch. 21.
27. "Revelation can prompt patching or network reconfiguration to block an attack, but this assumption is not always realistic. The attacker may have multiple pathways open or may have implanted malware that is difficult to remove in tactically meaningful timelines." Gartzke and Lindsay, "Thermonuclear Cyberwar," 44.
28. Gartzke and Lindsay, 42–43.
29. David E. Sanger and William J. Broad, "New Images of North Korea Buildup Confront Trump's Hopes for Disarmament," *New York Times*, March 9, 2019, https://www.nytimes.com/2019/03/09/world/asia/trump-north-korea-negotiations.html.
30. Lami Kim, "South Korea's Nuclear Hedging?," *Washington Quarterly*, Spring 2018, 115–33; Wade L. Huntley, "Speed Bump on the Road to Global Zero: US Nuclear Reductions and Extended Deterrence in East Asia," *Nonproliferation Review* 20, no. 2 (Summer 2013): 305–38.
31. See the discussion of cyber coercion in the concluding section of this chapter.
32. On the capacity of secret intelligence to reduce negotiating space and induce aggressive opportunism, see Aleksandar Matovski, "Strategic Intelligence and International Crisis Behavior," *Security Studies* 29, no. 5 (October–December 2020): 964–90, with appendix online at https://www.tandfonline.com/doi/full/10.1080/09636412.2020.1859128.
33. Huntley, "Speed Bump."
34. See Artyom Lukin, "Putin's Silk Road Gamble," *Washington Post*, February 8, 2018, https://www.washingtonpost.com/news/theworldpost/wp/2018/02/08/putin-china/; "China's Massive Belt and Road Initiative," Backgrounder, Council on Foreign Relations, January 28, 2020, https://www.cfr.org/backgrounder/chinas-massive-belt-and-road-initiative.
35. On the importance of positive rewards for compliance to the success of deterrence or coercion threats, see Schelling, *Arms and Influence*, 74–75.
36. The original draft of this scenario was composed prior to the 2020 US election. The inspiration for the persona of the president in the scenario is the character portrayed by Henry Fonda in the Sidney Lumet film *Fail-Safe*. "Shielding his face in

shame, he orders the unimaginable and takes full responsibility." Joshua Rothkopf, "When Our (Fictional) Presidents Are Tested by Their Moments," *New York Times*, March 26, 2020, https://www.nytimes.com/2020/03/26/movies/movie-presidents-virus.html.
37. The Riga city mayor from 2009 to 2019 was a leading Harmony party figure and the first person of Russian descent to hold that office since Latvia's restoration of sovereignty in 1991. He twice won reelection and previously ran for prime minister of the country. After removal in a 2019 corruption scandal, he won election to the European Parliament. The attitudes attributed to him in this scenario are purely fictional. See "Nils Ušakovs," Wikipedia, accessed September 1, 2021, https://en.wikipedia.org/wiki/Nils_U%C5%A1akovs.
38. See earlier reference to Klaipėda. The port city is located approximately sixty kilometers from the border of the Russian enclave of Kaliningrad.
39. Kenneth Waltz, "NATO's Days Are Not Numbered, but Its Years Are," *International Security* 18, no. 2 (Fall 1993): 76.
40. See Kathy Gilsinan, "Why Is Turkey in NATO Anyway?," *The Atlantic*, October 11, 2019, https://www.theatlantic.com/politics/archive/2019/10/turkey-and-nato-troubled-relationship/599890/.
41. On recent emergence of interest in nuclear weapons options in Germany, specifically as a response to perceived US infidelity to NATO and German security, see Ulrich Kühn and Tristan Volpe, "Keine Atombombe, Bitte: Why Germany Should Not Go Nuclear," *Foreign Affairs* 96, no. 4 (July/August 2017): 103–12, esp. 109–10. On the power considerations underlying this potential interest, see John J. Mearsheimer, "Back to the Future: Instability in Europe after the Cold War," *International Security* 15, no. 1 (Summer 1990); Tristan Volpe and Ulrich Kühn, "Germany's Nuclear Education: Why a Few Elites Are Testing a Taboo," *Washington Quarterly* 40, no. 3 (Fall 2017): 7–27.
42. US Government Accountability Office, *Defense Nuclear Enterprise: Processes to Monitor Progress on Implementing Recommendations and Managing Risks Could Be Improved*, Report to Congressional Requesters, GAO-18-144, October 2017, https://www.gao.gov/assets/690/687596.pdf; US Government Accountability Office, *Information Technology: Federal Agencies Need to Address Aging Legacy Systems*, Report to Congressional Requesters, GAO-16-486, May 2016, https://www.gao.gov/assets/680/677436.pdf, 15; Andrew Futter, "The Double-Edged Sword: US Nuclear Command and Control Modernization," *Bulletin of the Atomic Scientists*, June 29, 2016, https://thebulletin.org/2016/06/the-double-edged-sword-us-nuclear-command-and-control-modernization/; "ITT Exelis to Upgrade USAF's Strategic Automated Command Control System," *Air Force Technology*, May 8, 2013, https://www.airforce-technology.com/news/newsitt-exelis-to-upgrade-usafs-strategic-automated-command-control-system/. Cf. Steve Liewer, "Work on New $1.2 Billion StratCom HQ Will Soon Enter Phase 'Fraught with Risk,'" *Omaha World-Herald*, February 14, 2017, https://www.omaha.com/news/military/work-on-new-billion-stratcom-hq-will-soon-enter-phase/article_746a9ad1-3356-5db5-ae5c-b52ae765bb16.html; Tech. Sgt. Jarad A. Denton, "Minuteman III Receives Upgrade," 5th Bomb Wing public affairs release, October 2, 2017, https://www.af.mil/News/Article-Display/Article/1330869/minuteman-iii-receives-upgrade/; and "595th Command and Control Group," fact sheet, US Air Force

Global Strike Command, January 26, 2018, https://www.afgsc.af.mil/Library/Fact-Sheets/Display/Article/1424762/595th-command-and-control-group/.
43. "Coca-Cola Is Adding Wi-Fi to Its Vending Machines," *Digital Trends*, September 28, 2014, https://www.digitaltrends.com/cool-tech/coca-cola-adding-wi-fi-vending-machines/; US Strategic Command Public Affairs, "USSTRATCOM Announces Initial Operational Capability of NC3 Enterprise Center," April 3, 2019, https://www.stratcom.mil/Media/News/News-Article-View/article/1805006/usstratcom-announces-initial-operational-capability-of-nc3-enterprise-center/. The inspiration for this facet of the scenario comes from this iconic movie scene: "You're going to have to answer to the Coca-Cola company," clip from *Dr. Strangelove or: How I Learned to Stop Worrying and Love the Bomb*, directed by Stanley Kubrick (1964), https://www.youtube.com/watch?v=RZ9B7owHxMQ.
44. On the inevitability that complex systems will always contain flaws and vulnerabilities, see Scott Sagan, *The Limits of Safety: Organizations, Accidents, and Nuclear Weapons* (Princeton, NJ: Princeton University Press, 1993).
45. Gartzke and Lindsay, "Thermonuclear Cyberwar," 45.
46. On the requirement that US nuclear weapons *always* be available for authorized use and *never* be susceptible to unauthorized detonation, see the discussions in the prior chapter. For a depiction of recent surety and safety efforts in nuclear weapon design, see Sandia National Laboratories, "The Nexus of Always/Never," in *Always/Never: The Quest for Safety, Control, and Survivability; Part 3*, video, YouTube, 21:40–30:40, June 15, 2015, https://www.youtube.com/watch?v=0a1exo_vU_k.
47. For a seminal statement on the limitations of cyber capabilities in warfare, see Thomas Rid, *Cyber War Will Not Take Place* (Oxford: Oxford University Press, 2013).
48. On cyber resource perishability, see Wade L. Huntley, "Strategic Implications of Offense and Defense in Cyberwar," in *Proceedings of the 49th Hawaii International Conference on System Sciences* (IEEE Computer Society 2016), https://www.computer.org/csdl/proceedings-article/hicss/2016/5670f588/12OmNzahclv. On cyber coercion, see Erik Gartzke and Jon R. Lindsay, "The Cyber Commitment Problem and the Destabilization of Nuclear Deterrence," in *Bytes, Bombs, and Spies: The Strategic Dimensions of Offensive CyberOperations*, ed. Herbert S. Lin and Amy B. Zegart (Washington, DC: Brookings Institution Press, 2019); Brandon Valeriano, Benjamin M. Jensen, and Ryan C. Maness, *Cyber Strategy: The Evolving Character of Power and Coercion* (New York: Oxford University Press, 2018); Jon R. Lindsay and Erik Gartzke, "Coercion through Cyberspace: The Stability-Instability Paradox Revisited," in *Coercion: The Power to Hurt in International Politics*, ed. Kelly Greenhill and Peter J. Krause (New York: Oxford University Press, 2018); and Erica Borghard and Shawn Lonergan, "The Logic of Coercion in Cyberspace," *Security Studies* 26, no. 3 (2017): 452–81.
49. Gartzke and Lindsay, "Thermonuclear Cyberwar," 44.
50. See Erik Gartzke and Jon R. Lindsay, "Weaving Tangled Webs: Offense, Defense, and Deception in Cyberspace," *Security Studies* 24, no. 2 (2015): 316–48.
51. Also vital was US decision-makers' judgment that Russia credibly could be expected *not* to reveal the compromise if the US acquiesced to its wishes. On the importance that compliant behavior will not still be punished, see Schelling, *Arms and Influence*, 74–75.

52. On the distinction of perishability and obsolescence of cyberweapons, see Huntley, "Strategic Implications."
53. Matovski, "Strategic Intelligence," appendix, 4.
54. Autocrats have proven no less flawed. One may recall the adage, made famous by Winston Churchill, that "democracy is the worst form of Government except for all those other forms that have been tried," November 11, 1947, International Churchill Society, https://winstonchurchill.org/resources/quotes/the-worst-form-of-government/.
55. Francis Fukuyama, in his famous work at the end of the Cold War, traced to Hegel the idea that the quest for recognition is endemic to the human spirit. Francis Fukuyama, "The End of History?," *National Interest*, Summer 1989.
56. A recent analysis of data from twenty democratic countries indicates that public approval dynamics are more sensitive to outcomes on security issues for female presidents than for male presidents, and that female presidents are more systematically held accountable and electorally sanctioned for security failures than male presidents. See Ryan E. Carlin, Miguel Carreras, and Gregory J. Love, "Presidents' Sex and Popularity: Baselines, Dynamics and Policy Performance," *British Journal of Political Science* 50, no. 4 (October 2020): 1359–79.

PART IV

NINE

NC3 MODERNIZATION
PROGRESS AND REMAINING CHANGES

Michael S. Malley

In April 2019 US Strategic Command (STRATCOM) announced that its Nuclear Command, Control, and Communications Enterprise Center had reached "initial operational capability."[1] This marked the culmination of a rapid series of organizational changes at the direction of Secretary of Defense James Mattis, who "did not react well" when told during a visit to STRATCOM in September 2017 that a "committee" was in charge of nuclear command, control, and communications (NC3). According to the commander of US Strategic Command, Gen. John Hyten, Mattis made it clear that "I want somebody in charge. I want the commander in charge."[2] The new organization faced a long list of difficult challenges before it could begin the process of modernizing the NC3 system. As the center's new director remarked in 2019, "It's really kind of difficult to describe what NC3 is," adding, "We're just right now defining the architecture and then after the architecture, the blueprint" for a modernized NC3 system.[3] Modernizing the NC3 weapon system will be very different than modernizing the main nuclear delivery systems. Although Air Force and Navy leaders debate who should bear the cost of modernizing US nuclear forces, no one wonders which strike systems need to be replaced or what should replace them. Indeed, each major delivery system already has a named replacement and contracts have been awarded for the design or construction of new intercontinental ballistic missiles (ICBMs), heavy bombers, and nuclear-powered ballistic missile submarines (SSBNs). This progress has been possible because of a consensus about the need to modernize the US nuclear delivery systems that emerged among defense officials, members of Congress, and leaders of both political parties. This consensus also reflects a prior awareness of those high-profile nuclear systems, which are few in number, large in size and budget, and often featured in films, books, and other media.

The same can hardly be said about the NC3 system. Although it depends on a small number of large satellites, it consists mainly of dozens of terminals, radios, radars, and other components that are distributed across all services and are deployed on the land, in the air, at sea, and in space. None of these NC3 systems have names that are recognizable beyond the communities of technical specialists who design, build, maintain, and operate them. Until recently, even fewer people recognized them as constituting a single system, let alone one that deserved the attention or resources that major weapons systems typically attract. In the debate over nuclear modernization during the Barack Obama administration, little attention was paid to the NC3 system, much less the need to modernize its disparate elements. For example, the 2010 Nuclear Posture Review devoted only one paragraph to the topic of NC3, and the lengthy *Nuclear Matters Handbook* published by the Office of the Secretary of Defense in 2016 devoted only nine of its 280 pages to nuclear command and control (NC2)—and only two of those pages specifically described NC3.[4]

This chapter describes the emergence since 2012 of a broad consensus among defense planners that the various components of the US NC3 infrastructure should be acknowledged as a system equal in importance to any nuclear weapon or delivery capability and that the NC3 enterprise should be managed, funded, and modernized in the same way as other components of the US strategic deterrent. The chapter explains why this consensus embraces the organizational modernization of the NC3 system more than the development and deployment of new technologies for conducting NC3 operations. It also describes the challenges that lie ahead, keeping in mind that NC3 leaders themselves have acknowledged that modernization of the NC3 system cannot involve the simple replacement of existing components with newer ones, in the way the Navy can replace the *Ohio*-class SSBN with the *Columbia*-class SSBN. The emergence of new threats and the transition from analog to digital systems means that the entire NC3 architecture is being reexamined and substantial portions are likely to be redesigned rather than replaced.

The dynamic nature of NC3 modernization is reflected in the changes that have occurred since the NC3 enterprise center was established. Although nearly all details remain classified, military leaders have begun to discuss "NC3 Next Generation" not just as a goal but also as a set of incremental upgrades to the complex network of systems they manage.[5] According to Adm. Charles Richard, the commander of US Strategic Command, the first increment has been "defined," but subsequent increments have not yet been specified. His goal is not to deliver a single new system but to embrace an "evolutionary" approach that enables the system to be updated on a regular basis in response to technological changes and the emergence of new threats. In more colloquial terms, he told one audience, "A key thing to remember about NC3 Next Gen[eration] is that it's not a thing."[6]

GENERATING A CONSENSUS

In June 2012 the Senate Armed Services Committee published a report that drew attention to the dire condition of the NC3 system. It marked the beginning of a long process of raising political and bureaucratic awareness about the need to modernize NC3 governance to ensure that the system's individual elements were treated with the seriousness that the overall NC3 mission required. The committee acknowledged that the Department of Defense (DOD) was making efforts "to improve the reliability of the NC3 system" but then declared bluntly that it was "concerned that the Department's efforts are being pursued in a piecemeal fashion rather than part of a coherent system architecture and investment strategy with consistent leadership."[7]

The Senate Armed Services Committee's attention had been attracted by delays in an NC3 program that was little known beyond the circle of officials and contractors who dealt with space and satellite communications. Known as FAB-T (Family of Advanced Beyond-Line-of-Sight Terminals), the program was intended to produce terminals that would enable air and ground crews to take advantage of vastly higher data rates made possible by a new family of satellites. In 2001 the Air Force had awarded a contract to design the new Advanced Extremely High Frequency (AEHF) satellites with the aim of launching six during the 2010s. To ensure that the terminals were ready at roughly the same time that the satellites came into service, the Air Force awarded a contract in 2002 to Boeing for FAB-T development. Ten years later, however, Boeing still had not completed work on this project, and costs had risen from $235 million to $1.6 billion. In January 2012 the Air Force informed Congress that it intended to terminate the contract.[8] By that time, the first AEHF satellite had been launched, the second was set to launch, and the third was scheduled for launch in 2013.

Delays in the FAB-T program meant that end-users would only be able to communicate with the new satellites at the slower speeds supported by the old satellites that were being replaced. In particular, the Senate Armed Services Committee remarked that the delays meant "our strategic bombers, which can carry nuclear weapons, will not be able to use the very satellites designed for nuclear command and control," and the committee expressed its concern that the program "has veered off track and it may take years longer than expected before any of the needed capability becomes part of the NC3 system."[9] In response, the committee directed the Government Accountability Office (GAO) to conduct the first of several examinations of the NC3 system. Because they convey the committee's awareness that problems with FAB-T reflected much broader problems with NC3 as a whole, it is worth quoting its detailed directions to the researchers at the GAO:

The committee directs GAO to examine: 1) the DOD's efforts and activities underway or planned to upgrade and modernize the Nation's nuclear NC3 capabilities, including activities associated with cryptographic modernization; 2) the extent to which DOD's modernization and upgrade efforts are being coordinated as part of an overarching NC3 architecture and investment strategy; 3) whether there are NC3 gaps, shortcomings, technical challenges, or funding issues that need to be addressed currently; 4) the factors that caused the FAB–T program to go off track and the Air Force's plans to salvage the program, including how land and air platform integration challenges will be addressed; and 5) extent to which DOD has identified and addressed gaps or short-comings in the NC3 system through its inspections, training, and exercise programs.[10]

As the GAO commenced work on these issues, the RAND Corporation issued a report in 2013 that called attention to an anomaly in the way the Air Force managed the NC3 system. In contrast to all other nuclear systems, RAND found that "no single organization is responsible for the overall Air Force NC3 architecture, systems engineering, or sustaining engineering."[11] This "lack of stewardship" constituted a "glaring exception" to the way the Air Force managed all its other nuclear systems and was at the root of more serious problems. In the narrowest terms, it explained why the Air Force had "no life-cycle sustainment plan for NC3," let alone a plan for modernizing NC3. The RAND assessment called attention to the broader risks that stemmed from the Air Force's neglect of the NC3 system. Since the Air Force is responsible for three-quarters of the nation's NC3 system and because the system is a "vital node on which the rest of the nuclear mission system of systems relies," failure to sustain and modernize the system weakened the entire nuclear deterrent.

As evidence mounted that responsibility for NC3 had been diffused across various DOD and Air Force agencies, Congress directed the establishment of a high-level council to oversee the entire NC3 system and issued detailed requirements for reporting on the status of that system. In December 2013 Congress passed the FY 2014 National Defense Authorization Act, which established the Council on Oversight of the National Leadership Command, Control, and Communications System (NLC3S), whose chief responsibility would be "oversight of the command, control, and communications system for the national leadership of the United States, including nuclear command, control, and communications."[12] To ensure these issues received attention at the highest levels and across key agencies, Congress directed that the council would be cochaired by the undersecretary of defense for acquisition, technology, and logistics and the vice chairman of the Joint Chiefs of Staff and that its members should include the commander of Strategic Command, the director of the National Security Agency, and the DOD's chief information officer. The act imposed detailed reporting requirements on the council, the commander of Strategic Command, and the secretary of defense, including assessments of whether funding for NC3 was adequate and whether anomalies had occurred in the NC3 system. In order to identify the budgetary impact of the NC3 system's scattered elements, Congress also demanded that the council submit a report that included a "breakdown of each program element in such budget that relates to the system, including how such program element relates to the operation and sustainment, research and development, procurement, or other activity of the system."

Taken together, the 2012 Senate Armed Services Committee report, the 2013 RAND report, and the FY 2014 National Defense Authorization Act depicted an NC3 system whose contours were dimly understood and over which no one had been assigned clear responsibility. They also demonstrated a growing anxiety about the state of the NC3 system and a recognition that any efforts to reform the system would have to begin with the establishment of a governance structure that was charged with managing NC3 in a comprehensive fashion. And by highlighting problems in sustaining old equipment and making timely deliveries of new equipment, they illuminated the challenge of modernizing not just NC3 governance structures but also the platforms, assets, and technologies required to conduct NC3 operations.

Problems with the NC3 system reflected broader challenges that US nuclear forces, especially those in the Air Force, faced. Confronted with mounting evidence of trouble across the nuclear enterprise, in 2014 Secretary of Defense Chuck Hagel commissioned internal and external reviews of its condition. Both reviews were completed later the same year. Although the report of the internal review remains classified, an unclassified summary noted that its findings were "consistent with the findings and conclusions of the external review."[13] At least publicly, neither report explicitly addressed the NC3 system. Nevertheless, they both found deep systemic problems across the nuclear enterprise. External reviewers reported that they "did not find a coherent, integrated structure and synchronized set of activities that could be characterized as a DOD 'nuclear enterprise.'"[14] In the Navy, they found "elements of such an enterprise," but elsewhere in the DOD, the Air Force, and the Joint Staff, "the relevant activities are more accurately characterized as a loose federation of separate activities scattered across multiple organizations without clarity in responsibility and accountability."[15] Internal reviewers concurred with this assessment, saying that their study "echoed the finding of the external review regarding the absence, at the departmental level, of an integrated 'nuclear enterprise.'"[16]

To overcome these challenges, both reviews concluded that the most important changes would require modernization of the enterprise's governance.

As Madelyn Creedon, who cochaired the internal review, told the Senate Armed Services Committee in 2015, "The interdependent relationship of the problems identified within each Service, but particularly the Air Force, led to our conclusion that in many instances the ultimate solutions would have to be cultural and structural, and sustained over the long term."[17] Neither report recommended specific changes in the management or modernization of the NC3 system. Nor did any of the changes announced by Secretary Hagel in the wake of these reports concern NC3.[18] Nevertheless, Hagel did announce that Air Force Global Strike Command would be led by a four-star general and that the Air Force had reallocated more than $300 million in 2014 and 2015 to the command. These moves laid the foundation for Global Strike Command to assume leadership of NC3 in 2017.

Although these high-level reviews did not explicitly deal with NC3, Congress, Strategic Command, and Air Force leaders were keenly aware of the challenges NC3 faced and were moving quickly to identify ways of resolving them. From December 2013 to March 2014, the GAO issued three NC3-related reports that Congress had requested, including one on the status of the FAB-T program, another on operational assessments of the NC3 system, and another on the DOD's efforts to address weaknesses in the NC3 system.[19] Nearly everything about these reports was classified.

In early 2014 the commander of Strategic Command, Adm. Cecil Haney, told the Senate Armed Services Committee about the significant technological hurdles he confronted:

> Our challenges include operating aging legacy systems and addressing risks associated with today's digital security environment. Many NC3 systems require modernization, but it is not enough to simply build a new version of the old system—rather we must optimize the current architecture while leveraging new technologies so that our NC3 systems interoperate as the core of a broader, national command and control system. We are working to shift from point-to-point hardwired systems to a networked IP-based national C3 architecture that will balance survivability and endurability against a diverse range of threats, deliver relevant capabilities across the range of interdependent national missions, and ultimately enhance Presidential decision time and space.[20]

To meet these challenges, he said, a variety of programs were underway to deliver new or upgraded capabilities, such as the ones FAB-T was meant to provide.

In the summer of 2014 the Air Force Scientific Advisory Board reported the results of a study it had conducted into the capabilities and vulnerabilities of the Air Force portion of the NC3 system. Although this report also remains classified, an unclassified summary drew attention to a pair of challenges that any effort to modernize the system would confront. On the technical front, previous modernization efforts had resulted in a "system which is a hybrid of older and newer elements." Meanwhile, on the strategic front, "the range of scenarios that the NC3 system must operate in ha[d] greatly expanded since the end of the Cold War."[21] The board's findings reinforced Admiral Haney's view that modernization would require sustaining the old system while adopting radically new components in the face of changing threats.

In response to a growing sense of urgency, Air Force leaders initiated a process of organizational change to clarify roles and responsibilities for NC3 across the service's functional and geographic commands. In October 2014 the secretary of the Air Force issued a comprehensive instruction that established "policies, roles, and responsibilities" for the entire Air Force NC3 "enterprise."[22] Over the next three years, the Air Force unveiled an assortment of major changes in quick succession. In 2015 it designated Global Strike Command as the "mission area lead" for NC3. Later that same year, it designated a collection of more than sixty different systems spread across more than a dozen configuration elements (e.g., planes, satellites, and command posts) as a single "NC3 weapons system." And in 2017 it established the NC3 Center at Barksdale Air Force Base, Louisiana, to centralize operational support to the service's entire NC3 enterprise.[23]

For Congress, these changes did not appear to come quickly enough or reach far enough. In the FY 2016 National Defense Authorization Act, passed in November 2015, Congress urged the secretary of the Air Force to "consolidate ... under a major command commanded by a single general officer the responsibility, authority, accountability, and resources for carrying out all aspects of the nuclear deterrence mission of the Air Force, including ... the nuclear command, control, and communications system."[24] The following year, apparently still dissatisfied with progress on the FAB-T program, Congress inserted into the FY 2017 National Defense Authorization Act a specific requirement that the NLC3S Oversight Council assume responsibility for "space system architectures and associated user terminals and ground segments" as well as a host of other requirements that emphasized Congress's increasingly detailed understanding of the NC3 system's elements.[25] For instance, Congress directed the council to "determine whether the integrated tactical warning and attack assessment system and its command and control system have met all warfighter requirements for operational availability, survivability, and endurability." If the council found any shortcoming, Congress required that the secretary of defense and the chairman of the Joint Chiefs of Staff submit a report that explained the problem, describe efforts being taken to mitigate the problem, and outline a plan to eliminate the problem within a year.

In 2017 Gen. Robin Rand, the commander of Global Strike Command, described to the Senate Armed Services Committee the progress that had been made as a result of the Air Force's efforts since 2014 to improve its stewardship of NC3. He acknowledged that his command had "identified multiple areas that have atrophied through decades of low prioritization" and said that he had "advocated for funds specifically for NC3." Nevertheless, the amounts he mentioned were tiny, and the purposes were not obviously of the highest priority: "$16 million to improve long-haul communications, $8 million in telephony upgrades, and $2 million in radio upgrades."[26] His inability to report bigger achievements reflected the challenges the Air Force faced. Governance reforms, such as setting up a new NC3 Center, had just begun. And, as General Rand told an interviewer in late 2017, the Air Force still "had to figure out really what was the status of these different pieces that make up NC3, and that is what we have been doing."[27] A coordinated effort at sustainment and modernization could hardly proceed until the Air Force understood the extent and composition of its newest weapon system.

By late 2017 Congress began to hear a much more urgent message from senior officials and military officers about the need to modernize NC3 systems. General Hyten, the commander of Strategic Command, repeatedly emphasized the need to invest in a new NC3 architecture. In 2017 he told the House Armed Services Committee that in comparison to the main nuclear weapon delivery systems, NC3 was his "biggest concern" because it was "robust, resilient, and ancient" and therefore "very, very hard to recapitalize." Therefore, he said, NC3 was his "number one priority now inside the modernization piece to make sure we have a plan to modernize the nuclear command and control capability."[28] A month later, he reminded the Senate Armed Services Committee that "our nation's nuclear deterrent is only as effective as the command and control networks that enable it to function" and that "continued funding for NC3 modernization programs" was essential for this purpose.[29] A year later, he delivered a nearly identical message, telling the House Armed Services Committee that "sustainment, modernization, and recapitalization of key systems and capabilities throughout the NC3 architecture" was necessary for the credibility of the US nuclear deterrent.[30] The need for NC3 modernization, he said, stemmed not just from the age of existing technologies or a general need to compete with great-power adversaries. More pressing was the need to ensure compatibility between the NC3 systems and the new weapons platforms that will come into operation in the next decade. The new B-21 heavy bomber, the ground-based strategic deterrent, and the *Columbia*-class SSBN, he said, "are going to come in with a new command-and-control architecture. They are not going to build on the [19]60s architecture. They will have modern technology and have to plug into the new NC3 architecture."[31]

While General Hyten looked to the future, Congress continued to task the GAO with conducting in-depth assessment of existing NC3 systems and programs. In 2017 it completed a study of the Air Force's efforts to create a new, centralized structure to provide oversight of Air Force NC3 operations. Although the GAO acknowledged the Air Force had made progress, it remarked that the "focus has mainly been on short-term issues to sustain the current systems" rather than on longer-term efforts to modernize the system.[32] The GAO also recognized that the organizational changes had enabled the Air Force to "buil[d] up its understanding of the short-term sustainment needs for the 62 component systems" that made up the NC3 weapon system. When it reviewed the eight largest Air Force NC3 programs, however, the GAO found that half had "compressed schedules that could result in delays if any issues develop during development, production, or installation of the communication terminals," meaning that even sustainment of the current mission was at risk.

In a separate report, the GAO reported in 2017 that the DOD had made limited progress in its efforts to make similar changes. In 2015 the DOD had produced a classified report on NC3 that contained thirteen recommendations.[33] In its unclassified assessment of the DOD's progress in implementing these recommendations, the GAO noted that the DOD had "closed two of the 13 recommendations . . . and [was] making progress in implementing the remaining 11."[34] Among those eleven, the GAO was able to mention only one in its publicly released report. It was a recommendation that Strategic Command "review and validate the availability requirements of one of the NC3 systems," which the GAO said Strategic Command had done. Nevertheless, the GAO implied that the DOD may not have made substantial progress when it complained that its processes for measuring progress "do not identify performance measures, milestones, or risks," which makes it difficult to evaluate the extent to which the DOD has made progress and may conceal a lack of progress. DOD officials told GAO investigators that many of the eleven recommendations dealt with "enduring problems" and therefore could not be addressed quickly.[35]

By the end of 2017, Congress remained frustrated with the slow pace of DOD and Air Force efforts to improve management and sustainment of the NC3 system, let alone modernize it. In the FY 2018 National Defense Authorization Act, Congress mandated an array of detailed reporting requirements, institutional changes, and actions to address emerging threats. In response to persistent delays in NC3 acquisitions, Congress required the NLC3S Oversight Council to submit semiannual reports that identified delays of more than 180 days in any acquisition program that "materially contributes to the nuclear command, control, and communications systems of the United States."[36] In addition, it required the secretary of defense and the director of national intelligence to establish a fusion center "to effectively integrate and unify the protection of nuclear command, control, and communications programs, systems, and processes."[37]

NC3 IN AN ERA OF GREAT-POWER COMPETITION

Anxiety over the rising level of great-power competition fueled even greater concerns in Congress about the risks to the NC3 system. In recognition of emerging threats and their implications for the NC3 system, the FY 2018 National Defense Authorization Act required that the commanders of Strategic Command and Cyber Command annually "conduct an assessment of the sufficiency and resiliency of the nuclear command and control system to operate through a cyber attack from the Russian Federation [or] the People's Republic of China."[38] Similarly, Congress required the secretary of defense to conduct an assessment of NC3 supply-chain security and develop a plan to mitigate risks to the supply chain. More specifically, Congress directed the secretary to issue an instruction "establishing the prioritization of supply chain risk management programs . . . to ensure that acquisition and sustainment programs relating to [NC3] programs receive the highest priority."[39] Neither of these threats to the NC3 system had previously been the subject of congressional attention.

In 2018 Congress's determination to bring about major changes in NC3 governance, accelerate improvements in the NC3 system, and prepare for future threats to that system was finally matched by an equal commitment from the executive branch. The Donald Trump administration's almost simultaneous launch of a new National Defense Strategy and completion of a new Nuclear Posture Review emphasized the primacy of strategic competition with China and Russia and the need to modernize US nuclear forces. More specifically, the Nuclear Posture Review devoted unprecedent attention specifically to the need to modernize the entire range of NC3 capabilities, which it described as badly outdated in the face of emerging threats. In addition to developing and deploying new satellites, aircraft, and other assets, the Nuclear Posture Review declared that the Trump administration would move quickly to develop a plan to improve governance of the NC3 enterprise.[40]

General Rand of Global Strike Command returned to Capitol Hill in 2018, just a month after the administration released the Nuclear Posture Review and almost exactly a year after the Air Force NC3 Center had been established. In contrast to his testimony a year earlier, he was able to report significant achievements, including the allocation of $1.2 billion toward critical NC3 systems over the period FY 2019 to FY 2023. For example, he told the House Armed Services Committee the Air Force had allocated $275 million to modernize the E-4B aircraft, which serves as the National Airborne Operations Center in time of nuclear conflict, and more than $180 million to develop the E4-B's replacement. In addition, hundreds of millions of dollars had been allocated to develop, procure, and integrate various terminals (including FAB-T) that would enable Air Force command posts and aircraft to communicate with AEHF satellites.[41] His testimony indicated that the Air Force was making progress not just toward sustainment of existing NC3 systems but toward modernizing them as well. Rand also emphasized that these changes had been made by possible in large part by the NC3 governance reforms the Air Force had pursued over the previous three years.

Neither the Trump administration nor Congress was content with an NC3 governance structure that rested mainly on the Air Force's NC3 Center and a Pentagon-level oversight council. Both pushed for the creation of a national NC3 command structure centered on Strategic Command. In fact, the Senate's version of the FY 2019 National Defense Authorization Act contained a provision that would have required the secretary of defense to centralize responsibility over the NC3 system by "designat[ing] a single individual responsible for strategic portfolio management" and naming that person as head of the NLC3S Oversight Council.[42] The Trump administration objected to this provision on the grounds that it was already planning to make changes like those sought by the Senate.[43] The House version did not contain a similar provision, and in the face of administration objections the Senate agreed to remove it. In conference committee, however, the House and Senate conferees noted that they "expect[ed] to see clear improvements in lines of authority and decision-making that result in significant, rather than incremental, improvements over the status quo."[44]

In July 2018 the Pentagon announced the major organizational reforms that Congress had been seeking. Based on a review of NC3 governance that had been mandated by the 2018 Nuclear Posture Review, Secretary Mattis named the commander of Strategic Command as the "NC3 enterprise lead" and assigned the undersecretary of defense for acquisition and sustainment responsibility for NC3 resources and acquisition.[45] Under General Hyten, Strategic Command then began the process of creating an NC3 Enterprise Center, which reached initial operational capacity in April 2019. At the end of that year, the center's director, Elizabeth Durham-Ruiz, said she expected the center to reach full operational capacity within two years. In the meantime, the center's main task would be to construct a common-requirements document to guide the replacement and modernization of legacy NC3 systems across all services.[46]

The establishment of the NC3 Enterprise Center was a major milestone in the process of NC3 modernization. Seven years after Congress first called attention to delays in the development of FAB-T, the Air Force and DOD had begun to treat NC3 as equal in importance to heavy bombers, ICBMs, and submarine-launched ballistic missiles. Each had undertaken organizational reforms to centralize authority and responsibility for NC3 in high-level commands. Underlying these reforms was a broad consensus among defense planners in Congress, the Pentagon, and the Air Force that NC3 deserved greater attention and resources. But modernization of NC3 systems, apart from the governance of those systems, remained largely untouched, even as awareness of the need for modernization had grown.

MODERNIZING NC3 SYSTEMS

In Congress the debate over NC3 took an important turn during late 2019. With the House of Representatives under Democratic control for the first time in a decade, many observers wondered whether support for nuclear modernization would wane, especially since the new chairman of the House Armed Services Committee, Rep. Adam Smith, had taken strong stands against the 2018 Nuclear Posture Review and the Trump administration's nuclear policy more generally.[47] As many had expected, House Democrats announced priorities in negotiation over the FY 2020 National Defense Authorization Act that were sharply at odds with those of the administration, including cuts of more than $600 million from nuclear weapons programs, a sharp reduction in the production of plutonium pits, and a cutback of more than $100 million for the ground-based strategic deterrent. Yet, in contrast to those positions, the Democrats advocated an increase in funding for NC3.[48]

With Democratic support for the administration's NC3 priorities, Congress shifted its focus from demanding changes in NC3 governance to requiring "a plan on the future of the nuclear command, control, and communications systems."[49] Congress sought details on a wide range of fundamental issues, including the following:

- near- and long-term plans and options to recapitalize the NC3 systems to ensure the resilience of such systems
- requirements for such systems, including with respect to survivability and reliability
- the risks and benefits of replicating the current architecture for such systems as of the date of the plan
- the risks and benefits of using different architectures for such systems, including, at a minimum, using hosted payloads
- whether such architectures should be classified or unclassified
- timelines and general cost estimates for long-term investments in such systems.

These demands made clear that serious efforts at modernizing the NC3 system, unlike any leg of the triad, were just getting underway. Congress did not know what systems were needed, what the requirements for those systems would be, when they would be produced, how much they would cost, or even whether they would be classified.

Congress was hardly alone in this view. The leaders of the newly created NC3 Enterprise Center at Strategic Command emphatically agreed. In 2019 NC3 Enterprise Center director Durham-Ruiz told an interviewer that "continued upgrades or recapitalization efforts— that is, releasing a new version of the old thing—will not sufficiently meet 21st-century operational needs against 21st-century threats" and therefore "all architecture-design options are on the table."[50] To identify those options, one of the center's first initiatives was to issue a breathtakingly expansive call for ideas. It sought concepts regarding the roles, missions, and responsibilities the center "should undertake for the 2030 to 2080 timeframe."[51] It also sought "guiding principles on what technology and policy challenges must be overcome in order to design an NC3 enterprise architecture" that would enable the center's operations over the same half-century time horizon. To make certain that enterprise leaders' desire to rethink the NC3 system were not missed, they added that "it is our belief that a fundamental overhaul of the existing processes, from requirements definitions, to system engineering and integration, acquisition, and budgeting is needed."

The desire to rethink the entire NC3 system before embarking on its modernization reflects widespread appreciation of the challenges that must be overcome.[52] These challenges stem from fundamental changes that have occurred since each element in the NC3 system was designed and from the increasing pace at which these changes are occurring. One of these is the rapid development of antisatellite capabilities by potential adversaries. Apart from China's well-known ability to target satellites in low earth orbit with ground-based missiles, in 2019 the Defense Intelligence Agency concluded that China "is developing sophisticated on-orbit capabilities . . . [that] could also function as a weapon" and is probably developing other capabilities that would enable it to harm US satellites.[53] Some of these capabilities include the use of directed-energy weapons that would be able to "disrupt, degrade, or damage satellites and their sensors" and antisatellite weapons that could reach satellites in geosynchronous orbit more than twenty thousand miles from earth.[54] The Defense Intelligence Agency found that Russia, too, is developing similar capabilities and that even smaller countries, such as Iran and North Korea, have the capability to jam certain communications and Global Positioning System satellite signals.

Information technology presents another, perhaps even more obvious, technological challenge to NC3 modernization. Because future NC3 will be digital and networked, it will be vastly more capable than unconnected analog systems were. But it is also vulnerable to cyberattack. It is possible to design simpler, more easily defended information-technology products, but the pervasiveness of networked systems combined with the "system of systems" character of the NC3 system means that vulnerabilities themselves will be increasingly difficult to identify. As a result, it will become more and more difficult to guarantee the security of the system. As Eric Grosse put it, "Complexity is the enemy of security."[55] Avoiding such complexity is essential for a modernized NC3 system that still faces a requirement to provide survivable, secure, and enduring communication between the president and the nuclear forces in all threat scenarios.

Although the relationship between complexity and vulnerability is well understood, there are enormous pressures to build more complex systems because of the value that they are presumed to provide. This is most evident in the Pentagon's promotion of the Joint All Domain Command and Control (JADC2) system, which aims to link sensors in every domain (air, land, sea, space, and cyber) to users in every service through a common network. Secretary of Defense Mark Esper supported this initiative, saying, "The way we'll win in the future is being able to move data quickly."[56] In 2020 he asked Congress for funds to develop a "joint warfighting concept" based on JADC2.[57] General Hyten, who by then was serving as the vice chairman of the Joint Chiefs of Staff, acknowledged that JADC2 would be "intertwined" with NC3. In comments to a journalist in early 2020, he provided some of the only publicly available information on how the two systems would be related. He said, "NC3 will also operate in things that are separate from JADC2 because of the unique nature of the nuclear business, but it will operate in significant elements of JADC2. Therefore, NC3 has to inform JADC2 and JADC2 has to inform NC3. You have to have that interface back and forth, and that's been recognized."[58]

Since then, other senior leaders have said that the two systems will be so deeply connected that in many ways they may be indistinguishable. For example, the new director of the NC3 Enterprise Center, Rear Adm. Ronald R. Fritzemeier, said, "Fundamentally, JADC2 and NC3 Next-Gen will be . . . very closely interrelated. At some level, you would say, is that a JADC2 thing, or is that an NC3 thing, and the answer is yes."[59] The logic for linking these systems so closely was described by Gen. James Dawkins, the Air Force deputy chief of staff for strategic deterrence and nuclear integration, who said, "We've got to have an NC3 Enterprise Architecture that provides NC2 over assured [communications] for seamless integration of conventional and nuclear forces."[60]

While it is impossible to estimate how well two systems that have not yet been developed will work together, it is certainly clear each one will be a complicated amalgam of networked systems whose complexity will increase to the extent they are linked. And that complexity necessarily will increase the vulnerability of each system to cyberattacks, not to mention the ordinary challenges that arise when systems are connected. Nevertheless, the challenges are not merely technical. Blurring the lines between conventional and nuclear conflict raises even more complex questions about crisis management, escalation, and the maintenance of strategic stability.[61]

MODERNIZATION REQUIREMENTS FOR GREAT-POWER COMPETITION

Apart from these technological challenges to modernizing the NC3 system, planners must consider how the strategic environment has changed since the current system was created. During the Cold War, the United States faced a single adversary that was likely to launch a large number of nuclear-armed missiles simultaneously from a predictable direction, either as a "bolt from the blue" or as the culmination of a conflict that escalated from the conventional level. In response to this threat, the United States developed an NC3 system that would enable the president to quickly and reliably order a massive retaliatory attack. Today the threat environment is much different. Cold War–style attacks remain possible but seem less likely. Attacks may come from not just from Russia but also from China or North Korea. Attacks may be limited, either because Russia embraces a notion of "escalate to deescalate" or because a country possesses only a small number of nuclear weapons. Adversaries may choose not to launch a nuclear attack but instead to attack targets that are critical to the US ability to launch nuclear weapons, such as satellites that are part of the NC3 system. These are the concerns that are driving efforts to integrate conventional and nuclear command and control. As adversaries are increasingly inclined to blur the distinction between those two realms, US defense planners feel compelled to design systems that enable them to respond quickly to threats that cross the nuclear threshold. Conditions like these present architects of a modernized NC3 system with the challenge of designing a system that does more than maximize the time available to the president to make a launch decision. For instance, in the face of a limited strike or a nonnuclear attack on a nuclear-related target, twenty-first-century presidents may be reluctant to authorize a nuclear response without the benefit of the richly detailed real-time data that has become common in other walks of life.

While these challenges are studied and new architectures contemplated, some modernization programs are already underway. Most of these are simply intended to replace aging components in the NC3 system rather than contribute to a dramatically new system. For instance, the last two AEHF satellites, which provide faster, more secure communication links than their Military Strategic and Tactical Relay (MILSTAR) predecessors, were launched in 2019 and 2020. And the FAB-T program to develop terminals that enable air crews and ground forces to communicate at the higher speeds offered by AEHF satellites is continuing. Yet this oft-delayed program remains slowed by persistent technical challenges. In December 2019 the DOD found that the Air Force was "behind schedule delivering the FAB-T capability due to delays in resolving software deficiencies and the continued identification of new software deficiencies." As a result of these delays, a long list of core capabilities "would not be ready" until the next phase of testing. These capabilities included many that are essential to modernizing the entire NC3 system, such as the "Extended Data Rate capability, Presidential and National Voice Conferencing capability, the new FAB-T Airborne antenna, representative airborne platforms (E-4B and E-6B) employing the FAB-T, and the operationally representative CPT [command post terminal] with a ground transportable antenna."[62] In 2020 FAB-T terminals were installed at Schriever Air Force Base, Colorado, for use by the 4th Space Operations Squadron, but those meant to be installed on aircraft remained under development.[63] Together the AEHF and FAB-T programs provide constant reminders of the potential hurdles that more ambitious NC3 modernization efforts will face.

To modernize the early-warning capability that space-based infrared satellites currently provide, the Air Force has already begun development of a new satellite program known as Next-Generation Overhead Persistent Infrared (Next-Gen OPIR). This program is meant not just to replace an existing capability but also to demonstrate that modernization can be accomplished more quickly and more efficiently than in the past. Space-based infrared satellites have long been seen as a technology that was too expensive and took too long to deliver the capabilities it promised. In 2018 the Air Force decided not to fund the last two space-based infrared satellites it had planned to purchase. Instead, it began developing Next-Gen OPIR on a compressed timeline. To do so, the Space and Missile Systems Center, which is headquartered at Los Angeles Air Force Base in El Segundo, California, is taking advantage of section 804 in the 2016 National Defense Authorization Act, which authorized an acquisition approach for prototyping and fielding technologies in a two- to five-year time frame. General Hyten was among those who pressed the Air Force to move as quickly as possible to develop a successor to the constellation of space-based infrared satellites because of the need to respond to the rapidly increasing kinetic threats to US satellites.[64] In contrast to space-based infrared satellites, Next-Gen OPIR satellites are intended to be smaller, lighter, cheaper, and able to carry fuel so "they could move to a different orbit or deploy countermeasures if attacked."[65]

Although Air Force leaders remain optimistic that they can launch the first Next-Gen OPIR satellite as soon as 2025, Congress slowed the process in 2020 by requiring the Air Force and the newly formed Space Development

Agency to provide "a detailed blueprint of how they will coordinate on space systems research, development and procurement" before fully funding the program.[66] The underlying challenge is how to meet rapidly evolving threats and mission requirements. The emerging response highlights yet again the fundamental ways in which elements of the NC3 system are being rethought rather than simply replaced. Two of the most pressing threats stem from adversaries' deployment of counterspace capabilities and their development of maneuverable hypersonic missiles. Each of these makes reliance on a small number of geosynchronous satellites a less attractive proposition than in the past. Hence, planners are considering the possibility that the Next-Gen OPIR satellites will be placed in a range of orbits. As the head of the Space and Missile Systems Center said in 2020, "I think all orbital regimes are on the table."[67]

Other modernization programs remain at much earlier stages of study. For instance, in the late 2010s, the Air Force began to examine an AEHF replacement that it calls "evolved strategic satellite communications." Like the Next-Gen OPIR satellite, it is intended to cope with potential adversaries' growing abilities to jam and directly threaten US satellites. But unlike with the Next-Gen OPIR satellite, the Air Force is considering the possibility that the evolved strategic satellite system will include its own satellites as well as payloads hosted by commercial satellites.[68] In each case, the Air Force is aiming to save money and expedite delivery by increasing the use of common components. For instance, in 2019 it issued a request for information on "spacecraft buses" that could be used for the evolved strategic satellite system, the Next-Gen OPIR satellite, and other missions.[69] As this request indicates, however, development of the evolved strategic satellite system remains at a very early stage. Air Force and industry leaders have suggested that the first satellites are not likely to be delivered until the 2030s.

Another major modernization project under study is a replacement for the Air Force E-4B and the Navy E-6B, which provide similar NC3 airborne command center capabilities. The effort to design a replacement illustrates the obstacles to rapid NC3 modernization as well as the opportunities to reimagine the fundamental elements in that system. In 2015 an analysis conducted by the Joint Chiefs of Staff "suggested potential programmatic, platform, and/or mission system synergies across and between fleet recapitalization programs" that included not just the two airframes used for the NC3 mission but also the "executive airlift" role provided by the C-32.[70] A few years later, the Air Force began leading the effort to develop a single aircraft known as the "survivable airborne operations center." In 2018 it published a request for information that sought "solutions to accomplish the missions performed by the E-4B, E-6B, and C-32A," with the intent of "acquiring a single common platform or a combination of platforms that do not sacrifice operational effectiveness or increase the overall cost."[71] At that time, it budgeted more than $600 million over five years for research and development costs of the new aircraft. The challenge was not simply to design a new airframe but also to rethink the missions that the existing aircraft performed. According to an Air Force spokesperson, the program did "not yet have a technical baseline, formal requirements, a service cost position or concept of operations."[72]

Yet just two years later, the Air Force and Navy developed new plans to develop separate aircraft. This was not simply as case of two services designing direct replacements for existing platforms. The Air Force remained focused on acquiring a new aircraft that was similar in size and capabilities to the existing E-4B, while the Navy made a surprising announcement. In a procurement notice, the Navy explained that its "Analysis of Alternatives (AoA) results indicated that the four-engine, militarized C-130J-30 is optimally configured aircraft for performing the TACAMO [Take Charge and Move Out] mission."[73] Implicitly, the Navy seemed to indicate that it no longer sought a new aircraft that would be capable of serving as an airborne command post. In early 2021 Admiral Richard, the head of Strategic Command, not only confirmed that the Navy was moving in this direction but highlighted this decision as an example of how the services are rethinking the way they fulfill the NC3 mission. He recalled that the TACAMO and command post missions had not always been combined on one aircraft, and "that's the direction Navy is headed in right now."[74] When asked if he expected the Air Force to acquire a new fleet to fulfill the launch-control mission, he suggested that major changes were under consideration. "The goal," he said, "is a survivable command post and maybe it's in the air and maybe it's not, as long as it's survivable, right?" The he added, "we're trying to achieve old standard [sic] by new ways to do it both better and probably cheaper."[75]

CONCLUSION

This chapter illustrates the many challenges that Strategic Command and NC3 Enterprise Center leaders have identified and confronted in their quest to modernize and adapt NC3 to meet a changing technological and strategic environment. The fact that NC3 modernization is occurring in the digital setting of the information revolution further complicates matters; the introduction of new digital systems tends to accelerate the obsolescence of existing systems. Systems such as space-based infrared satellites, for instance, cannot simply be replaced. Nor can the acquisition processes that produced space-based infrared satellites be reused. New systems must be developed, and they need to be designed, tested, and delivered on a faster timeline than in the past. But doing so is difficult for familiar reasons. Even if satellites can adopt a common bus or airborne command posts can be built on a common airframe, they must confront the complexity of building the communication systems that make satellites and aircraft valuable. In this regard, FAB-T stands as a stark reminder of how large this challenge is. Nearly two decades since the start of that program, all AEHF satellites have been launched and are in orbit, but the terminals required to communicate with them are bedeviled by software problems.

Designing new architecture is a tall challenge. Executing it may be even harder. But a consensus has finally emerged within the highest levels of the US government that the time has come to begin the process.

NOTES

1. "USSTRATCOM Announces Initial Operational Capability of NC3 Enterprise Center," US Strategic Command, April 3, 2019, https://www.stratcom.mil/Media/News/News-Article-View/Article/1805006/usstratcom-announces-initial-operational-capability-of-nc3-enterprise-center/.
2. Barbara Starr, "Mattis and Dunford Call for Classified Nuclear Changes," CNN, July 20, 2019, https://www.cnn.com/2018/07/19/politics/mattis-dunford-nuclear-changes/index.html.
3. Rachel S. Cohen, "STRATCOM's New NC3 Center Suggests Program Changes," *Air Force Magazine*, May 6, 2019, http://airforcemag.com/Features/Pages/2019/May%202019/STRATCOMs-New-NC3-Center-Suggests-Program-Changes.aspx.
4. Office of the Secretary of Defense (Nuclear Matters), *Nuclear Matters Handbook 2016*, 80–81, https://web.archive.org/web/20190206214107/https://www.acq.osd.mil/ncbdp/nm/NMHB/docs/NMHB2016_Ch6_web.pdf.
5. Rachel S. Cohen, "STRATCOM Hopes Experiments Will Speed Nuclear Command Upgrades," *Air Force Magazine*, September 30, 2020, https://www.airforcemag.com/stratcom-hopes-experiments-will-speed-nuclear-command-upgrades/; Theresa Hitchens, "Congress Fears DoD Not Prepared for NC3 Cyber Attacks," *Breaking Defense*, December 11, 2020, https://breakingdefense.com/2020/12/congress-fears-dod-not-prepared-for-nc3-cyber-attacks/.
6. "Interview with the Defense Writers Group," US Strategic Command, January 8, 2021, https://www.stratcom.mil/Media/Speeches/Article/2466803/interview-with-the-defense-writers-group/.
7. US Congress, Senate, Committee on Armed Services, *National Defense Authorization Act for Fiscal Year 2013: Report (to Accompany S. 3254)*, 112th Cong., 2nd sess., 2012, S. Rep. 112–173, 199, https://www.congress.gov/112/crpt/srpt173/CRPT-112srpt173.pdf.
8. Andrea Shalal-Esa, "Pentagon Weighs Boeing Fate on Satellite Terminals," Reuters, February 17, 2012, https://www.reuters.com/article/boeing-space/pentagon-weighs-boeing-fate-on-satellite-terminals-idUSL2E8DHCWZ20120217.
9. Senate Committee on Armed Services, *National Defense Authorization Act for Fiscal Year 2013: Report (to Accompany S. 3254)*, 199.
10. Senate Committee on Armed Services, 199.

11. All quotations in this paragraph are found in Don Snyder, Sarah A. Nowak, Mahyar A. Amouzegar, Julie Kim, and Richard Mesic, *Sustaining the U.S. Air Force Nuclear Mission* (Santa Monica, CA: RAND Corp., 2013), 11–12.
12. All quotations in this paragraph are found in National Defense Authorization Act for Fiscal Year 2014, Pub. L. 113–66, December 26, 2013, https://www.congress.gov/113/plaws/publ66/PLAW-113publ66.pdf.
13. "Summary of DoD Internal Nuclear Enterprise Review," DOD, May 1, 2014, 1, https://dod.defense.gov/Portals/1/Documents/pubs/Summary-Internal-NER.pdf.
14. "Independent Review of the Department of Defense Nuclear Enterprise," DOD, June 2, 2014, 6, https://dod.defense.gov/Portals/1/Documents/pubs/Independent-Nuclear-Enterprise-Review-Report-30-June-2014.pdf.
15. "Independent Review of the Department of Defense Nuclear Enterprise," DOD, June 2, 2014, 18, https://dod.defense.gov/Portals/1/Documents/pubs/Independent-Nuclear-Enterprise-Review-Report-30-June-2014.pdf.
16. "Summary of DoD Internal Nuclear Enterprise Review," DOD, May 1, 2014, 2, https://dod.defense.gov/Portals/1/Documents/pubs/Summary-Internal-NER.pdf.
17. "Statement of the Honorable Madelyn Creedon, Co-Chair of the Department of Defense's Internal Nuclear Enterprise Review and Principal Deputy Administrator, National Nuclear Security Administration, U.S. Department of Energy, on the Air Force and Navy Nuclear Programs Implementation of the Nuclear Enterprise Review Recommendations, before the Subcommittee on Strategic Forces Senate Committee on Armed Services," Senate Armed Services Committee, April 22, 2015, https://www.armed-services.senate.gov/imo/media/doc/Creedon_04-22-15.pdf.
18. See Jim Garamone, "Hagel Announces Changes to U.S. Nuclear Deterrent Enterprise," DOD News, November 14, 2014; "Fact Sheet: Implementing Changes to the Nuclear Enterprise," DOD, n.d., https://archive.defense.gov/pubs/ner-fact-sheet.pdf.
19. GAO, "Nuclear Command, Control, and Communications: Review of DOD's Current Modernization Efforts," March 18, 2014, GAO-14-414R, https://www.gao.gov/assets/670/661752.pdf.
20. "Statement of Admiral C. D. Haney, Commander United States Strategic Command, before the Senate Committee on Armed Services," February 27, 2014, 9, https://fas.org/irp/congress/2014_hr/022714haney.pdf.
21. "USAF Scientific Advisory Board Study, Nuclear Command, Control, and Communications, Study Abstract," Inside Defense, July 2, 2014, https://insidedefense.com/sites/insidedefense.com/files/documents/jul2014/07312014_sab2.pdf.
22. Air Force Instruction 13-550, October 2, 2014, https://fas.org/irp/doddir/usaf/afi13-550-2014.pdf.
23. Carla Pampe, "AFGSC Stands Up Air Force NC3 Center," Air Force Global Strike Command Public Affairs, April 3, 2017, https://www.kirtland.af.mil/News/Article/1139359/afgsc-stands-up-air-force-nc3-center/.
24. National Defense Authorization Act for Fiscal Year 2016, Pub. L. 114–92, November 25, 2015, https://www.congress.gov/114/plaws/publ92/PLAW-114publ92.pdf.
25. National Defense Authorization Act for Fiscal Year 2017, Pub. L. 114-328, December 23, 2016, https://www.congress.gov/114/plaws/publ328/PLAW-114publ328.pdf.
26. Gen. Robin Rand, "Presentation to the Senate Armed Services Committee: Strategic Forces Subcommittee," June 7, 2017, 11, https://www.armed-services.senate.gov/imo/media/doc/Rand_06-07-17.pdf.

27. Stew Magnuson, "Exclusive: Interview with Gen. Robin Rand, Head of Air Force Global Strike Command," *National Defense*, November 14, 2017, https://www.nationaldefensemagazine.org/articles/2017/11/14/global-strike-command-tackles-atrophying-nuclear-command-control-systems.
28. "Transcript of Hearing on Military Assessment of Nuclear Deterrence Requirements," DOD, March 8, 2017, https://dod.defense.gov/Portals/1/features/2017/0917_nuclear-deterrence/docs/Transcript-HASC-Hearing-on-Nuclear-Deterrence-8-March-2017.pdf.
29. "Statement of John E. Hyten, Commander, United States Strategic Command, before the Senate Committee on Armed Services," April 4, 2017, 6, https://www.armed-services.senate.gov/imo/media/doc/Hyten_04-04-17.pdf.
30. "Statement of John E. Hyten, Commander, United States Strategic Command, before the House Committee on Armed Services," March 7, 2017, 8, https://docs.house.gov/meetings/AS/AS29/20180307/106941/HHRG-115-AS29-Wstate-HytenJ-20180307.pdf.
31. Sandra Erwin, "Q&A: Air Force Gen. John Hyten Says U.S. Space Strategy, Budget Moving 'Down the Right Path,'" *SpaceNews*, April 3, 2018, https://spacenews.com/qa-air-force-gen-john-hyten-says-u-s-space-strategy-budget-moving-down-the-right-path/.
32. All quotations in this paragraph are found in GAO, *Nuclear Command, Control, and Communications: Update on Air Force Oversight Effort and Selected Acquisition Programs*, GAO-17-641R, October 27, 2017, 2.
33. The classified report is mentioned in the GAO's unclassified report *Defense Nuclear Enterprise: Processes to Monitor Progress on Implementing Recommendations and Managing Risks Could Be Improved*, GAO-18-144, October 2017, 1. The review that produced this report is mentioned in "Statement of Robert Work, Deputy Secretary of Defense, and Admiral James Winnefeld, Vice Chairman of the Joint Chiefs of Staff, before the House Committee on Armed Services," June 25, 2015, 7, https://docs.house.gov/meetings/AS/AS00/20150625/103669/HHRG-114-AS00-Wstate-WorkR-20150625.pdf.
34. GAO, *Defense Nuclear Enterprise: Processes to Monitor Progress on Implementing Recommendations and Managing Risks Could Be Improved*, GAO-18-144, October 2017, 11.
35. GAO, 19.
36. National Defense Authorization Act for Fiscal Year 2018, Pub. L. 115-91, 1759, December 12, 2017, https://www.congress.gov/115/plaws/publ91/PLAW-115publ91.pdf.
37. National Defense Authorization Act for Fiscal Year 2018, 1760.
38. National Defense Authorization Act for Fiscal Year 2018, 1756.
39. National Defense Authorization Act for Fiscal Year 2018, 1764–65.
40. DOD, *Nuclear Posture Review: 2081*, 56–58, https://media.defense.gov/2018/Feb/02/2001872886/-1/-1/1/2018-NUCLEAR-POSTURE-REVIEW-FINAL-REPORT.PDF.
41. Gen. Robin Rand, "Presentation to the House Armed Services Committee: Strategic Forces Subcommittee," March 22, 2018, 16, https://docs.house.gov/meetings/AS/AS29/20180322/108035/HHRG-115-AS29-Wstate-RandR-20180322.pdf.
42. US Congress, Senate, S. 2987, Report No. 115–262, June 15, 2018, 777–82, https://www.congress.gov/115/bills/s2987/BILLS-115s2987pcs.pdf.

43. US Office of Management and Budget, "Follow-On to Statement of Administration Policy," White House, June 26, 2018, 5, https://www.whitehouse.gov/wp-content/uploads/2018/06/saps2987s_20180626.pdf.
44. US Congress, House of Representatives, Conference Report to Accompany H.R. 5515, John S. McCain National Defense Authorization Act for Fiscal Year 2019, 115th Cong., Rep. 115-874, July 25, 2018, 1078, https://www.congress.gov/115/crpt/hrpt874/CRPT-115hrpt874.pdf.
45. Sandra Erwin, "U.S. STRATCOM to Take Over Responsibility for Nuclear Command, Control and Communications," *SpaceNews*, July 23, 2018, https://spacenews.com/u-s-stratcom-to-take-over-responsibility-for-nuclear-command-control-and-communications/.
46. Sara Sirota, "NC3 Enterprise Center Outlines Requirements, Explores Readiness and Cost," *Inside Defense*, December 11, 2019, https://insidedefense.com/daily-news/nc3-enterprise-center-outlines-requirements-explores-readiness-and-cost.
47. See, e.g., Kingston Reif, "Smith, Inhofe Clash on Nukes," *Arms Control Today*, January/February 2019, https://www.armscontrol.org/act/2019-01/news/smith-inhofe-clash-nukes.
48. US House of Representatives, House Committee on Armed Services, "Democratic Priorities in the FY20 NDAA," https://armedservices.house.gov/_cache/files/b/9/b9940805-15aa-4a0a-9593-f2e2708ea926/F3A097D3DE2B5A16821BA36A316EEF1A.democratic-priorities-in-the-fy20-ndaa.pdf.
49. National Defense Authorization Act for Fiscal Year 2020, Pub. L. 116-92, December 20, 2019, https://www.congress.gov/bill/116th-congress/senate-bill/1790/text.
50. Kevin Dehoff, "Modernizing the US Nuclear Deterrent: An Interview with Elizabeth Ruiz-Durham," McKinsey & Company, June 2019, 3–4, https://www.mckinsey.com/industries/aerospace-and-defense/our-insights/modernizing-the-us-nuclear-deterrent-an-interview-with-elizabeth-durham-ruiz.
51. All quotations in this paragraph regarding the call for ideas are found in "Next Generation NC3 Enterprise Challenge," November 27, 2018, originally posted at https://www.fbo.gov/notices/390609791364842047d3ab34aa7d1441 and now archived at http://www.fbodaily.com/archive/2018/11-November/29-Nov-2018/FBO-05160025.htm.
52. See, e.g., DOD, *Nuclear Posture Review: 2018*; "Statement of Charles A. Richard, Commander, United States Strategic Command, before the Senate Committee on Armed Services," US Strategic Command, February 13, 2020, 17, https://www.stratcom.mil/Portals/8/Documents/2020_USSTRATCOM_Posture_Statement_SASC_Final.pdf; Jon R. Lindsay, "Cyber Operations and Nuclear Weapons," Tech4GS Special Reports, June 20, 2019, https://www.tech4gs.org/nc3-systems-and-strategic-stability-a-global-overview.html; Eric Grosse, "Security at Extreme Scales," Tech4GS Special Reports, May 30, 2019, https://www.tech4gs.org/nc3-systems-and-strategic-stability-a-global-overview.html; Paul Bracken, "NC3 in a Multipolar Nuclear World: Big Structures and Large Processes," Tech4GS Special Reports, May 14, 2019, https://www.tech4gs.org/nc3-systems-and-strategic-stability-a-global-overview.html.
53. Defense Intelligence Agency, "Challenges to Security in Space," February 2019, 20, https://www.dia.mil/Portals/27/Documents/News/Military%20Power%20Publications/Space_Threat_V14_020119_sm.pdf.
54. Defense Intelligence Agency, 21.

55. Grosse, "Security at Extreme Scale," 2.
56. Aaron Mehta, "Mark Esper on the 'Big Pivot Point' That Will Define the 2022 Budget," *Defense News*, February 10, 2020, https://www.defensenews.com/smr/federal-budget/2020/02/10/mark-esper-on-the-big-pivot-point-that-will-define-the-2022-budget/.
57. "Secretary of Defense Mark T. Esper, Department of Defense Posture Statement, Senate Armed Services Committee," March 4, 2020, 7, https://www.armed-services.senate.gov/imo/media/doc/Esper_03-04-20.pdf.
58. Colin Clark, "Nuclear C3 Goes All Domain: Gen. Hyten," *Breaking Defense*, February 20, 2020, https://breakingdefense.com/2020/02/nuclear-c3-goes-all-domain-gen-hyten/.
59. Rachel Cohen, "STRATCOM Hopes Experiments Will Speed Nuclear Command Upgrades," *Air Force Magazine*, September 30, 2020, https://www.airforcemag.com/stratcom-hopes-experiments-will-speed-nuclear-command-upgrades/.
60. Theresa Hitchens, "Congress Fears DoD Not Prepared for NC3 Cyber Attacks," *Breaking Defense*, December 11, 2020, https://breakingdefense.com/2020/12/congress-fears-dod-not-prepared-for-nc3-cyber-attacks/.
61. Rebecca K. C. Hersman and Reja Younis, "Surveillance, Situational Awareness, and Warning at the Conventional-Strategic Interface," Project on Nuclear Issues, January 15, 2021, http://defense360.csis.org/wp-content/uploads/2021/01/Hersman-and-Younis-ISR-Nuclear-Nexus.pdf.
62. Director, Operational Test and Evaluation (DOT&E), FY 2019 Annual Report, December 20, 2019, 188, https://www.dote.osd.mil/Portals/97/pub/reports/FY2019/af/2019fab-t.pdf?ver=2020-01-30-115238-347. The CPT is an element of FAB-T modernization.
63. Nathan Strout, "Space Force Squadron Gets New Advanced Terminal for Secure Communications," C4ISRNet, July 14, 2020, https://www.c4isrnet.com/battlefield-tech/space/2020/07/14/space-force-squadron-gets-new-advanced-terminal-for-secure-communications/.
64. Sandra Erwin, "The End of SBIRS: Air Force Says It's Time to Move On," *SpaceNews*, February 19, 2018, https://spacenews.com/the-end-of-sbirs-air-force-says-its-time-to-move-on/.
65. Sandra Erwin, "Plan to Modernize Air and Space Systems Takes Air Force out of Its Comfort Zone," *SpaceNews*, February 19, 2018, https://spacenews.com/plan-to-modernize-air-and-space-systems-takes-air-force-out-of-its-comfort-zone/.
66. Theresa Hitchens, "OPIR Missile Warning Sats Plow Ahead amid $$ Turmoil," *Breaking Defense*, June 19, 2019, https://breakingdefense.com/2019/06/opir-missile-warning-sats-plow-ahead-amid-turmoil/.
67. Courtney Albon, "OPIR Architecture Report Designates MDA as Lead for HBTSS, Reveals New Interagency AQ Team," *Inside Defense*, December 22, 2020, https://insidedefense-com/daily-news/opir-architecture-report-designates-mda-lead-hbtss-reveals-new-interagency-aq-team. See also Theresa Hitchens, "Shifting Gears, DoD Moves to LEO for Future OPIR Sats," *Breaking Defense*, June 18, 2020, https://breakingdefense.com/2020/06/shifting-gears-dod-moves-to-leo-for-future-opir-sats/.
68. Vivienne Machi, "Air Force, Industry Considering Future of Protected Satcom," *National Defense*, January 19, 2018, https://www.nationaldefensemagazine.org/articles/2018/1/19/air-force-industry-considering-future-of-protected-satcom.

69. "SMC Modular Enterprise Spacecraft Bus Procurement Request for Information," March 6, 2019, https://www.fbo.gov/spg/USAF/AFSC/SMCSMSC/SMCModularEnterpriseBus/listing.html.
70. US Air Force, "Department of Defense Fiscal Year (FY) 2021 Budget Estimates," vol. 2, February 2020, 157, https://www.saffm.hq.af.mil/Portals/84/documents/FY21/RDTE_/FY21%20Air%20Force%20Research%20Development%20Test%20and%20Evaluation%20Vol%20II.pdf?ver=2020-02-12-145218-377.
71. DOD, "National Airborne Operations Center (NAOC), Executive Airlift, Airborne Command Post (ABNCP), Take Charge and Move Out (TACAMO) (NEAT)," July 31, 2018, https://beta.sam.gov/opp/e8d7f4fbc5a4f9f3c19e666df17f071d/view?keywords=NAOC.
72. Sara Sirota, "E-4B NAOC Replacement Program Eyeing Multicontract Award for Pre-EMD Work in FY-21," *Inside Defense*, February 13, 2020, https://insidedefense.com/daily-news/e-4b-naoc-replacement-program-eyeing-multicontract-award-pre-emd-work-fy-21; Theresa Hitchens, "Air Force to Kick Off E-4B Replacement Competition in 2021," *Breaking Defense*, February 14, 2020, https://breakingdefense.com/2020/02/air-force-to-kick-off-e4-b-replacement-competition-in-2021/.
73. "Navy TACAMO Program Office: Green/Test C-130J-30 Aircraft and Associated Airframe Analysis," December 18, 2020, https://beta.sam.gov/opp/74fc6f2df4064b209f8c546b364deecc/view; "The Survivable Airborne Operations Center (SAOC) Weapon System," December 18, 2020, https://beta.sam.gov/opp/e3a93a32c0844775a5ba7c9cce09e767/view.
74. "Interview with the Defense Writers Group," January 8, 2021, US Strategic Command, https://www.stratcom.mil/Media/Speeches/Article/2466803/interview-with-the-defense-writers-group/.
75. "Interview with the Defense Writers Group."

CONCLUSION

US NC3 AT A CRITICAL JUNCTURE

Jeffrey A. Larsen

The US government has committed itself over the next two decades to pursue the costly replacement of all three legs of its strategic nuclear triad—the delivery systems for nuclear weapons that provide a secure second-strike capability against any threat and thereby provide the ultimate deterrent guarantee against adversary attack. None of those delivery systems is usable, however, without a reliable and robust nuclear command, control, and communications (NC3) system that can identify a threat, provide information to the country's decision-makers, and send the orders of the president to the forces in the field, all in a timely manner even under the most dire circumstances. This is a tall order. Yet that system is facing a perfect storm of challenges. The NC3 system has not been truly updated in nearly forty years. New types of delivery systems are in the procurement pipeline that must be able to synch with the existing system for the coming fifty years. The United States faces new adversaries with advanced capabilities that can threaten its deterrent force as well as its NC3 system. Moreover, all of this is happening in a digital world for which legacy NC3 systems were not designed. And the existing architecture must continue to work flawlessly while a new system is put in place.

This volume has described NC3, how the system works, how it relates to broader command and control, and what components make up the system of systems. The authors described how concerns about NC3 shaped the evolution of the US nuclear force posture, the challenges facing the system today, and some of the requirements for modernizing the National Military Command System. Our contributors filled a niche that allowed the reader to better understand not only how NC3 contributes to national security strategy but also the challenges facing the National Military Command System in today's more complex cyber era.

The literature on NC3 is sparse, and most of the publications that do exist are quite similar in their approach due to the limited amount of publicly available information about this understandably esoteric subject. As one book on US nuclear forces put it, "For all that has been written about nuclear weapons strategy and theory, there is surprisingly little that describes the procedure for how nuclear weapons would actually be used."[1] In one of the few recent publications on NC3, retired Lieutenant General David Deptula introduced a report on NC3 modernization by saying that "it is these systems that define an architecture that coalesces in a coherent fashion all the activities, processes, and procedures performed by military commanders and support personnel that, through the chain of command, allow for senior-level decisions on nuclear weapons employment."[2] The US military is reluctant to discuss the system, its shortfalls, possible modernization plans, or much else about NC3, although various government documents do explain its basic functions. The authors of this volume understand that reticence, but they also recognize the need for public awareness and discourse about NC3 and the overdue necessity for modernization of the system. This book serves as an unclassified primer on America's NC3 system and the way forward toward a modernized, twenty-first-century backbone of deterrence.

It is hard to believe that despite all the advances in recent decades in computers, data processing, communications, remote sensing, satellites, space architecture, and other advanced technologies, America's system for command and control over its ultimate deterrent force still relies on systems largely put in place nearly forty years ago. Granted, after the unanticipated and surprisingly peaceful end of the Cold War, the world shared a collective sigh of relief, with subjects such as deterrence, nuclear forces, and NC3 largely consigned to the dustbin of history—at least in the public eye. Unfortunately, the need for deterrence never fully disappeared, and in the past decade that requirement has returned with a vengeance. As a result, the United States is late starting the modernization effort that it needs to undertake to bring NC3 into the twenty-first century.

This chapter highlights several themes that carried across the volume and provides a summary of key concepts raised by our authors.

NC3 IS THE UNDERAPPRECIATED BACKBONE OF AMERICAN DETERRENCE

In the early 1980s Gen. Richard Ellis, commander of Strategic Air Command, testified before Congress and identified the minimum responsibilities of an NC3 system. These requirements still hold today. In his words, NC3 had to "recognize that we are under attack, characterize that attack, get a decision from the President, and disseminate that decision to the forces prior to the first weapon impacting upon the United States."[3]

While the United States relies on its NC3 system for early warning, communications, and its deterrence strategy, there are problems within the complex systems that control nuclear forces. Perhaps most important is that NC3 does not get much respect. It is not glamorous in the way of strategic bombers, ballistic missile submarines, or intercontinental ballistic missiles (ICBMs). Yet NC3 serves as the backbone of deterrence. Sometimes called the "fifth leg" of America's nuclear deterrent triad (the fourth leg being the warheads themselves), NC3 is absolutely critical to the proper functioning of the other legs. Without command, control, or communications, no nuclear weapon would reach its target—or, for that matter, even receive a message to launch.

Among the most vital problems facing NC3 is the age of most of its components. It is based on analog systems, whereas the challenges it faces today are digital and cyber in nature. On paper NC3 is a simple concept; in reality, however, it is a huge and diverse system of systems that must serve a single customer and that has but a single purpose: deterrence of attack on the United States, its allies, and its vital national interests. And for our sake, it cannot fail.

All accidents and mishaps involving nuclear weapons and their associated delivery vehicles over the past seventy-five years have constituted some sort of breakdown in NC3. As James J. Wirtz pointed out in his introduction to this volume, "NC3 itself did not create this Pandora's box of nuclear accidents, inadvertent nuclear war, human incompetence, treachery, and organizational pathologies. NC3, however, is the key that can keep that box closed." The four close calls for NC3 that opened chapter 4 of this volume, for example, took place across six decades, including one just a few short years ago. The problems remain, and they must be addressed.

As pointed out by several of this book's authors, NC3 is the means to execute the five mission-essential functions embodied in nuclear command and control.[4] An open-source Air Force instruction describes NC3 as "an integrated system comprised of facilities, equipment, communications, procedures, and personnel."[5] It forms the core of the National Military Command System, which maintains continuous, survivable, secure command and control of nuclear forces. NC3 is the key enabler of any effort to incorporate nuclear weapons into a national defense strategy because it provides both positive and negative control of nuclear forces.

Nevertheless, despite this important mission, the US NC3 system is a system of systems that has been cobbled together over the decades with little regard for simplicity or interoperability and is thus in dire need of overhaul, modernization, and rationalization. Concerns about the security of nuclear forces and command and control systems are not new, of course. As our authors noted, during the Cold War observers worried that nuclear infrastructure and command networks could be penetrated, corrupted, destroyed, or spoofed, leading to a loss of positive control or negative control. Nuclear arsenals, deterrent policies, and an analog NC3 system were all designed without cyberthreats in mind.

Embracing deterrence as a strategy involves a good deal more than just possessing a weapons system—it also involves developing and preserving accurate situational assessments in peacetime, during crises, and during war itself. NC3 is thus a critical enabler of deterrence because it provides the capability necessary to execute deterrence threats. Without effective NC3, deterrence lacks credibility. Furthermore, in the face of a limited strike or a nonnuclear attack on a nuclear-related target, twenty-first-century presidents who have grown up in the computer age may be reluctant to authorize a nuclear response without first reviewing the richly detailed, real-time data that has become common in other walks of life. The emergence of new threats and the transition from analog to digital systems means that the entire NC3 architecture is being reexamined. Substantial portions are likely to be redesigned rather than simply replaced.

AMERICA LEARNED THE VALUE AND SHORTCOMINGS OF A ROBUST NC3 SYSTEM AS THE RESULT OF REGULARLY OCCURRING NUCLEAR CRISES

The "tasks" of NC3 have remained essentially the same throughout the Cold War, although the methods and technologies that operationalized those tasks were updated about every twenty years. NC3 operators have always been responsible for trying to provide adequate early warning of nuclear attack to allow national decision-makers (particularly the president) to reach an informed decision on whether and how to retaliate. The Soviet threat changed over time, from manned bombers armed with fission weapons to much faster long-range missiles with more destructive hydrogen bombs and later to missiles carrying multiple nuclear warheads. Each of these changes reduced the time available for decision-making and complicated response options. In addition, adversary weapons began to target components of the US NC3 system itself, which raised other concerns, such as the viability of early-warning, targeting, and communication systems before or during a crisis. NC3 operators are responsible for transmitting the orders of the president to US military units armed with nuclear weapons. This was made more difficult by interservice rivalries that plagued the NC3 system, as each branch tried to assert the requirement to maintain its own authorities and systems and to reject efforts to create a unified nuclear command.

The vast expansion of the US arsenal under President Dwight Eisenhower in the 1950s exacerbated early NC3 challenges, given the rapidly increasing variation in the size of weapons, their delivery systems, and the types of units that operated them. This same dynamic affected NC3 during President Ronald Reagan's buildup of the 1980s. In both periods, dramatic increases in the destructive capability of nuclear weapons, the speed of their delivery, and the resultant vulnerability of US nuclear forces required significant changes in NC3. While the essential tasks of NC3 remained the same, the sharp decline in warning time meant that an adversary's surprise attack might appear more effective and therefore more tempting, thus reducing crisis stability. Advances in automated communications, computing, and launch detection increased capabilities on both sides but also introduced complexities and errors within the NC3 system. Throughout the Cold War the NC3 network struggled to meet new technological demands to operate effectively against an ever-increasing Soviet nuclear arsenal.

The increasing number of Soviet warheads from 1960 to the mid-1980s also raised concerns about the survivability of US NC3 systems. As James Clay Moltz pointed out in chapter 3 of this volume, a classified study conducted in the 1970s concluded that a focused nuclear strike by just 1 percent of the Soviet arsenal on US NC3 nodes could take out 80 percent of America's political-military nuclear command structure. This was not good news for deterrence or for those who expressed concern over possible solutions to this threat that might make nuclear war even more likely (such as adopting a "launch-on-warning" policy).

Technological innovations such as electronic miniaturization, the shrinking size and increasing power of computers, and ongoing advances in satellite technologies interacted synergistically to allow considerable improvements in America's NC3 system over the decades. These were critical upgrades, given the diversification of the US nuclear force structure and the increasingly complex war plans in the missile age. All these changes placed new and more challenging requirements on NC3 in terms of situation monitoring, early warning, message trafficking to and from national security leaders, and tracking and coordinating strike forces. And many of the improvements slowed down or were canceled after the end of the Cold War, putting the United States in the demanding situation it faces today.

NC3 HAS BEEN SLOW TO CATCH UP WITH TECHNOLOGICAL AND DOCTRINAL CHANGES

The high cost of NC3 technologies, which often required long lead times for construction of new transmission equipment, radars, and other facilities, meant that budgets for needed upgrades often proved inadequate or were spread out over many years. In some cases, the systems were obsolete before they could be completed, thus starting another cycle of attempting to catch up to newly emerging threats.

As a result, the US NC3 system has always stood at the intersection of the changing foreign nuclear threat, the evolving US nuclear arsenal, and the makeup and policy preferences of political leaders. During the Cold War, these determinants were in constant flux even as NC3 operators struggled to keep the nuclear arsenal safe, ready, and responsive, often with outdated equipment and inadequate funding.

Many close calls and NC3 errors occurred during periods of transition to a new doctrine or policy. For example, the nearly disastrous false alarms of 1979 and 1980 were caused by computer upgrades to existing NC3 systems at North American Air Defense Command. These close calls all turned out to be the result of internal mistakes or errors. Today, however, the effects experienced in each of those cases could potentially be generated by external actors using cyber means.

Nearly thirty years ago, analysts such as Bruce Blair and Scott Sagan were writing separately about accidents, near misses, close calls, and other interesting but frightening stories from the Cold War, leading them to the conclusion that the country needed to modernize NC3 in the wake of that conflict. Blair was particularly worried about the inflexibility of the NC3 system during the Cold War. He said, "The U.S. command and control system requires major modifications to bring it into proper alignment with the international context in which it operates. . . . [It] needs to be modified to handle threats of inadvertence."[6] The "cyber context" of today is raising similar concerns and is likely to complicate efforts to modernize NC3.

THE LACK OF COHESION IN NC3 HAS BEEN DUE IN LARGE PART TO A LACK OF PROPER GOVERNANCE

The increasing Soviet threat during the Cold War forced the United States to episodically increase its efforts to improve readiness, reduce vulnerabilities, and build survivable communications and command posts. This was not always easy. For instance, the Navy successfully argued for its own control over its ballistic missile submarines, leading to continued frictions and coordination problems with the Air Force that lasted through the end of the Cold War. The Army also retained separate command over its battlefield weapons, causing other difficulties. The creation of a Joint Strategic Target Planning Staff and Single Integrated Operational Plan tried to reconcile and deconflict such problems, but it took years to succeed—and then only following the end of the Cold War and the creation of US Strategic Command (STRATCOM).

Over the years, the Air Force and Navy simply added new NC3 capabilities whenever a requirement was identified, resulting in a large set of early-warning and communication networks that often worked independently of one another. Additions to the system occurred when deemed necessary, without the benefit of a master plan. The rationale for every system was legitimate and fulfilled an identified operational need, but the resulting panoply of systems was often inefficient and redundant.

As the US nuclear force structure diversified, new types of delivery systems presented their own operational requirements and conflicting time constraints on NC3 systems and procedures. Increasingly complex war plans, including a variety of target "withholds" (targets not attacked in the initial response but held hostage to follow-on strikes) and attack options for protracted nuclear conflict, also placed new and challenging requirements on NC3, which had to retain significant functionality well into a nuclear exchange—a big change from the "one-shot" war plans of the early nuclear era.

America's NC3 system is a vintage system, created in a predigital world and in an ad hoc manner that had no master plan or deliberate design. In fact, NC3 is a collection of parts and pieces that were simply added as they came online, reflecting new systems that were created to address new needs as they arose rather than an organized and efficient system of systems. As a recent study explained, "There is no one NC3 system. The NC3 system as it exists today is a patchwork of disparate systems, each with its own characteristics. There is no one operating system or coding language."[7] This is the antiquated system on which American security rests today. As if that were not enough, following the end of the Cold War, America's NC3 systems faced the same twenty years of neglect as did nuclear forces and deterrence thinking in general.

THE CYBER ERA AND LEFT-OF-LAUNCH THREATS ARE PLACING EVEN GREATER STRAINS ON THE ANTIQUATED NC3 SYSTEM OF SYSTEMS

Today most analysts recognize a number of contemporary challenges confronting the NC3 weapons system produced by accelerating technologies. These include cyberthreats and the cyber world of today, insider threats, principle-agent problems created by a breakdown of organizational routines and individual discipline, direct threats against elements of the NC3 system or its supporting infrastructure, and information overload that undermines the development and maintenance of accurate situational awareness. There are even newer technologies, such as artificial intelligence, big data, continuous global surveillance, and quantum computing, that have not yet been fully evaluated in the NC3 context. Simply refurbishing old systems and reinforcing adherence to existing procedures and protocols might not be the best way forward given this changing strategic and technological environment.

Threats to the integrity of the NC3 systems appear to be moving "left of launch." Preserving the integrity of NC3 now involves more than surviving a nuclear attack in order to ensure a viable secure second-strike capability in a postattack environment. Cyberattacks against critical communication hubs or command centers today occur on an ongoing basis. In fact, such attacks show that NC3 may be the Achilles' heel of nuclear deterrence. It might not be possible to destroy all the weapons in a large nuclear arsenal to avoid second-strike nuclear retaliation, but it might be possible to destroy an opponent's ability to fire those weapons in a timely manner by disrupting or destroying its NC3 early-warning, communication, or command and control capabilities. This can be accomplished against either space-based or terrestrial assets.

No matter the vintage of NC3 technology, adversaries will always have incentives to penetrate it to gain intelligence in peacetime or military advantage in wartime. NC3 now incorporates digital technologies to enhance the efficiency and reliability of the strategic deterrent. This development increases the complexity of NC3 systems and the number of attack vectors that must be guarded, now and into the future. Cybersecurity is thus emerging as a critical factor in NC3. Adversaries that may have an interest in compromising US NC3 can utilize a variety of means to identify vulnerabilities and devise exploitations. Not coincidentally, states with the requisite organizational capacity for sophisticated cyber operations also happen to be nuclear weapons states.

As Wade Huntley described in chapter 7, a Department of Defense (DOD) cyber exercise in 1997 concluded that the department was almost completely unprepared and defenseless against cyberattacks. The adversary in that exercise was restricted from using more sophisticated offensive capabilities that were available, and those capabilities have advanced even further in the twenty-five years since that exercise. Any nuclear actor faces the daunting challenge of maintaining defensive vigilance when the most dangerous threats are also the most invisible. Huntley's scenario in chapter 8 showed that while achieving cyber coercion by NC3 infiltration may indeed be difficult, its effects can be decisive—and thus possibly worth the effort.

MULTIPLE LINES OF EFFORT ARE UNDERWAY TO MODERNIZE NC3, BUT THEY LACK A MASTER VISION IN THE FACE OF AN UNCERTAIN FUTURE

Given the time since the last major upgrades and the return of great-power competition, the need for a major reconsideration of how best to organize US NC3 is obvious. This vital system of systems needs to be revamped, but simply adding more capabilities without trying to rationalize the existing system would be throwing good money after bad. Eventually the system will become so complicated and burdensome that its effectiveness will be called into question. Within the US government there is a growing consensus on the need to modernize NC3—but so far primarily only in organizations and governance.

Many US NC3 systems are outdated and require modernization or replacement. Senior government leaders have recognized this deficiency for more than a decade. All three legs of the US strategic nuclear triad are scheduled to be replaced with modernized systems in the next ten to fifteen years, with costly research and development programs underway. As noted by all our authors, however, nuclear delivery systems are of no value without a functioning, operational NC3 system. NC3 modernization will not be inexpensive. Nevertheless, it will cost less than replacing any one of the legs of the triad, and none of those legs will work as planned without modernized NC3. Updating the US system to be fully integrated with its new triad will require new communication links and possibly new NC3 systems.

Some progress has been made in recent years. The formation of Global Strike Command, the creation of its NC3 Center, the designation of NC3 as a weapons system, and naming STRATCOM as the lead for the entire NC3 enterprise highlight efforts to emphasize the nuclear deterrence mission in US national security strategy.

Yet the current responsibility for NC3 missions, equipment, personnel, training, acquisition, and maintenance remains dispersed across numerous DOD, Navy, and Air Force agencies and commands. The complexity and challenge of trying to rationalize this broad but diffuse oversight was one reason for the recurring demand in official reports over the past decade that the DOD needed to reform the governance of the NC3 system. This process began several years ago, after similar recognition by the Air Force—which remains the lead authority for some 70 percent of all NC3 systems—that the system was basically a mess of parallel, overlapping, and complex parts that had little oversight or common vision. On top of all that, the world has transitioned from analog to digital, yet the US NC3 system remains primarily analog.

Since 2012 a broad consensus has emerged among defense planners and members of Congress that the various components of the US NC3 infrastructure should be acknowledged as a system equal in importance to any nuclear weapon or delivery capability and that the NC3 enterprise should be managed, funded, and modernized in the same way as other components of the US strategic deterrent. But so far this consensus embraces only the organization of the NC3 system rather than the development and deployment of new technologies for conducting NC3 operations. That is certainly understandable. In 2019 the director of STRATCOM's new NC3 Enterprise Center said, "It's really kind of difficult to describe what NC3 is. We're just now defining the architecture and then after the architecture, the blueprint" for a modernized NC3 system.[8]

A June 2012 Senate Armed Services Committee report about problems within the NC3 system marked the beginning of a long process of raising political and bureaucratic awareness regarding the need to modernize NC3 governance to ensure that the system's individual elements are treated with the seriousness that the overall NC3 mission requires. As explained in chapters 4 and 9 of this volume, recognition of the need to modernize initially arose from delays and problems in the Family of Advanced Beyond-Line-of-Sight Terminals program. As STRATCOM commander Adm. Cecil Haney said, "Many NC3 systems require modernization, but it is not enough to simply build a new version of the old system—rather; we must optimize the current architecture while leveraging new technologies so that our NC3 systems interoperate as the core of a broader, national command and control system."[9] The need for NC3 modernization, he said, stemmed not just from the old age of existing technologies or a general need to compete with great-power adversaries. More pressing was the need to ensure compatibility between the NC3 systems and the new weapons platforms that will come into operation in the next decade.

Seven years after Congress first called attention to delays in the development of the Family of Advanced Beyond-Line-of-Sight Terminals program, the Air Force and the DOD finally began to treat NC3 as equal in importance to heavy bombers, ICBMs, and submarine-launched ballistic missiles. Each military service has undertaken organizational reforms to centralize authority and responsibility for NC3 in high-level commands. Underlying these reforms is a broad consensus among defense planners in Congress, the Pentagon, and the Air Force that NC3 deserves greater attention and resources. But modernization of NC3 systems, apart from the governance of those systems, has remained largely untouched, even as awareness of the need for modernization has grown. As a recent STRATCOM request for proposal put it, "continued upgrades or recapitalization efforts—that is, releasing a new version of the old thing—will not sufficiently meet 21st-century operational needs against 21st-century threats" and therefore "all architecture-design options are on the table."[10] STRATCOM's call for new ideas, including the desire to rethink the entire NC3 system before embarking on its modernization, reflects widespread appreciation of the challenges that must be overcome in designing a twenty-first-century NC3 replacement.

CONCLUSION

America's NC3 system faces multiple operational and policy challenges. Operationally, there have been persistent challenges to mission fulfillment, including inadequate warning and response time, evolving threats, survival of the chain of command, ensuring the timely delivery of orders, conducting poststrike assessment, and communicating with follow-on forces during a conflict. The NC3 system has faced the impact of interservice rivalries and suspicions, the high cost of survivable NC3 systems, long lead times for deployment of new systems, changes in the nature of America's adversaries, uneven federal budgets, low and diminishing interest in national security affairs by the nation's leaders, changes in US strategies, interallied politics, and extended-deterrence commitments. Many of these challenges have come together in the past decade to increase the level of interest and sense of priority in fixing the legacy system on which national security rests. The system is too big to continue patching and hoping for the best and too critical to the nation's survival to get wrong.

As Michael S. Malley said in the conclusion to chapter 9, designing new architecture is a tall challenge. Executing it may be even harder. But a consensus has finally emerged within the highest levels of the US government that the time has come to begin the process. To quote James J. Wirtz once again, this time from chapter 1, "The ultimate challenge facing those responsible for NC3 might in fact be the need to adapt the system continuously to a world of accelerating change while preserving the stability and predictability of the NC3 weapons system itself."

NOTES

1. Nathan Hodge and Sharon Weinberger, *A Nuclear Family Vacation: Travels in the World of Atomic Weaponry* (New York: Bloomsbury, 2008), 90.
2. David Deptula, "Foreword," in Deptula and William LaPlante, *Modernizing US Nuclear Command, Control, and Communications*, Mitchell Institute Report, MITRE Corp., February 2019, http://docs.wixstatic.com/ugd/a2dd91_ed45cfd71de2457eba3bcce4d0657196.pdf.
3. Gen. Richard Ellis, quoted in Eric Schlosser, *Command and Control: Nuclear Weapons, the Damascus Incident, and the Illusion of Safety* (New York: Penguin, 2013), 442. For an in-depth look at NC3 during the Reagan buildup, see Ashton Carter, John Steinbruner, and Charles Zraket, eds., *Managing Nuclear Operations* (Washington, DC: Brookings Institution, 1987), esp. chaps. 7–15.
4. The five widely acknowledged mission-essential functions of NC3 are force management, planning, maintaining situational awareness, decision-making, and force direction. See Secretary of the Air Force, "Nuclear, Space, Missile Command and Control: Air Force Nuclear Command, Control and Communications (NC3)," Air Force Instruction 13-550, April 16, 2019, 4, https://irp.fas.org/doddir/usaf/afi13-550.pdf.
5. Secretary of the Air Force, 4.
6. Bruce Blair, *The Logic of Accidental Nuclear War* (Washington, DC: Brookings Institution, 1993), 90–91. See also Scott Sagan, *The Limits of Safety: Organizations, Accidents, and Nuclear Weapons* (Princeton, NJ: Princeton University Press,

1993); and Bruce Blair, *Strategic Command and Control: Redefining the Nuclear Threat* (Washington, DC: Brookings Institution, 1985).
7. "Nuclear Command, Control, and Communications System Operational Assessment Program Solicitation, Number HC10471DR4009," Defense Information Systems Agency, Procurement Directorate, August 4, 2010, https://www.fbo.gov/index?s=opportunity&mode=form&id=ca9ed977f427844fb095c1e170a579ee&tab=core&_cview=1.
8. Rachel S. Cohen, "STRATCOM's New NC3 Center Suggests Program Changes," *Air Force Magazine,* May 6, 2019, http://airforcemag.com/Features/Pages/2019/May%202019/STRATCOMs-New-NC3-Center-Suggests-Program-Changes.aspx.
9. "Statement of Admiral Cecil Haney, Commander United States Strategic Command, before the Senate Committee on Armed Services," February 27, 2014, 9, https://fas.org/irp/congress/2014_hr/022714haney.pdf.
10. Kevin Dehoff, "Modernizing the US Nuclear Deterrent: An Interview with Elizabeth Durham-Ruiz," McKinsey & Company, June 2019, 3–4, https://www.mckinsey.com/industries/aerospace-and-defense/our-insights/modernizing-the-us-nuclear-deterrent-an-interview-with-elizabeth-durham-ruiz.

CONTRIBUTORS

MATTHEW R. CROOK is a lecturer in the Space Systems Academic Group, Naval Postgraduate School, Monterey, California. He served as an officer aboard ballistic missile and attack submarines from 2003 to 2011. He also served as a wargame director at the US Naval War College from 2012 to 2015. As a member of the military faculty at the Naval Postgraduate School, he received the Military Officers Association of America Joint Service Warfare Faculty Award.

REBECCA K. C. HERSMAN is a senior adviser in the International Security Program at the Center for Strategic and International Studies (CSIS) and director of the Project on Nuclear Issues—the preeminent program for developing next-generation nuclear policy expertise. She cochairs the CSIS Trilateral Dialogues on Nuclear Issues with peers from France and the United Kingdom. A leading expert on nuclear, chemical, and biological weapons policy, Ms. Hersman has authored numerous studies and reports on deterrence, nonproliferation, crisis management, global health security, emerging technologies, and strategic stability. She served as deputy assistant secretary of defense for countering weapons of mass destruction (WMD) and holds an MA in Arab studies from Georgetown University.

WADE L. HUNTLEY holds a joint appointment in the National Security Affairs Department and the Cyber Academic Group at the Naval Postgraduate School. He teaches courses on cyber policy and strategy, international politics, and WMD proliferation and has completed projects for US Cyber Command, US Marine Corps Forces Cyberspace Command, and Department of Energy national laboratories. His background includes a PhD in political science from the University of California, Berkeley, computer science training, and work at the intersection of technology and strategy in other policy areas.

JEFFREY A. LARSEN is a research professor in the Department of National Security Affairs, Naval Postgraduate School, and president of Larsen Consulting Group in Colorado Springs, Colorado. He was director of the Research Division at the NATO Defense College, Rome, from 2013 to 2018 and previously served as a senior policy analyst with Science Applications International

Corporation. He also was a command pilot in the US Air Force. Dr. Larsen was NATO's 2005 Manfred Wörner Fellow and is the author or editor of more than 150 books, journal articles, chapters, and monographs, including *On Limited Nuclear War in the 21st Century*. He earned a PhD in politics from Princeton University.

JON R. LINDSAY is an associate professor at the School of Cybersecurity and Privacy and in the Sam Nunn School of International Affairs at the Georgia Institute of Technology. He is the author of *Information Technology and Military Power* and editor of *Cross-Domain Deterrence* and *China and Cybersecurity*. He holds a PhD in political science from the Massachusetts Institute of Technology and an MS in computer science from Stanford University. He served in the US Navy.

MICHAEL S. MALLEY is a lecturer in the Department of National Security Affairs at the Naval Postgraduate School. From 2017 to 2019 he directed a project that developed a curriculum on nuclear command, control, and communications for the US Air Force. From 2012 to 2017 he was executive director of the Project on Advanced Systems and Concepts for Countering Weapons of Mass Destruction for the Defense Threat Reduction Agency. His work has been published in *Asian Survey*, *Democratization*, the *Nonproliferation Review*, and a variety of edited volumes. He earned degrees from Georgetown University, Cornell University, and the University of Wisconsin.

JAMES CLAY MOLTZ is dean of the School of International and Defense Studies at the Naval Postgraduate School. He is the author, coauthor, or editor of a number of books on space and nuclear issues as well as over fifty articles and book chapters. From 2012 to 2016 he directed the Project on Advanced Systems and Concepts for Countering Weapons of Mass Destruction for the Defense Threat Reduction Agency. He also served as deputy director of the Center for Nonproliferation Studies at the Middlebury Institute of International Studies, where he founded the *Nonproliferation Review*. He holds a PhD in political science from the University of California, Berkeley.

JAMES J. WIRTZ is a professor in the Department of National Security Affairs at the Naval Postgraduate School. He is the author of *Understanding Intelligence Failure: Warning, Response and Deterrence* and coeditor of *Strategy in the Contemporary World*. In March 2016 he was recognized as a distinguished scholar by the Intelligence Studies Section of the International Studies Association. He received his PhD in political science from Columbia University.

INDEX

Figures and tables are indicated by page numbers in *italics*.

1990 Base Reduction and Closure Act, 65
4th Space Operations Squadron, 109, 200

Able Archer, 4, 62, 72
Acheson-Lilienthal Committee, 40
Advanced Extremely High Frequency (AEHF) satellite, 110–12, 187, 195, 199–201, 203
Advisory Committee on Uranium, 37
Aegis, 80
Air Force Instruction 13-550, 5
Air Force Materiel Command, 84
Air Force Nuclear Weapons Center, 84
Air Force Scientific Advisory Board, 84, 190
Air Research Development Command, 51
air-gapped, 155, 172
Alaska, 45, 53, 76, 80, 93, 112–14
Aleutian Islands, 44, 75
Alternative for Germany (party), 162
Alternative National Military Command System Command Post, 76
Always-never dilemma, 21, 32, 39, 85, 88, 125, 129, 145, 148, 150, 173
AN/FPS-120 Radar, 114
AN/FPS-123 Solid State Phased Array Radar System, 113
AN/FPS-132 Radar, 114
AN/USQ-225, 79
analog (computer context), 8, 10, 22, 28, 78, 86, 115, 186, 197, 211–12, 217
Andrews Air Force Base, 146–47
Andropov, Yuri, 63

Anti-Ballistic Missile Treaty, 57, 62, 78
Arctic Ocean, 162
Army Air Forces, 41
Army Satellite Operations Brigade, 109
Army/Navy Transportable Radar Surveillance and Control Model 2 (AN/TPY-2), 80
Atlas missile, 51
Atomic Energy Act of 1946, 40
Atomic Energy Commission (AEC), 40–43, 54

B-1 bomber, 59, 61
B-2 bomber, 82
B-21 bomber, 192
B-29 bomber, 38–39, 41, 93
B-47 bomber, 1
B-52 bomber, 2, 26, 51, 71, 82, 92n32, 111
Baggott, Jim, 42
Ballistic Missile Early Warning System, 53, 76, 80, 101, 113–14
ballistic missile submarines (SSBN), 52, 83, 85, 89, 113, 185–86, 192, 211, 214
Baltics, 64, 162–66, 168–71, 176
Barksdale Air Force Base, xiii, 26, 77, 84, 92n32, 191
Base Reduction and Closure Act, 65
battle-damage assessment, 36
Beale Air Force Base, 113–14
Bedford Incident, The 2, 5, 22
Belarus, 64–65
Belt and Road Initiative, 169
Berdyansk, 162
Berlin Airlift, 41

223

224 INDEX

Berlin Crisis, 41, 46, 54
Biden, Joseph, 177n7
Blainey, Geoffrey, 30
Blair, Bruce, 214
bolt-from-the-blue, xi, 3, *137*, 140, 199
boosted fission bomb, 42–43
Bracken, Paul, 3
Brexit, 162
Brezhnev, Leonid, 59, 63
Brown, Harold, 60
Bruntingthorpe Air Base, United Kingdom, 1
Brzezinski, Zbigniew, 60, 146–47, 155, 157n7
Bush, George H.W., 64, 66

C-135 aircraft, 3, 51
C-32 aircraft, 201
Canada, 44, 74–76, 93, 112
Canopy Wing, 126
Carter, Jimmy, 58–60, 62, 77, 146–47, 157n7
Cavalier Air Force Base, 114
Central Intelligence Agency, 133
Challenger disaster, 4
Chernenko, Konstantin, 63
Chernobyl, 4
Cheyenne Mountain Complex, 71, 74, 76, 82, 114
Chiles Commission, 25
China, xi, 41, 44, 63, 134, *135*, 136, 162, 168, 170, 194, 197, 199
Chukotka Peninsula, 54
Churchill, Winston, 182n54
Clear Air Force Base, 53, 76, 113–114
Cohen, Avner, 26
Cold War 1, 3, 8–9, 17, 21–26, 28, 35–37, 39, 50, 52, 56, 63–67, 73–75, 77–78, 85, 87, 89, 113, 126, 134, 155, 182n55, 191, 210
Columbia-class fleet ballistic submarine, 186, 192
Combined Space Operations Center, 114

Command, Control, Battle Management, and Communications (C2BMC), 80
Command Post Terminal, 111, 200, 207n62
Comprehensive Nuclear Test Ban Treaty, 66
Congressional Research Service, 78
Cooperative Threat Reduction Program, 65
Corporal missile, 45
Council on Oversight of the National Leadership Command, Control, and communications system, 78, 188, 191, 193, 195
Creedon, Madelyn, 190
Crook, Matthew R., 91n22
Cuban Missile Crisis, *25*, 36, 50, 55, 61, 71
cyber assault, 115
Cyber Command, 129, 294
cyber commitment problem, 130, *131*, *137*, 139–49
cyber context, 8–9, 23, 86, 115
cyber effects, 134, 161
cyber intrusions, 23, 130, 149, 162, 172–73
cyber operations, 8, 23, 122–26, *128*, 128–41, 175, 216
cyber strategy, 174–75
cyber warfare, 67, 127, 129, 139
cyberattack, 5, 22–23, 86, 115, 126, 130, *131*, 136, *137*, 138–39, 149, 198–99
cybersecurity, 87, 122, 127, *137*, 155, 216; alarmism, 149
cyberspace, ix, 134, 138, 150, 152, 175

damage limitation, *137*, 139, 140
Daugavpils, 163, 165, 177n9, 177n11
Dawkins, James, 198
dead man's switch, 22
decapitation strike, 3, 19, 101
Defense Intelligence Agency, 197
Defense Logistics Agency, 26

INDEX

Defense Satellite Communications System, 57, 109–10
Defense Science Board, 148
Defense Support Program, 57, 62, 76, 80, 102
Delicate Balance of Terror, The 17
demonstration shot, 39, 128
Department of Defense; Defense Department, xiii, 25–27, 44–45, 55–56, 63, 65, 83–85, 89, 101, 147–51, 154, 156n3, 172, 187–90, 193, 195, 200, 216–18
Department of Energy, 65, 82
Deptula, David, 210
détente era, 36, 50, 56, 58, 60–61
DEW Line, 45, 53, 75–76, 112
distributed denial-of-service attack (DdoS), 152
Dr. Strangelove, 2, 49; character, 122
dual phenomenology, 74, 101–2, 113–14
Dulles, John Foster, 45
Durham-Ruiz, Elizabeth, 195, 197

E-4 aircraft, 83; E-4B, 150, 194, 200–202
E-6B aircraft, 7, 150, 200–201; E-6, 83
Eighth Air Force, 92n32
Einstein, Albert, 93
Eisenhower, Dwight D., 44–45, 47, 51–53, 55, 75, 213
Eligible Receiver Exercise, 97 148–49, 153
Elksnins, Andrejs, 177n11
Elugelab, 43
Emergency Action Management Agency, 72
emergency action message, 7, 74, 150, 171
Emergency Rocket Communications System, 56
Electromagnetic pulse (EMP), 23, 28, 30, 53, 57–58, 60, 77, 81, 86, 111
Enhanced Polar System, 111–12
enhanced-radiation nuclear weapon, 59

Esper, Mark, 198
European Phased Adaptive Approach, 80
extended deterrence, 30, 134, *135*, 168–69, 219
extremely high frequency, 103–11

F-106 aircraft, 71
F-15 aircraft, 62
FAB-T (Family of Advanced Beyond Line-of-Sight Terminals), 111, 187–88, 190–91, 195, 199–200, 203, 207n62, 216
fail deadly, 21, 23
Fail-Safe, 2, 49, 179n36
false alarm, 2–3, 20, 71–72, 101–2, 113, 146–47, 157n7
FB-111 bomber, 71
Federal Advisory Committee Nuclear Command and Control System Comprehensive Review, 78
first strike, 50, 54, 58, 62, 74, 85, *137*, 139, 157n7, 169
Fleet Satellite Communications system, 62, 108
flexible response, 36, 52–53
football, the, 7, 75
Ford, Gerald R., 58–59
Fort Ritchie, 45, 76
France, 30, *135*, 162, 171, 221
Fritzemeier, Ronald R., 198
Fukuyama, Francis, 182
Futter, Andrew, 8
Fylingdales Moor, 53, 76, 114

Galileo satellite system, 97
Gartzke, Erik, 174
Gates, Robert, 26
Gavin, James M., 48n34
General Advisory Committee, 42–43
geostationary orbit, *96*, 97–98, 108, 111
geosynchronous orbit (GEO), *96*, 97–98, 102–3, 108, 110–11, 197, 201
Global Cybersecurity Index (GCI), *135*

Global Navigation Satellite System (GLONASS), 97
Global Positioning System (GPS), 77, 97, 197
Global Strike Command, 27, 77, 84, 92n32, 190–92, 194, 217
Gorbachev, Mikhail, 50, 63–64
Governance Improvement Implementation Plan, 88
Government Accountability Office (GAO), 84, 151, 158n16, 187–88, 190, 193
Grand Forks Air Force Base, 57
"Grand Slam" conventional bomb, 47n7
gray zone, 17
Greenland, 44, 53, 75–76, 112, 114
Gregg, Walter, 1
Grosse, Eric, 198
ground launched cruise missile, 59, 61, 63
Ground Observer Corps, 46
Groves, Leslie, 37, 40
gun-type device, 38

Hagel, Chuck, 189–90
hair trigger, 3, 21, 54
Haney, Cecil, 190–91, 218
Hanford, Washington, 37
Harmony (party), 163
Hart, Gary, 147
Hartinger, James, 147
Harvey, John, 25
highly elliptical orbit (HEO), 97–98, 102–3, 111–12
Hiroshima, 39, 93
Honest John missile, 45
hotline, 55, 127
House Armed Services Committee, 192, 194, 196
Hunter Air Force Base, 1
Huntley, Wade, 218
hydrogen bomb, 35–36, 42–43, 45, 49, 51, 212

hypersonic weapons, 5, 86; missiles, 201
Hyten, John E., 84, 185, 192–93, 195, 198, 200

Imperial Japan, 35, 38–39
implosion device, 38
India, 66, 134, *135*
Information Age, 9, 18, 28
information revolution, 10, 20, 202
Integrated Tactical Warning and Attack Assessment system, 88, 101, 114, 150, 191
intercontinental ballistic missile (ICBM), 24, 27, 49, 52, 54, 56–58, 60, 64, 71–72, 74–75, 82–84, 92n32, 94, 98, 100–103, 113–14, 166–67, 169–70, 185, 196, 211, 218
Interim Polar System, 111–12
Intermediate-Range Nuclear Forces Treaty (INF), 63, 166
International Telecommunications Union, 103
internet, 67, 86, 129–30
Iran, 60, 66, 123, 133–34, *135*, 140, 162, 197

Jablow, Mark, 27
jamming, 105–6, 109–10
Joint All Domain Command and Control (JADC2), 198
Joint Chiefs of Staff, 27, 52, 84, 88, 147–48, 165, 188, 191, 198, 201
Joint Comprehensive Plan of Action, 134
Joint Publication 3-0, 79
Joint Strategic Target Planning Staff, 52, 66, 76, 214
Jupiter missile, 51

Kaliningrad, 180n38
Kazakhstan, 64–65
KB-50 tanker, 45
KC-135 tanker, 71, 90n2
KC-97 tanker, 45

Kennedy, John F., 52–55
Kenney, George, 41, 48n18
Khrushchev, Nikita, 52, 54
King test, 43
Kissinger, Henry, 56
Klaipeda, 163, 171, 180n38
Koehler, Earl, 1
Korean Air Lines, 62, 71
Kubrick, Stanley, 2, 11n7
Kulka, Bruce, 1, 10n1

launch facility down, 166–67, 169, 171–72
launch-on-warning, 3, 213
Lawrence, Ernest, 43
Law and Justice (party), 162
Lawrence Livermore National Laboratory, 65
left-of-launch, 5, 22, 28, 33n17, 86, 126, 129, 215–16
LeMay, Curtis, 41–43
Lewis, Jeffrey, 7
light detection and ranging (LIDAR), 112
Little Boy, 38
Long-Range Discriminating Radar, 80
Los Alamos National Laboratory, 37–38, 65
low earth orbit (LEO), 94, *96*, 96–97, 100
Lugar, Richard, 65

MacArthur, Douglas, 44
Malley, Michael S., 219
Malmstrom Air Force Base, Montana, 27–28
malware, 122, 153, 172, 179n27
Manhattan Project, 37–38
Mao Zedong, 44
Mariupol, 162
Mark 3 "Fat Man" atomic bomb, 38, 40
Mark 6 atomic bomb, 1
Mars Bluff, South Carolina, 1–2
Material Protection, Control, and Accounting Program (MPCA), 65

Mattis, James, 84, 185, 195
McNamara, Robert, 53, 56
medium earth orbit (MEO), *96*, 96–97
Merkel, Angela, 162
Mike test, 43
Military Air Transport Service, 41
Military Strategic and Tactical Relay (MILSTAR), 110–11, 199
Minihan, Kenneth, 148
Minimum Essential Emergency Communications Network, 75
Minot Air Force Base, 26, 166, 171
Minuteman III, 26, 51, 54, 56–57, 82, 166; silos, 61
Missile Defense Agency, 80
Missile Defense Alarm System, 102
Missile Warning Center, 114
Mobile User Objective System, 108–9
Moltz, James Clay, 90n6, 213
Moore's law, 32
Morocco, 42
Multiple independently targetable reentry vehicles (MIRV), 50, 56–62
mutual assured destruction, 3, 36, 50, 55–56, *131*
MX missile, 59, 61

Nagasaki, 39, 93
National Airborne Operations Center, 83, 150, 195
National Command and Control System. *See* National Military Command System (NMCS)
National Command Authority 53, 75, *128*
National Defense Authorization Act, 83–84, 188–89, 181, 191, 193–96, 200
National Defense Reorganization Act, 75
National Defense Research Council, 37
National Emergency Airborne Command Post, 51, 60, 146–47
National Emergency Command Post Afloat, 51

National Military Command Center, 74, 82, 146
National Military Command System (NMCS), 6–10, 15, 19–20, 22, 27, 31–32, 75–77, 82, 124, 145–55, 161, 172, 190, 209, 211, 218; command post at Fort Ritchie, Maryland, 76
National Nuclear Security Administration, 25
National Security Agency, 133, 148–49, 189
National Security Council Document, 162/2, 45
National Security Decision Document, (NSDD-13), 61
National Security Strategy, 9–10, 16, 27–28, 87, 209, 217
Navy NC3 Executive Steering Committee, 83
Navy Space Operations Center, 107
Nazi Germany, 38–39
NC3 Analysis Directorate, 84
NC3 Center, xiii, 27–28, 32, 80, 84, 191–92, 194–95, 217
NC3 Integration Directorate, 84
NC3 Next Generation, 186
negative control, xi, 2, 7–10, 21–24, 28, 31, 39, 55, 85, 211–12
neutron bomb, 59
New Look strategy, 45
New START Treaty, 24
Next-Generation Overhead Persistent Infrared (Next-Gen OPIR), 200–201
Nixon, Richard, 56–58
NLC3S Oversight Council. *See* Council on Oversight of the National Leadership Command, Control, and Communications System
no-first-use pledge, 61, 134, *135*
normal accident, 1, 4, 8, 22–23, 28, 127, 147
North American Air/Aerospace Defense Command (NORAD), 46, 71, 76, 146–47, 157n9, 157n11, 158n16, 214

North Atlantic Ocean, 76
North Atlantic Treaty Article, 5 165, 168–69, 171
North Atlantic Treaty Organization (NATO), 58, 60–63, 72, 80, 162, 164–66, 168–71, 180n41; Council, 165–67, 169–70; nuclear exercise, 4
North Korea, xi, 44, 66, 126, *135*, 136, 168–69, 197, 199
North Pole, 72, 102–3
North Warning System, 45, 112
nuclear command and control (NC2), 6, 8, 10, 73, 82, 149, 186, 198; defined, 5–6, 79, 156n1
Nuclear Command and Control System, xi, 78, *81*, 194
Nuclear Command, Control, and Communications Enterprise Center, 185–86, 195, 197–98, 202
Nuclear Detonation Detection System, 80
nuclear freeze, 52
Nuclear Matters Handbook, 79, 101, 150, 186
Nuclear Oversight Board, 27
Nuclear Posture Review (NPR), 10; 2001, 25; 2010, 83, 186; 2018, 27, 78, 86–87, 131, 194–96
Nuclear Weapons Employment Policy (NUWEP), 63
Nunn, Sam, 65
Nunn-Lugar program, 65

Oak Ridge National Laboratory, 37
Obama, Barack administration, 10, 85, 186
Odom, William, 146, 157n7
Off Tackle war plan, 42
Offutt Air Force Base, 82, 147, 150, 172
Ohio-class fleet ballistic submarine, 82, 186
one-shot war, 53, 215
Oppenheimer, J. Robert, 37–38, 40, 42
Out-of-spec, 4, 22, 28–29, 33n19

INDEX 229

Pacific theater, 37
Partial Nuclear Test Ban Treaty, 55
Patriot missile defense, 80
Pearl Harbor, 3, 37
Perimeter Acquisition Radar Attack Characterization System, 80
Permissive Action Links, 56
Perry, William, 76
Pershing II missile, 59–61, 63
Peterson Air Force Base, 109
phased-array ground radar, 98
Pinetree Line, 44–45, 112
Plutonium, 7, 37–39, 42, 93
positive control, xi, 7–10, 19, 21–24, 28, 31, 39, 55, 85, 211–12
Powers, Thomas, 54
Precision Acquisition Radar Attack Characterization System, 114
Precision Acquisition Vehicle Entry Phased Array Warning System (PAVE PAWS) 77, 80, 113
precision-strike capabilities, 5, 28
Presidential Directive, 59, 60, 77
principle-agent relations, 4, 28, 32, 215
Protected EHF band satellites, 107, 110–11

R-7 missile, 50
Rand, Robin, 192, 194–95
RAND Corporation, 17, 83, 188–89
Ratcheting effect, 3–4, 22
Reagan, Ronald, 4, 50, 60–63, 77, 213, 219n3
red lines, 16, 18, 20, 29
Regulus cruise missile, 45
Reykjavík summit, 63
Richard, Charles, xi, 186, 202
Rickover, Hyman, 51
Riga, 164–65, 171, 180n37
Robbins Air Force Base, 113
rogue regimes, 31
Roosevelt, Franklin D., 37–38, 93
Russia, ix, 24, 44, 64–65, 97, 134, *135*, 136, 153, 162–75, 176n2, 177n7,
177n11, 178n14, 180n37, 180n38, 181n51, 194, 197, 199

Safeguard, 114
Sagan, Scott, 55, 214
salami tactics, 18
Sandia National Laboratories, 65
Schelling, Thomas, 17, 139
Schlosser, Eric, 55
Schriever Space Force Base, 107, 109, 200
Schriever, Bernard, 51
Scowcroft Commission Nuclear Command and Control System End-to-End Review, 78
Sea of Azov, 162
second strike mode, 24, 85; capability 17, 31, 74, 82, 124, 209, 216
Semi-Automatic Ground Environment network (SAGE), 53, 76
Senate Armed Services Committee, 83, 187, 189–90, 192, 218
Shalikashvili, John, 148
Single Integrated Operational Plan (SIOP), 52, 55, 63, 76, 214
Sino-British Joint Declaration, 168
Situation Room, 165, 167
Si vis pacem para bellum, 17
Smith, Adam, 196
Solid State Phased Array Radar System, 113–14
South Korea, 44, 46, 168, 171
South Pole, 97, 102–3
Soviet Military Power, 61
Soviet Union, 2, 24, 35–36, 39, 41–46, 50–51, 54, 56–60, 62–65, 71, 94, 100–101, 113, 147, 157n7
Space and Missile Systems Center, 200–201
Space-Based Infrared System (SBIRS), 76, 80, 100, 103, 200, 202
Space Development Agency, 200
Special Operations Command, 165
Spetznaz attacks, 8
SS-18 ICBM, 58

SS-20 missile, 58, 61, 63
Strategic Arms Reduction (START) Treaty 1991, 24
Strategic Air Command (SAC), 2, 17, 41–46, 51–54, 66, 71, 146–47, 210; alert 90n2; headquarters 74–78
Strategic Arms Limitation Treaty (SALT); the SALT agreement, 56–61
Strategic Automated Command Control System, 150–52, 171
Strategic Defense Initiative (SDI), 50, 62–63
Strategic Systems Programs, 83
Stuxnet, 126, 133, 140
submarine launched ballistic missile (SLBM), 7–8, 24, 52, 56–59, 61, 75–76, 82, 85, 94, 103, 168, 196, 218
Sun Tzu, 33n2
super high frequency, 103–11
survivable airborne operations center, 201
survival launch, 71
Sweeney, Charles W., 39
Szilard, Leo, 93

Take Charge and Move Out (TACAMO) Airborne Command Post, 56, 83, 91n24, 150, 202
Tallinn, 171
target "withholds," 66, 215
Task Force on DOD Nuclear Weapons Management, 26
Teller, Edward, 43
Terminal High Altitude Area Defense (THAAD), 80
Terminator, 2
Tertrais, Bruno, 7
Texas Towers, 46, 76
thick line, 106–7, 150
thin line, 74, 106–7, 110, 114, 150
Third Generation Infrared Sensors, 80
Three Mile Island, 4
Tibbets, Paul, 39

Tinian Island, 38–39
Titan ICBM, 51
Tous azimuts, 31, 34n36
Trinity test, 38, 47n7
Truman, Harry S., 38–41, 43
Trump, Donald, administration, 10, 131, 134, 194–96
Tunner, William H., 41

Ukraine, 4, 64–65, 162, 164–65, 177n7
ultra-high frequency, 103–11
Ultra High Frequency Follow-On system, 108
United Kingdom, 39, 42, 51, 53, 76, 114, *135*, 162
United Nations, 40, 56, 62
Uranium, 35, 37, 42, 54–55
US Nuclear Detonation Detection System, 80
US Space Surveillance Network, 114
US Strategic Command (STRATCOM), xi, 7, 27–28, 32, 66, 73, 77–78, 80, 82–85, 88–89, 92n32, 126, 150, 172, 185–86, 189–90, 192–95, 197, 202, 214, 217
USS *Northampton*, 51
USS *Wright*, 51

Vance, Cyrus, 60
Vandenberg Air Force Base, 54; Space Force Base 114
Vladivostok, 58,
Volk Field, 71

W80 nuclear warhead, 26
War Department, 38
War Games, 2, 126
Warsaw Pact, 43, 61, 63–64, 126
weapon of mass destruction, 31, 55
Weinberger, Caspar, 63
Wideband Code Division Multiple Access (WCDMA), 108–9
Wideband Global Satellite Communication System, 109–10

window of vulnerability, 60; opportunity 139
Wirtz, James J., 211, 219
Wohlstetter, Albert, 17
Wohlstetter, Roberta, 3
World War I, 3
World War II, 37, 46, 47n7, 64, 72, 93

Worldwide Military Command and Control System (WMCCS), 53, 75

Yeltsin, Boris, 64

zero-day vulnerability, 152–53
Zilupe, 164–65

www.ingramcontent.com/pod-product-compliance
Lightning Source LLC
Chambersburg PA
CBHW032039300426
44117CB00009B/1113